Working the Skies

Working the Skies

The Fast-Paced, Disorienting World of the Flight Attendant

Drew Whitelegg

NEW YORK UNIVERSITY PRESS
New York and London

NEW YORK UNIVERSITY PRESS
New York and London
www.nyupress.org

Library of Congress Cataloging-in-Publication Data
Working the skies : the fast-paced, disorienting world of the
flight attendant / Drew Whitelegg.
p. cm.
Includes bibliographical references and index.
ISBN-13: 978-0-8147-9407-4 (cloth : alk. paper)
ISBN-10: 0-8147-9407-6 (cloth : alk. paper)
ISBN-13: 978-0-8147-9408-1 (pbk. : alk. paper)
ISBN-10: 0-8147-9408-4 (pbk. : alk. paper)
1. Flight attendants—United States. 2. Flight attendants—
United States—Anecdotes. I. Title.
HD8039.A432U69 2007
387.7'364—dc22
2006101773

New York University Press books are printed on acid-free paper,
and their binding materials are chosen for strength and durability.

Manufactured in the United States of America

c 10 9 8 7 6 5 4 3 2 1
p 10 9 8 7 6 5 4 3 2 1

For Lisa, and Maya

People on the airplane will look at us and they'll go, "Do you always just live out of that suitcase?" I go, "No, I have a house in Atlanta. I cut the grass. I get the trash out. I have friends. I teach Sunday school." And they'll go, "Flight attendants do things like that?" They think all we own is a uniform and a suitcase.

—Claudette, Delta flight attendant

It makes a difference when you do what you like. I've had jobs that I've hated and did not want to get in the car in the morning and go to work, and that's what I told the children as they were going through school: whatever the pay is, do what you love. I remember going by the airport because I lived there. I remember this big old Delta jet going over my head one time and I said, "Damn it, I'm going to do that one day, damn it!" And I did, and so no matter my age, although I thought, I'm too old, I did it and I'm proud of it.

—Jill, Air Tran flight attendant

Contents

All illustrations appear as a group following p. 148.

Acknowledgments

I once heard Harry Belafonte say that if you can't give someone a hand up, don't give them a push down. While researching this
book, I have been struck by the generosity of numerous people prepared
to share time, offer support, and give help in equal measure. First and
foremost, I would like to thank all those flight attendants who sat down
with me in their homes, in coffeehouses, and in airport lobbies to tell
me their stories. Without them this book would simply not exist, and
though confidentiality concerns prevent me from mentioning any individuals by name, they know who they are.

At NYU Press, Ilene Kalish, my editor, from our first conversation,
saw value in this project and at the same time consistently forced me to
think deeper about it. Working with Ilene has been a pleasure. I would
also like to thank Salwa Jabado for answering my numerous technical
queries.

The book emerged from research supported by the Alfred P. Sloan
Foundation and conducted at the Emory Center for Myth and Ritual in
American Life (MARIAL) in Atlanta. MARIAL provided a stimulating
and supportive community. I cannot thank my colleagues there enough,
especially Bradd Shore, Marshall Duke, Robyn Fivush, Donna Mote,
Jennifer Bohanek, and Kelly Marin. I would like particularly to thank
Carla Freeman, Beth Kurylo, and Donna Day.

I have been very lucky to exchange phone calls and e-mails with
other academics and students working on the topic of flight attendants.
There are not that many of us, and I have been touched by the spirit
with which we have circulated information and ideas. In particular I
would like thank Terri Ballard, Leslie Macdonald, Ellen Heuven, Alyce
Desrosiers, Katie Barry, Christine Yano, Takeda Atsushi, and Lauren
Westbrook. Heather Healy, Candace Kolander, Dawn Deeks, and Corey
Caldwell answered my various questions at the Association of Flight Attendants, as did Lonny Glover at the Association of Professional Flight

Attendants. Sarah Finke and Shane Enright of the International Transport Workers' Federation have always been a great support. Special thanks are also due to the Alteon Company of Long Beach, California, which provided hospitality and space for two focus groups conducted there.

My thinking about flight attendants has been considerably improved by numerous conference presentations and invited talks. Angel Kwolek-Folland at the University of Florida provided an early venue for my ideas, showed me the Gainesville "prairie," with its cattle egrets and alligators, and helped considerably with draft proposals for this book. Similarly, the brilliant labor historian Michelle Brattain invited me to speak to her class at Georgia State University. I have benefited especially from sharing ideas at the annual Sloan Working Families conferences in, respectively, Los Angeles, Boston, and Chicago. From these I would like to thank Joan Williams, Elinor Ochs, Ann Bookman, Juliet Bourke, Leah Wingard, Heather Willihnganz, Tamar Kremer-Sadlik, Chuck Darrah, Tom Fricke, Brian Hoey, and Pete Richardson for their interest in my work.

I would also like to acknowledge the feedback provided by anonymous referees both for this book and for journal articles I have submitted elsewhere on flight attendants. When conducted properly, the peer review system is, to my mind, second to none for sharpening one's thoughts, and I would like to thank the editors of *Southern Cultures, Antipode,* and the *Journal of Transport History* collectively. Special mention should go to those at *Gender, Place and Culture,* in which I published an earlier, much different, form of chapter 6.

I also thank Karyn Lacy, a constant source of encouragement; Peter Lyth, my fellow airline obsessive; Meika Loe, who helped me think about Hooters; Parker Nolen, another airline expert; my old Cambridge colleague, Mo Fitzgerald; my geography mentors and urbanists Chris Hamnett and Andy Merrifield; and the teachers who have inspired me: Jim Potter, Eric Mottram, and Chris Jordan.

Ian Plendeleith and Conny, Nina, and Natascha Lotze gave me some great reasons to keep going back to Washington. Susie Johnson put me up in Cambridge and has been a lifelong friend, as has Kevin Sheedy. Paul, Vanessa, Jack, and Louise McCloskey made sure the soul-fire flame kept burning even when at times it got a bit dim. Duane and Arline Dillman were a constant source of support, as were my parents. Brian Whitelegg died suddenly, shortly before I finished this book. With his dislike of airplanes and, shall we say, "traditional" views on women, he may not have really grasped it; Joy Whitelegg, teacher, mom, and an emotional laborer if ever there was one, most certainly will.

There are three women, however, without whom I can safely say this book would never have happened. Bobbie Sullivan is a flight attendant expert second to none. She read every word I have written here, offered criticism and encouragement in equal measures, and never once failed to answer the many, many questions I have had over the past few years. Though any mistakes in interpretation are mine, I do not think it presumptive to say that Bobbie is as responsible for this book as I am.

Maggie Walsh first interviewed me when I was the tender age of seventeen and was applying to go to Birmingham University, England. She told me at the time she "didn't think I'd to bother turn up," and in many ways she was almost right. Our interests in gender and transport have gravitated toward each other over the ensuing twenty-five years. Maggie has been a first port of call on numerous academic and professional issues, but what she has given me most is the greatest thing a teacher can give to a student: the confidence to believe he or she can do it.

Finally, my ex-partner Lisa Dillman towers above these pages. With her astonishing intellectual and linguistic ability, often expressed in red ink in the margin of my work (normally as "Huh???" or "*What* is your argument?"), she taught me truly how to connect the thoughts in my head to the way I expressed them on the page. Before I met Lisa, I was, like the Coen Brothers' eponymous Barton Fink, just a tourist with a typewriter. This book is for her more than anyone else.

Introduction

"We're Here to Save Your Ass, Not Kiss It"

At 7:11 A.M. on Tuesday, September 11, 2001, American Airlines flight attendant Amy Sweeney, on board Flight 11 from Boston to Los Angeles, took advantage of a slight delay in departure to phone home. She was hoping to apologize to her five-year-old daughter for not being there to put her on the bus for kindergarten that morning. Like many flight attendant mothers—especially those with young children—Sweeney preferred to work only on weekends, allowing her to be with her family the rest of the time. She had only volunteered to fly that Tuesday as a bonus—one of the job's perks being the ability to "pick up" additional flights at relatively short notice—and had arranged to have lunch with an old friend in California, possibly at her favorite Mexican restaurant on the West Coast (she had another favorite on the East). Amy's stepmother told a local newspaper, "She just happened to pick up an extra day, and today happened to be the day." Sweeney had only recently gone back to work following the birth of her son. According to her husband, Michael, Amy's return was partly determined by her desire to keep flying the Boston-L.A. route. Like many flight attendants, she appreciated the space this trip provided.[1]

Just over an hour later, Sweeney made another call, this time to American's flight service center in Boston, to report her airplane had been hijacked. She told the manager where the hijackers had been sitting, that she had been shown a bomb, and that two of her colleagues and a passenger had been stabbed (a claim made by fellow flight attendant Betty Ong in another call, which was aired during the 9/11 Commission hearings).[2] Her information, which should have revealed Mohamed Atta's name on the flight manifest in one of the ascribed seats, would—according to 9/11 Commission member Bob Kerrey—have enabled American Airlines to identify a suspected Al Qaeda operative at the heart of the hijacking, still too late to prevent Flight 11 becoming the first plane to hit the World Trade Center.[3] Boston's flight manager reported Sweeney's last words as, "I see water. I see buildings. We're flying low. We're flying way too low. Oh, my god."[4] In losing her life that morning, Amy Sweeney would be joined by twenty-four other flight attendants. She was thirty-five years old and had worked for American for twelve years.

Post-9/11 Nostalgia

Society has become increasingly nostalgic for the air travel of yesteryear. Instead of the modern-day hell of long airport lines, exhausting security procedures, and bankrupt airlines unexpectedly canceling flights, American popular culture has fixated on the days when flying was fun and the nation secure. In 2003, the centenary of the Wright Brothers' first flight at Kitty Hawk reminded the United States of its technological achievements; a year later in Atlanta, Delta Air Lines dusted down an old 1940s Douglas DC-3 and pointed it skyward to celebrate the carrier's seventy-fifth anniversary. Authors delved into the past in an attempt to recapture the days when air travel had its grip on the imagination. One of the key post-9/11 novels, Philip Roth's *The Plot against America,* places the original flying hero, Charles Lindbergh, at its core.[5] Movies such as *The Aviator* depict the hubristic accomplishments of pioneering airmen such as Howard Hughes.

Nostalgia is defined as "an acute longing for familiar surroundings," and because its etymological roots lie in pain, it is unsurprising that Americans should have experienced such longing in the wake of 9/11.[6] They were "yearning for yesterday," in the words of sociologist Fred Davis, seeking a "past imbued with special qualities which, moreover, acquires its significance from the particular way we juxtapose it to certain features of our present lives."[7]

When it comes to flight attendants, nostalgia has followed a curious path. It played little part in 9/11's immediate aftermath, when Americans came to view them in a new light: passengers paid more attention during safety briefings; they made eye contact when handing the attendants their trash; they thanked them more sincerely at the end of a flight. As Suzanne, a Los Angeles–based flight attendant with United Airlines since 1984, observes: "[Just after] September 11 was the only time I didn't feel unappreciated. I had people that would come up, passengers, 'Thank you so much.' It was great to be noticed. They noticed me. 'Thank you for coming to work, thank you for being here, for what you do.' "[8] But things have changed. Now that the initial impact of 9/11 has receded, flight attendants report that passengers are back to their rude old selves, treating them as if they were invisible.

The industry has also embarked upon one of the most savage restructuring efforts in its short history, with roughly 10,000 fewer flight attendants nationwide out of a pre-9/11 total of 110,000.[9] Whereas once flight attendants used the job to "space-out," as I call it, creating a world that considerably expanded their personal autonomy, they now face a "squeeze-in," where such autonomy is being constricted, inch by inch. Meanwhile empathy for modern flight attendants has been replaced by nostalgia for an image they thought they had seen the back of.

The "Nostalgic Flight Attendant" in Popular Culture

Popular culture has yearned for "yesterday's" flight attendants rather ruthlessly. Whereas in the real world passengers complain about increasingly grumpy workers, in magazines and paperback aisles, the alluring, sexy, smiling "stewardess" is back. In October 2002, *Vanity Fair* talked of the days of "glamour with attitude," when workers strutted the cabin with style and panache.[10] Penguin Books republished the notorious best-selling 1960s sex-and-frolics exposé, *Coffee, Tea or Me?*, in which two fictional ex-Eastern stewardesses encapsulate the decade's archetypal "Barbie Doll" icon. According to the publisher, this "hilarious jet-age journal offers a gold mine of anecdotes from the aerial to the amorous lives of those busty, lusty, adventurous young 'stews' of the swinging sixties."[11] Though less racy, Ernestine Bradley's autobiography, *The Way Home*, recalls her time as a glamorous Pan American Airways (Pan Am) stewardess.[12] Meanwhile, on stage, a hit at the 2005 New York Musical Theatre Festival was *Plane Crazy*, heralded on its author's Web site as "an engaging story that follows two young stews who are learning about love and life in the high-flying airline business circa 1965, a time 'When Stews Were Sexy and the World Was Sexist.' "[13] On television's *Sex and the City* the character of Miranda Hobbs improved her speed-dating possibilities by pretending she was a flight attendant rather than a Harvard-trained lawyer.

The "nostalgic flight attendant" made her greatest splash at the movies. Opening on Christmas Day 2002, Steven Spielberg's *Catch Me If You Can* provided the perfect antidote to jet travel's modern nightmare, as blue gabardine–clad Pan Am stewardesses escorted Leonardo DiCaprio through the Miami terminal to the tune of Frank Sinatra's carefree "Come Fly with Me." Pan Am, no longer in existence, was once as great a symbol of optimistic U.S. cultural imperialism as Coca-Cola. Its cosmopolitan, multilingual stewardesses served as ambassadors for a confident, dynamic nation. They were the cream of the crop. According to one former worker, in 1965, "being a Pan Am stewardess was truly one of the most desirable occupations you could land."[14] In the 1960s spoof *Down with Love* (2003), the airline's stewardesses are also simultaneously sophisticated and salacious, as they provide sexual interest for lothario Ewan McGregor's character whenever they happen to drop into town.

In *View from the Top* (2003), Hollywood A-lister Gwyneth Paltrow sports a "Royalty Airlines" uniform and dreams wistfully of flying "Paris: First Class International." Unluckily for her, but probably more accurately, she ends up on the Cleveland shuttle, that is, before the kindly intervention of "superstew" Candice Bergen. In the end she deems the career incompatible with a stable domestic relationship (airlines used this conservative argument to uphold marriage bans until the late 1960s) and then miraculously (and rather counterintuitively) becomes a Royalty Boeing 737 pilot.

Steven Spielberg was back in 2004 with *The Terminal,* in which flight attendant Catherine Zeta-Jones befriends a stranded émigré Tom Hanks at New York's JFK airport while working for United. Another alluring transient dependent upon a married man's whimsical affection, Zeta-Jones, too, fitted the nostalgic flight attendant bill. Hollywood's younger starlets have also gotten in on the act: quirky Kirsten Dunst cropped up in *Elizabethtown* (2005) as a flight attendant. Finally, even *The Aviary* (2005), an independent movie actually written by a flight attendant, regurgitated stereotypes of footloose and fancy-free contemporary workers, suggesting nothing had really changed much since the 1960s.

Most real-life flight attendants did not think much of these movies, if their reactions on such online forums as flightattendants.org or airline crew.net were anything to go by.[15] I was invited to watch the Atlanta press screening of *View from the Top* with two ex-Delta fliers, who spent most of their time laughing (and I spent most of mine laughing at them laughing) yet were dismissive of the movie. "That was really dumb," one declared as we headed for the escalators after the screening. "Yeah, stupid," said the other, criticizing both the farcical plot and the general trivialization of her former profession. Flight attendant unions have endorsed their views. Heather Healy, director of the Association of Flight Attendants (AFA) Employee Assistance Program (EAP), told me, "Whenever a film like that comes out it is like flight attendants go back twenty years."[16]

Nostalgia and the Airlines

Yet nostalgia sells, and airlines themselves have picked up on the trend. In a somewhat postmodern example of life imitating art imitating life, Song Airlines (Delta's low-cost spin-off) announced its intention to "put the fun back into travel" by recruiting the bubbliest flight attendants it could find among Delta's existing pool of workers, christening them "Song Talents" and getting them to entertain like their 1960s antecedents. In their Kate Spade–designed uniforms, they also look like their colleagues from yesteryear. Style is a "huge signature" of the Song brand, the carrier's president claims, while for the chief executive officer flying has become "boring" and Song Talents could liven things up a bit.[17]

"Why Song?" one Talent asked over the Boeing 757's public address system as I was settling into my refurbished leather seat en route from JFK to Atlanta in June 2003. "Songs are a part of everyone's life. Songs are about choice and self-expression. Like food: you can make indulgent choices like Snickers or Pringles or simple salads. We are so proud of this cool airline." She went on to tell us all about her "audition" for the job. It transpires that workers, whose primary responsibility is to save passenger lives in an emergency situation, do not "interview" for employment at Song but undergo an "audition," part of which, logically, requires the performance of a musical ditty or other short theatrical routine. I am not suggesting that Song skimps on safety—no carrier would risk such a reputation. I do suggest, though, that the iconography of Song Talents is a long way from that of the safety professionals these flight attendants really are.

Hooters Air, which launched service between Atlanta and Myrtle Beach in 2003, has cranked up the entertainment factor on board a notch further. Its trademark large-breasted "Hooters Girls"—the signature of the national restaurant chain—run trivia games and hand out prizes in skimpy white tank tops emblazoned with the slogan "Delightfully Tacky." These women are *not* flight attendants, I should stress. The onboard flight attendants are provided by Pace Airlines and sport sober, plain uniforms. Hooters Girls have no safety function at all, though in an emergency passengers may not realize this, especially because the onboard safety cards have a Hooters Girl—and not a Pace flight attendant—on the cover.

In the charter airline market, Beverly Hills–based Ecstasky Air recently took to the sky. For about $40,000 passengers choose their own flight attendants from a list and dress them in teddies, merry widows, or bikinis. The flight attendants also offer pedicures, shoulder massages, and foot rubs to bachelor parties and high rollers flying the airline's Lear jets and Gulfstreams.[18]

The combination of sex and style in the cabin, considered by many flight attendants as belonging to another era, has not been confined to low-cost and holiday or charter carriers. Richard Branson, head of the Virgin operation, and never one to miss a trick when it comes to publicity, cheerfully told reporters that his flight attendants were instructed not to disturb couples locking themselves in the lavatory with the intention of joining the "mile-high club." His comments came at a gala unveiling Virgin's new Airbus A380, on which Branson hopes to put beds, in which people will have "lots of room to innovate," he said. "You can do it on a cruise ship, you can do it at home, why can't you do it in the air?"[19]

In 2004, Delta employed another top designer, Los Angeles–based Richard Tyler, to remodel its uniforms. "I want them to look sexy and great," declared Tyler.[20] Uniform revamps became part of an industry trend among numerous big international carriers, including British Airways, Air France, and Korean Air. Airlines entrusted their company image to top-range designers in a manner not seen since the early 1970s, though some—notably American and United—claimed financial pressures limited their capacity to update uniforms. One of the star attractions for Delta's new look is a red silk taffeta wrap dress, perhaps inspired by the company's onetime global alliance partner Singapore International Airlines (SIA), which has constructed its entire brand around traditional two-piece *sarong kebaya*–wearing "Singapore Girls."[21] Indeed, in an increasingly global market, the Singapore Girl—long revered by passengers—has become something of an ideal to which other airlines aspire, conveniently ignoring the "Girls'" employment conditions, which, with their age limits, are more resonant of U.S. carriers before civil rights took hold in the late 1960s.[22]

Resexing the Cabin

Maybe this reinvestment in flight attendant image, the move to songs and sex appeal, and the notion that "boring" air travel needs some excitement are a subtle distraction to calm jumpy American passengers. As one male flier recently admitted to the *New York Daily News,* "When I'm flying, I'd rather be checking out the flight attendants than thinking about terrorism."[23] After all, an oxymoronic combination of relieving boredom and alleviating fear was the main reason airlines employed flight attendants in the first place. In the 1930s, when carriers such as United and American established themselves, it soon dawned on them that once up in the air there really was not much for passengers to do, other than worry about crashing. Employing trained nurses as flight attendants reduced passenger fear and provided the almost-ubiquitous male customer on board with something to "look at." Flight attendants quickly became a central pillar of airline advertising, a trend that reached its apex (or nadir) in the sex-charged innuendo campaigns of the *Coffee, Tea or Me?* era of the 1960s.[24]

Even if the confluence of nostalgic flight attendant images is more a product of coincidence than conspiracy, some airline iconography does appear to be heading back several decades to a period when "stews" were sexy and the world was indeed sexist. JetBlue, for instance, dresses both airplanes and flight attendants in nostalgic, retro and "mod" sixties tones, passed off as "Prada-esque" in airline press releases. Indeed, Song's attempt to establish its brand through stylish uniforms clearly mirrored JetBlue.[25] Yet you cannot divorce images from the social conditions that created them. No doubt highly chic, the era being resurrected also predates the full impact of the women's movement and recalls a time when men unhesitatingly controlled the skies and airlines divided labor along gendered lines.[26] Men with "the right stuff," as Tom Wolfe described it, were largely in charge of the "hardware"—the machines, the technology, and the capital.[27] Despite the presence of 1920s flying heroines such as Amelia Earhart, U.S. airlines would not entrust one of their airplanes to a female pilot until the 1970s.[28] Piloting —and certainly owning an airline—was men's business.[29]

In contrast, carriers consigned women to look after the "software," the cabin in particular. But, as the nostalgic flight attendant should remind us, men exerted control here, too. Those sexy 1960s stewardesses may be the leitmotif of an era, but they were also subjected to draconian restrictions affecting their ability to marry, work beyond a certain age, and have children, not to mention regulations regarding weight, makeup, hair, fingernails, and a host of other issues. They were also almost uniformly white. Though these women sought to create spaces for themselves—subtly challenging hemlines and hairstyles, for instance—they did so within a male-dominated environment.[30] If one subtext of the journey back to when flying was fun is that in those days America was safe, another is that in those days (white) men were in the driver's seat (and of course the two are connected). Within this testosterone-driven mind-set, today's airplane cabin becomes a metaphor for society itself. Society is dominated by feminism and women have too much power, and look at the disastrous results. The nostalgic flight attendant resurrects the days when women chose to work in the air under male-imposed conditions, before workers "spaced-out" and exerted autonomy: underneath the nostalgic flight attendant, it would not be out of place to inscribe the word "backlash."[31]

Women and Men Passengers

However, the world *has* changed since the 1960s in the sense that there are now many more women passengers, as well as male and older female flight attendants in this once male-controlled space. As regards passengers, U.S. airlines cannot turn back the clock, or surely they run the risk of alienating a good chunk of their customer base.[32] For example, when I flew on Hooters Air in the summer of 2005, at least half the passengers were female.

Quite what they thought of the Hooters Girls' performance is anyone's guess, though in an online debate in the *Atlanta Journal-Constitution*, most female contributors attacked the airline's objectification of women.[33] So far as I could see, none of the women passengers joined in the trivia competition, suggesting that, as sociologist Meika Loe concluded in her ethnographic research on a Hooters restaurant, they felt uncomfortable or intimidated—or perhaps plain embarrassed.[34] Hooters' own strategy is more about in-your-face brand building for its restaurant chain, and it makes no apologies for its use of women workers. "If you don't like Hooters Air," claimed the company's president, Mark Peterson, "don't fly it."[35]

Prior to 9/11, most American carriers pursued gender-neutral marketing campaigns, largely due to flight attendants fighting sexist imagery in the 1970s. Yet they did so in the face of overseas competitors, most significantly Southeast Asian airlines milking images of sex and servitude—wrapped in the guise of "Orientalism"—for all their worth. Undoubtedly, the targets of these images—easily found on a weekly basis in journals such as *Business Week*—have been the male businessmen, not women, of the emerging Pacific Rim. Though U.S. airlines have often formed strategic alliances with such carriers, and thereby have acquiesced in imagery that would be impossible at their own companies, the smiling, deferential "Oriental" flight attendant—most famously Singapore Girl—compares unfavorably in the minds of passengers with their own workforce.[36]

Singapore Girl is the only marketing creation to be embodied in wax at London's famous Madame Tussauds museum, where she stands with Marilyn Monroe and Madonna as female icons of her age. In terms of global iconography, Southeast Asian carrier flight attendants set a global benchmark against which all other flight attendants are compared. That said, one of the features of globalization is that such comparisons permeate down to the local level. Flight attendant imagery even in U.S. markets half saturated with women is often determined by Pacific Rim markets long saturated with men.[37] So even with more women passengers on board, many airlines still implicitly view the male passenger as the most important.[38] From Singapore Girl to Song Talent, flight attendant imagery coalesces around the idea of these workers as entertainers and not safety professionals.

Excluded Workers

One group for whom the nostalgic flight attendant would appear to have little relevance is male cabin crew. Constituting about 20 percent of U.S. flight attendants, men have been employed constantly in the profession from its earliest days, albeit in small numbers. Their presence grew substantially in the 1970s following implementation of the Civil Rights Act of 1964. Even earlier, men had been influential, especially in the development of flight attendant trade unions.[39]

The relationship between male workers and the nostalgic flight attendant is complicated by common assumptions that men working on board are inevitably gay, to the annoyance of straight and gay males alike.[40] However, with the profession's gay subculture hardly a secret, evoking the "glamour days" would appear to reimpose heterosexuality as the *only* form of sexuality allowed at 35,000 feet, and to reconnect the job with the times when airlines marketed it as something akin to a dating service for future (straight) marriage partners.[41] Gay men—as opposed to the promise of straight young women—have never been a feature of airline marketing, though little evidence exists that airlines have considered their presence in the cabin a problem.[42] Though pilots, especially, no doubt concerned for their own sexuality, subjected male flight attendants to homophobic comments and behavior in the "early days" (i.e., the 1970s), reports of such attitudes among fellow flight attendants and passengers are fairly rare.[43] In fact, given the new security fears, many passengers may now find the presence of *any* men—presumed gay or straight—reassuring. Even though excluded from the nostalgic flight attendant image, male workers have not been subjected to company policies that effectively drive them from the industry.

The same cannot be said of "older" women workers. This is the group, I would argue, that is most excluded from the nostalgic flight attendant image. As scholar Carol Pollard has noted, "With flight attendants staying on the job longer, one of the more poignant concerns is that of reconciling aging in a profession that is known for its image of youth and beauty."[44] Some might suggest that older women—not gay men—are responsible for the absence of sexuality in the cabin. Healthy heterosexual hormones in the skies are the very things that older women presumably lack, their biological clocks having expired. In a society in which hetero*sexual* relations between older people are possibly regarded as more taboo than homosexuality, older women tend to be shunted to the sidelines, as any ex-Hollywood A-lister knows.[45] Yet here they are, still on board, bringing you your 7-Up. In a double blow, the nostalgic flight attendant not only juxtaposes today's flight attendants with those of yesterday but also holds a mirror up to reveal their former selves in the process. They had all once looked as glamorous as those Pan Am stewardesses on the arms of Leonardo DiCaprio.

What this does for the morale of older workers can be discerned in the comments of at least two fifty-year-old women who told me they quit because they "didn't feel comfortable" in the cabin any more. When one journalist writes, "Airlines are betting millions that Fifth Avenue or Paris style can help them stand apart from frumpy rivals," it does not take a rocket scientist to figure out just who symbolizes that frumpiness in the cabin.[46] According to one Delta flight attendant in her late forties (hardly "old" in societal terms these days), those new Kate Spade uniforms at Song only come in "small sizes." She had got the message: when Song recruited from Delta's existing pool of workers, the "frumps" did not apply.

Alongside real-life Southeast Asian flight attendants, the nostalgic version provides a model against which older women workers can be judged. As Bruce Handy, writing for *Vanity Fair,* suggests: "Stewardesses are what flight attendants were called once upon a time when they were uniformly young, single, slim, attractive and female."[47] The not-so-subtle message here is that today's crop is not really any of these things. "Why are they all so *old?*" a fellow British man asked me about transatlantic workers, clearly miffed at the absence of Catherine Zeta-Jones look-alikes in the cabin, a comment I have heard echoed by American men and women when I tell them about my research. Having won battles over forced retirement in the late 1960s, career-minded flight attendants became one of the most high-profile representatives of older women workers and were consistently in the public eye. Now they are being squeezed—sometimes literally—out of the space they created for themselves.

Back to the Sixties

There is an ultimate irony connected with the rise of the nostalgic flight attendant. The airline industry actually *is* trying to take the profession back to the 1960s, though in ways that have little to do with nostalgia. Airlines wanting to get rid of older women in the cabin are not basing their thinking around absent sexuality, though they may claim to be responding to passenger demand: rather, the problem is that these women are paid too much and have helped turn the job into a permanent career. Creating an image from which older women feel excluded is a handy human resources device to slash labor costs. As the geographer David Harvey has argued, underneath the cloak of post-modernity's web of images and nostalgic playfulness, hard political and economic forces are at work.[48] Before civil rights legislation came into force during the late 1960s and 1970s, the key thing that marked the flight attendant profession was its short tenure, with workers lasting on average eighteen months.[49] After the legislative impact of court decisions, workers could effectively stay indefinitely, as flight attendants turned the profession from a short-term position between college and marriage into a full-time vocation. In doing so, workers "spaced-out," as I call it, exerting considerable control over their lives, and amassed sizable pension obligations on the part of airlines to boot.

A permanent workforce in which women worked for in excess of thirty years was the last thing airlines wanted. Amid the current industry turmoil, with four of the top five U.S. carriers under Chapter 11 bankruptcy protection, they have a vested interest in going back to the transient 1960s. Of course, U.S. airlines can no longer overtly discriminate along the lines of gender, sexuality, age, or race. What they can do is create a job in which workers will not hang around for that long. As one flight attendant at low-cost carrier Air Tran said to me, "It's cheaper to train [us] than to keep [us]." Either burn workers out, or let them know that there is no pot of gold at the end of the rainbow. The profession is thus being subjected to what I term a "squeeze-in," whereby the very spaces that flight attendants have created for themselves—including the size of the uniform—are being seriously eroded. Stress levels will become too high, perks and externalities of the job too few, and pensions will be nonexistent. This may not get rid of "older women" per se; it will reduce the number of workers trying to make a career out of the job. And, as is the custom in industrial relations, the quicker the turnover of the labor force, the weaker that labor force is in terms of industrial muscle. It is no accident that the golden years of flight attendant activism—the 1970s—coincided with the job's establishment as a permanent career.[50] As Pat Friend, president of the Association of Flight Attendants commented to me, "I could tell you clearly that our employers would like to create an environment that makes it a short-term proposition. . . . It's the sixties all over again."[51]

In an industry that was among the pioneers of the most recent bout of globalization, U.S. flight attendants find themselves caught between the rock of massive structural changes at home and the hard place of competition from overseas-based crews.[52] At the moment, flight attendants at Chapter 11 Northwest Airlines have announced their fears that their airline intends to transfer all international flights to foreign-based crew. Outsourcing is on the march at the airlines as much as in other industries. As their male counterparts in heavy industry have experienced, flight attendants face a highly uncertain future in which the job *as a way of life* has changed, and will change, irrevocably. The nostalgic flight attendant, far from being a harmless vehicle to put the fun back into flying, is a harbinger of the profession's demise.

Space Matters

This book chronicles how a group of predominantly women workers turned a short-term, exploitative, and restrictive job with an image of triviality into a long-term professional career with almost unparalleled mobility and autonomy. I analyze how, just as they attained this, flight attendants have been confronted with forces driven by the dynamics of capitalism that have sought to undermine their achievement.

I concentrate mainly on female flight attendants, partly because the overwhelming majority—about 80 percent—of U.S. flight attendants are women. The job falls under what some have called "women's work" —the commercialized caring and service activities carried out for centuries by women in the domestic sphere. Examining the profession through the prism of gender sharpens the analysis.[53] Of course, what constitutes "gender" or, more precisely, normative gender expectations, is for the most part not naturally proscribed. In other words, women were not born to be flight attendants and men to be pilots. These gender expectations are, in sociological parlance, "socially constructed," not the product of biology. And, as such, they can therefore be challenged and changed. One of this book's stories is how flight attendants *contested* their prescribed gender roles both in the workplace and in society as a whole.

This is also a book about space. One of the benefits in thinking about flight attendants is that it allows us to think about space in practical—as opposed to abstract—terms and to appreciate its importance in our lives. Our lives are shaped by space at the same time that we, in turn, shape space. Often without actually realizing it, we engage continuously in spatial projects and adjustments: rearranging the furniture in our home, putting our seat back on a flight, figuring out a quicker route to work, deciding to embark on the South Beach Diet (thereby address-ing the "space" of our own bodies). We take a break from relationships to "get some space," possibly because one's partner is "cramping our space." We need to get "distance" on things; we climb up high build-ings to get a better view of the space around us. Anyone knows that the spatial act of "stepping back"—both literally and metaphorically—changes our perspective.

Space over Time

Space is often taken for granted. When it is juxtaposed with "time," it comes off the poor relation. Here is writer Jeremy Rifkin, for exam-ple: "All of our perceptions of self and the world are mediated by the way we imagine, explain, use and implement time."[54] It is true we live in a time-fixated society: try typing "time" into Google, and you will get more than a billion hits, three times the number for "space" and about the same number as for "space," "place," "food," and "sex" combined. Time obsession stalks the pages of self-help and lifestyle magazines, where families are given tips on how to save themselves from collapse through creating "quality time" and "downtime" with their kids.[55] We live in a world of "time binds" and "time crunches" and "24-hour rolling coverage," the latter de rigueur for any serious news network. On television, the series *24*, with its "real time" back-drop, a continuously running clock, has high ratings and has won nu-merous awards. Wal-Mart looks out for "time theft" among its employ-ees, a policy resonant of Michael Ende's children's fantasy *Momo*, in which the "time thieves" are on the loose and stealing from the inno-cent.[56] To redress economic and social imbalances in the United States, writes economist Juliet Schor in *The Overworked American*, "I . . . ad-vocate mandatory increases in free time."[57]

I am not disputing time's significance. As the old Pink Floyd song "Time" goes, "Every day is getting shorter, no one seems to find the time." But time obsession negates space's importance, or at least con-ceals the fact that every temporal problem has a spatial dimension, too. Americans are in a time bind, for instance, because they spend too much time traveling across space, driving between a series of disparate locations. In addition to advocating the increase in "free time," we should perhaps be suggesting things get built in closer proximity to one another. As well as "quality time," families lack "quality spaces" where they can all be together, hopefully something more substantial than the dystopian mealtime table portrayed in films such as *American Beauty* and *The Ice Storm*.

Space's position within a capitalist society has also often been taken for granted. The use of the "speedup" to increase worker exploitation is well known; the use of the "squeeze-in" is less recognized. Even Marx was guilty of assuming that space was a blank sheet over which essentially temporal battles—rooted in the old adage that "time is money"—between bosses and workers would be fought.[58] For instance, Marx's theory of surplus value—the difference between the value of a product and the actual price paid to labor in the form of wages—which forms the core of his analysis of capitalist profit making, is predicated on time, namely, how much *free time* the boss can extract from the worker.[59] Throughout the world, histories of the labor movement have documented struggles for limitations on working hours.[60] Less written about is the fact that all those struggles and meetings required a space in which to be held. Not only did workers want time to eat their lunch; they also wanted some*where* to eat it.

In recent years, geographers have begun to think more about the role of space within the process of capitalism.[61] Along the way, they have established that space—as much as time—has been fought over and contested, and that capitalism exploits and creates space in much the same way that it exploits and creates time. In his famous work, *The Production of Space,* the French philosopher Henri Lefebvre argues that every society produces its own space.[62] In other words, a society's spatial dimensions vary: compare, for instance, the spatial horizons of pre-Columbian Europe with those of today; or, for that matter, those of a child growing up in contemporary rural Angola with those of one growing up in suburban Los Angeles. Lefebvre transforms space from a dead, abstract concept to something alive and dynamic. Far from a neutral blank slate, space, like time—and indeed gender—can be conceptualized as a social construction determined and shaped by human beings. Thus, if things are constructed by human beings, they are never permanent or fixed in stone. Other human beings can, and often will, do something to change them. In a further example, the great wilderness areas of the national park system exist because of human decisions made in the early twentieth century, not because of "natural forces." And equally, today, as human priorities change, they are once more under threat.

When trying to find a group of women workers for whom space is of manifest importance, one need look no further than flight attendants. No other comparable income group travels the physical spaces of the planet to such an extent. In twenty-one years, for instance, flight attendant Diana Fairechild logged more than 10 million miles with Pan Am. Flight attendants can unaffectedly reel off the places and spaces of the globe they have been to, rather like a bartender listing cocktails.[63] But there is more to space than geographic distance.

The Three Phases of the "Space-Out"

My argument is that for most flight attendants, the job's main rewards have come in the form of what I call "spatial remuneration" as opposed to financial remuneration. Being a flight attendant has opened up new spatial experiences for women entering the profession, providing them with almost unique mobility. The rewards of freedom, flexibility, and control are what keep flight attendants in the job, even when the job itself is arduous, emotionally exhausting, disorienting, and often thankless.

The expression "space-out" describes how flight attendants have used the job through the years to earn "spatial remuneration." I choose the term "space-out" purposefully. It is a phrasal verb implying flight attendants are the active—and not passive—subject. It is also a nice reappropriation of an idiom normally associated with "airheadedness," just as this book seeks to reinterpret a group of workers stereotypically viewed as "ditzy Barbie Dolls." Finally, it partly resurrects the verb "to space" in its original, now obsolete, meaning, which was "to roam," a wonderfully mobile concept that is in keeping with the peripatetic nature of flight attendants' lives.

Chronologically, flight attendants "spaced-out" in three broad phases. In the "predestination phase," found in the very early years, from 1930 until the outbreak of World War II, flight attendants joined the profession as part of a wider group of middle-class women seeking to take advantage of new travel opportunities to step outside the home. Mobility per se, for this group of women, was subversive, as they used the automobile, especially, to reshape their spatial movements and general behavior patterns. Women flight attendants, who were all qualified nurses, took the mobility bug to another level, often because they—like many women at the time—were fascinated by flying. Most did not stay in the job long, perhaps a year at best. For them, "spatial remuneration" came from the job itself—the novelty of flight and sense of liberation it offered—*not* from the very limited list of destination cities on offer.

In the "destination phase," between the 1940s and the early 1970s, flight attendants were drawn to the career by the exotic lifestyle it offered.[64] Planes were flying more smoothly to far more destinations both in the United States and overseas. After the mid-1950s, jet travel added a further element of glamour. Women became flight attendants as a "stopgap," often straight out of college and wanting to see the world before settling down to marriage. Airlines encouraged them to conceptualize the profession thus, and most lasted about eighteen months before leaving. For them, "spatial remuneration" came from the spaces the job opened up to them in the form of destinations that were beyond the reach of their peer group at home. Simply moving around was no longer an end in itself, and where you went mattered.

The third phase of the "space-out," the "postdestination phase," runs from the early 1970s to the present. Women flight attendants have reshaped the career from stopgap to full-time profession. They are fascinated not so much with the job itself but with all the things they can do *outside* of the job. With the increasing importance of seniority, women are able to control their lives to a far greater degree than previously, setting their spatial schedules according to where they need to be and when. The average tenure of flight attendants is now about ten years. "Spatial remuneration" comes not from the job itself but from the sense of control it gives attendants over their lives. Like the first phase, destination is largely unimportant, but not for lack of choice. These flight attendants simply arrange their schedules to maximize time away from the job. Since 9/11 there have been increasing signs within the industry that the profession is moving back to the conditions associated with the destination phase, with the job reverting to a short-term, temporary status, staffed by people wanting to travel and then move on to other things.

For many flight attendants, the job's rewards came from the spaces it provided more than the income it returned. This is not to say that money was unimportant. Before deregulation in 1978, flight attendants could earn good money, though their pay has declined in relative terms since. Also, like many jobs these days, especially for parents, benefits are an increasingly important factor. But collective action by flight attendants—reasonably common through the years—has as often as not been about issues *other* than wages and, I would argue, has often been spatial in origin. Such action has ranged from fighting sexist advertising, and therefore taking control of the spaces of their bodies, to establishing rest periods, and somewhere to rest, on long-haul flights. And though airlines have never stopped thinking about the bottom line— and have consistently chipped away at flight attendant salaries—their current attempts to shed workers after 9/11 have revolved more around closing down those spaces of remuneration rather than hitting them with pay cuts. It is in this sense that the industry is currently implementing a "squeeze-in," whereby worker autonomy has become restricted.

Women fought to achieve this autonomy. They forged an identity through work, broke down gendered roles in the domestic and work spheres, practiced a geographic mobility hitherto largely reserved for men, and changed the image of their position from Barbie Doll to safety professional. In short, women redefined the job as a full-time career, not a stopgap, and exerted power in a previously male-controlled environment. Women, not men, would choose when they retired, had babies, and got married. Where airlines would prefer to market them as attractive service providers on board, flight attendants fought to establish themselves as first and foremost safety workers, here to "save asses, not kiss them," as they often like to say. This alone countered gendered assumptions that women were no good in a crisis. In creating an identity of safety professional, these women created a space that enhanced pride, confidence, and self-reliance, attributes that women have supposedly—and sometimes in actuality—historically lacked.[65]

The "Space-Out" in Action

To develop some of these points more fully, let us return to the tragic tale of Amy Sweeney, on Flight 11 on the morning of September 11, 2001. Amy was, first of all, a working mom. Like most working moms, she felt an element of guilt that morning for not being at home for her kids and wanted to let her daughter know she was sorry for not putting her on the kindergarten bus. Had Amy been flying in the days depicted by *Catch Me If You Can* or *Down with Love,* she would not have been faced with such a dilemma, because flight attendants were not allowed to have children or be married. American Airlines also would have considered Amy, at thirty-five, over the hill and would have given her a desk job or forced her out of the company altogether. So the autonomy in Amy's life, the choice to *be* a working mom and the space that comes with that—though perhaps tempered by guilt—was a product of her predecessor flight attendant sisters fighting to improve their working conditions.

In being a flight attendant and a working mom, however, Amy also inevitably worked at great distances from home, while her husband was left behind literally holding the baby. Though working moms are hardly a new phenomenon (indeed, they have been around for as long as paid work has existed) and modern households reflect a greater gender balance—but nonetheless still an imbalance—in domestic and child care responsibilities, flight attendants buck the trend in several respects. For one, women who work in other jobs, unlike flight attendants, still tend to do so in closer geographic proximity to home than their husbands, especially those employed in women-dominated professions.[66] Men are far more likely to clock up nights in faraway hotels than their wives are. Second, flight attendant moms are regularly away from home for longer periods than their counterparts in most other jobs. They are not just working late at the office or the store, comfortable in the knowledge that in a real emergency they could drop everything. They are in another city, another state, another country, and often another continent. In this scenario, their partners take on primary care tasks and become more heavily involved in their children's upbringing than most husbands. In other words, male spouses of flight attendants inevitably become house husbands for more substantial periods of time than with other employment groups. If this sounds like a happy working through of radical feminism's advocacy of androgyny, it is also a recipe for conflict as flight attendant moms often return home to suspect that dad has not been quite as good a mom as mom herself would have been. Still, in all the moving tributes to be found from friends on Internet obituary boards about Amy Sweeney, not one suggested that her husband, Michael, could not cope with raising their two children without her—perhaps because as a flight attendant's husband he had had more practice than most.

Amy had returned to work after the premature birth of her son. She took off the maximum amount of allowed time but, according to Michael, had "had to go back that fall to hold the Boston-L.A. trip." Here Amy "spaced-out" in two ways: first, given decent seniority—her twelve years would have provided reasonable collateral at a smallish base such as American's at Boston—she could command and control not only when she flew but where. She could even "pick up" an extra trip, perhaps making a little extra money in preparation for the holiday season. Amy could have picked other routes, but the transcontinental flights are among the most popular for flight attendants because they earn the "biggest bang for their buck," as one told me. Flight attendants have to fly a certain number of hours per month: for many, logic dictates that it is far preferable to do so in the minimum number of trips possible. One Boston-L.A. round trip on the weekend would be the rough equivalent of four round trips to New York dotted all over the week.

In short, Amy could manipulate her schedule to create space *away* from the job. Flying the minimum number of trips maximized the space in which she could do other things, like be at home with her family. And—crucially—her ability to control her schedule increased as she moved up the seniority list: when on "reserve," flight attendants have virtually no say over when and where they work. Indeed, even Amy Sweeney's autonomy was limited—she *had* to go back to work or she would have lost her place in line on the popular transcontinental route.[67]

"Well," one may ask, "couldn't she have just flown somewhere else?" This misses the point. Flying the Boston-L.A. route on weekends gave Amy Sweeney the space to become someone other than a mom for a small and limited part of her life. She had to go back to hold that route for none other than herself. And here is the second way she "spaced-out." If the first was to maximize her space at home—away from the job—the second was to maximize her space *away from home*. Being a flight attendant gives workers an alternative identity to that associated with home. From the tributes paid to Amy Sweeney, it was clear that it was the flight attendant *lifestyle*, not just a job, she loved, and for more than just money. It was a lifestyle that enabled her to have friends on both sides of the country who she could meet for lunch. It was a lifestyle that she clearly found addictive—with twelve years' seniority, Amy had gone through the traditional burnout points at which many flight attendants tend to quit.[68] Finally, it was a lifestyle that, guilt or no guilt, allowed her to get away temporarily from the kids and husband and to find her own space.

The Safety Professional

The last point in Amy Sweeney's story concerns the issue for which she became famous. In making that phone call from hijacked Flight 11, she, along with Betty Ong, has been rightly lauded. Her actions led to the state of Massachusetts establishing the Madeline Amy Sweeney Award for Civilian Bravery for state residents demonstrating "exceptional bravery, without regard for personal safety, in an effort to save the life or lives of another or others in actual imminent danger."[69] She also posthumously received the FBI's highest civilian honor, the Exceptional Public Service Award.

None of what I say here is meant to detract from the undoubted heroic actions of these women. Yet the most honest appraisal of Amy Sweeney's role in the horrific drama of Flight 11 came from her ex–police officer husband: "She would have said she was just doing her job."[70] Endless commentators have cited how Sweeney and Ong displayed "remarkable calmness" and "retained their professionalism" in making those phone calls. In fact, these are backhanded compliments, the suggestion being that this is somehow surprising. In moments of panic, according to traditional gendered stereotypes, women are supposed to become hysterical while men with the right stuff act with cool, detached rationality. The most famous catchphrase to emerge from 9/11, uttered by a male passenger on the ill-fated United Flight 93 as he led male passengers in their alleged conquest of the cockpit, was "Let's roll." Numerous flight attendants have expressed resentment that the documented actions of their colleagues on that flight, boiling water to throw on the terrorists, assembling ice hammers for use as weapons, were lost in the folklore of American men coming to the rescue.

Not one flight attendant I have spoken to registered amazement that Sweeney and Ong remained calm, confident, and professional under duress. If anything, they have been offended by people who have assumed it would have been anything different. They expressed admiration, empathy, sadness, and pride. But without ever saying the words, flight attendants communicated to me one thing: "This is what we do."

Compare that to the general astonishment among the public, with its eulogies to Sweeney's and Ong's "calmness." But when the dominant image the public has of flight attendants is continually stuck on entertainment figures from the 1960s, who can blame them? Readers will be able to think of plenty of flight attendants becoming hysterical in movies, including Gwyneth Paltrow in her first flight in *View from the Top*. They will struggle hard to recall images of flight attendants evacuating airplanes or saving lives, which is, in fact, why they are on board. The safety professional is a figure completely at odds with the nostalgic flight attendant of popular culture, and yet flight attendants still struggle to impose their gravitas, especially when the likes of Song and Hooters Air are taking flight attendant imagery backward.

The Ties That Bind: The Flight Attendant Community

The permanent status that being a full-time safety professional conferred on the job provided flight attendants with a footing from which they could "space-out" in the postdestination phase. In so doing, however, and in creating a strong work identity, flight attendants grapple with several psychological issues. On the one hand, numerous women claim the job has given them confidence. Training, especially, and the need to give clear and concise commands provided them with belief in their ability to "do things" from as serious as fighting an onboard fire to as mundane as learning how to drive on the "wrong" side of the road when in Ireland. That identity also cemented a space in which they could receive empathy from their fellow workers, an understanding based largely on the supposition that, as I have often been told, "no one else actually does understand us." On the jump seat, on those transcontinental flights, workers create space in which to find solace and support from other members of the flight attendant "family" (as it is often called) in such routines as "jump seat therapy," when the most intimate details are exchanged on a regular basis.

This sense of community is reinforced by a distinctive flight attendant vernacular. With their arcane terminology, flight attendants often sound as if they are talking another language entirely—small wonder no one else understands them. It is not just a question of specialist terms—many professions have these. There is also something distinctive about the way flight attendants speak that I began to appreciate when spending time with them. They are assertive and confident, but they also often speak in a "machine-gun" fashion, as though every sentence needs to be finished as rapidly as possible. And they often run ideas together in a peculiar way, as if trying to actually cram the thoughts needed for three completely different topics into the space of one sentence.

In the transformation from shyness to confidence, a flight attendant can seemingly become another person altogether, and attendants spend a good deal of their lives acting out roles, as they freely admit. As sociologist Arlie Hochschild has written, this transformation can sometimes be so complete that one is no longer sure where the acting stops and the "real" person begins.[71] Flight attendants are still subjected to such strict supervision that their very emotions and emotional responses become part of the passenger service. The core of what Hochschild calls "emotional labor," the smiles, the "thank-yous," and the codependent behavior, becomes a strain for workers, who can end up feeling numb and desensitized, especially when they finally arrive home exhausted and find that they have used up on their passengers all the love they have for their nearest and dearest. While one of the benefits of jump seat therapy is that it usually takes place among complete strangers—workers who have never met before and will not do so in the future—the career lends itself to a whole pattern of deep yet transient bonding, like a lifetime full of summer flings that ultimately becomes meaningless. Among this huge, close-knit family, quite a few flight attendants paradoxically feel dreadfully lonely. Finally, though flight attendants live peculiarly spatial lives, they also have an intensified relationship with time. They constantly project forward, consuming time in "chunks" or "sections" between which they sometimes switch roles and characters (this, again, is manifested in the way they speak). They spend so much effort projecting into the future, one wonders sometimes how they cope with the here and now.

Yet despite the drawbacks, flight attendants often establish a deep-rooted occupational identity that is difficult to shake.[72] When "no one else understands you," the chances are that bonds and loyalties will run thick, even after you have left the profession—an echo of other safety workers in male-dominated jobs such as firefighting. A nice example of this can be found in the monthly meetings of organizations such as Clipped Wings, groups of long-standing or retired flight attendants who get together to chew the fat, eat, raise money for charity, hear guest speakers, and reaffirm that, deep down, they are still flight attendants.[73]

One woman I met at a Delta Clipped Wings meeting in Atlanta had stopped flying in the 1950s, but she still thought of herself in such terms. "Once it's in your blood," she told me, "it never goes away." This deep sense of occupational identity spans generations: though retirees may complain about the standards of new hires, and, of course, younger workers do things today that older ones "would never have gotten away with," one only needs to spend time with a group of cross-generation flight attendants to witness this bonding in action. As sociologist Roberta Lessor points out: "The job itself has not escaped transformation, and [workers] have a lot to say about how different working is now from when they first started. However, the differences more specifically concern the conditions under which the work is done than the work itself."[74] This point still holds. Flight attendants tell me about changes in work conditions, especially about having less time for passengers and fewer flight attendants on board. But at the same time, the intrinsic qualities they find in the job, especially freedom and camaraderie, have remained essentially unchanged from the start of the profession. Airlines have realized this, and since 9/11 have targeted these qualities in an attempt to shed staff, especially older workers.

Modern Workers in a Postmodern World

Without being too grandiose, it would not be out of place to think of flight attendants inhabiting a quintessentially postmodern world. Postmodernism, perhaps best illustrated in films such as *Memento* and *Blade Runner*, celebrates and embraces the fleeting, the transient, and the superficial. It revels in kaleidoscopes of imagery, jumbled constructions of time and space, and consequent disorientation.[75] Flight attendants live in a world of constant coming and going, shifting characters and time zones, in airports and hotels that look almost identical the world over, forming relationships with workers and passengers alike that end as soon as they have begun, smiling at people whom they might actually sooner slap in the face, working within a family that is often more supportive than their real families back home, never quite sure when they will get wherever it is that they are heading, arriving in cities at an earlier time than they took off from the last one, and invariably running late.

And yet, though they may live in a postmodern world, flight attendants can also be thought of as quintessentially modern workers. Modernity, as the Marxist writer Marshall Berman reminds us, is a condition in which human beings try to construct something stable and comprehensible amid a sea of continual change, something solid even if everything we build melts into air before our very eyes.[76] This seems to me a pretty fair way of thinking about flight attendants who, having "spaced-out" their lives through their jobs and created a career and work identity that had purpose, suddenly find all those spaces being "squeezed-in," as their autonomy, their layovers, and their pensions dissolve into nothingness.

I am not suggesting that flight attendants are the *only* women workers who have created spaces for themselves in their jobs and who now find these spaces being squeezed.[77] The flight attendant experience is an *extreme* form of this phenomenon. I would argue that flight attendants had a greater uphill battle in establishing their job as a profession, experience more disorienting time and space patterns, juggle a larger number of sometimes conflicting roles, and have a greater sense of occupational identity than any other group of women workers. Studying them allows us to appreciate the role of the spatial "squeeze-in" within capitalism, as opposed to the more familiar temporal "speedup."

In the distance between "spacing-out" and the "squeeze-in," flight attendants therefore represent modern women workers in a postmodern world. As full-time safety professionals, flight attendants achieved a sense of indispensability, which fed their sense of autonomy; but as short-term workers, an arrangement the industry seems to be heading back toward, flight attendants once more enter the world of permanent impermanence. The sad irony is that the very things—the spaces—that Amy Sweeney loved about her job, and that led her to a cruel and premature death, are now the very things that are being squeezed from the colleagues she left behind.

The Flight Attendant Odyssey

This book is structured around a flight attendant's journey, including preparation, departure, flight, layover, and return. In chapter 1, I provide an overview of the job's history from its early nursing days, through the period when airlines depicted women as mother or sex goddess, respectively, and into the post-1978 deregulation period and beyond. I explore how flight attendants continually attempted to build something solid in an industry characterized by almost permanent technological and structural flux, and how their efforts culminated in the emergence of a full-time professional career.

In chapter 2, I explain how flight attendants bid for trips and the importance of seniority. More than half of U.S. flight attendants have dependent care responsibilities—either children or aging parents—and they thus juggle the job's needs with those of home.[78] Though they welcome the chance to pass on caring tasks to other family members, normally their spouse, flight attendants still find leaving for work emotionally taxing. They often follow tried-and-true routines, culminating in the switch into "flight attendant mode" in which their character takes on the identity of the job. However, they cannot escape home entirely, often trying to micromanage their families in advance preparation for their absence.

Establishing the job as a safety profession was imperative if flight attendants were to "space-out" in the postdestination phase. In chapter 3, I look at various safety issues in which these workers have become embroiled, from fatigue to air rage. I argue that attitudes toward safety have been—and continue to be—gendered in the sense that flight attendants have had to fight continuously to be taken seriously. Paradoxically, after 9/11, flight attendants finally won certification as safety professionals at exactly the time when their jobs were most under threat. At the time of writing, they remain outside the ambit of Occupational Safety and Health legislation, an indication that they still face challenges in being treated as safety workers first and foremost.

Chapter 4 follows on from this discussion of safety, dealing with flight attendant challenges to clichéd and stereotypical imagery used by airlines in marketing campaigns. As I argue, the spaces of flight attendants' bodies have been fair game for airlines, which not only attempted to exploit women's sexuality—as some Asian airlines still do—but also historically have placed severe bodily controls on their workers. Flight attendants have constantly had to battle airlines over such controls, especially weight, which reimpose gender hierarchies. Yet at the same time, as historian Cathleen Dooley argues, while flight attendants objected to airlines exploiting their bodies for their own ends, they also often felt empowered by their ability to conform to a dominant heterosexual construction of beauty. Rather than battling the "beauty myth" per se, flight attendants battled for control over it, paradoxically subverting their position of centrality within airline marketing.[79]

In chapter 5, we take to the air, with a discussion of flight attendant routines on board. Here flight attendants engage in rituals such as jump seat therapy, exchanging all sorts of advice and confidential counseling with workers who may be complete strangers. I argue that flight attendants have created an "occupational community," whereby they bond closely with anyone else who wears the uniform. This bonding finds expression in the strong solidarity shown by flight attendant unions, one of the reasons airlines have sought to undermine it.

Chapter 6 deals with one of the job's most important aspects: the layover. It is here that flight attendants create the space of an alternative home to which they can escape from the pressures of their real ones. Despite guilt at leaving their families, flight attendants with small children, for instance, relish the opportunity to sleep in, take long baths, watch television, read, or do a host of other things that would be impossible if they were needed for parenting duties. For women, especially, the confidence that comes from training enables them to negotiate unfamiliar places and cities and fuels their sense of geographic liberation and mobility. There is also the issue of keeping in touch with home, however. Flight attendant mothers, especially, inhabit a double bind of enjoying getting away and yet feeling guilty once they do. The shared experiences and camaraderie of their fellow workers help in this regard, though flight attendants also suffer from disorientation and loneliness. Their response is to create an alternative home, populated by an alternative family, that is more relaxing than the home or family they have left behind. Flight attendants often claim that being able to get away keeps a marriage fresh and contributes to the relatively low rates of divorce in the profession.[80]

No matter how happy they have been while away, all flight attendants must eventually return to their real homes. Chapter 7 looks at how they do this. Just as they go through set departure routines, so they often go through a series of rituals on return. Most come home tired and disoriented, and many have problems being immediately intimate with their loved ones. The potential for deferred conflict and unresolved issues is high, and flight attendant parents can also overcompensate for their absences. There is an ultimate paradox in that the job's peculiar demands can place so much pressure on the home front that flight attendants' only escape route is to go back to the job again. In other words, the job becomes a safety valve from the problems it actually helps to create.

In the concluding chapter I examine specifically the "squeeze-in." Airlines have increasingly squeezed flight attendant autonomy since 9/11 in a major industry restructuring. Carriers have sought to undermine the notion of the career as a long-term prospect and to force senior flight attendants out of the industry. The power of seniority, one of the ways in which flight attendants gained control of their spatial movements, will become eroded. Flight attendants will increasingly "space-out" in conditions akin to the destination, not postdestination, phase, and turnover rates will increase, reducing union power in the process. In short, the lifestyle that flight attendants created will become increasingly a thing of the past. That said, I suggest how flight attendants can continue to shape their job, through stressing their safety role and increasing their emphasis on certification, much as nurses have done over the last few years.

Pizza with Ellen

Prior to beginning the research for this book, I had already explored flight attendant labor and gender issues in the United Kingdom (where workers are more accurately called "cabin crew"). However, my earlier studies involved talking to union leaders and cabin service managers, and I had little contact with flight attendants themselves. In the fall of 2002, I set off to meet my first real-life flight attendant interviewee.

Ellen had recently retired from Delta, where she had worked since the early 1970s. On the way to our meeting at a local pizza place in Atlanta, I realized I had no idea what she looked like. But I had no difficulty recognizing her: about five feet two inches high, with a neat graying bob, she was both staring straight ahead and simultaneously taking in everything going on in her peripheral vision. In fact, rather like a hawk, she had spotted me long before I spotted her. "You must be Drew," she said in her southern drawl. "Well, hey!"

Two things struck me during that initial meeting. First, though I had turned up fully expecting to hear tales of labor and gender exploitation, Ellen's opening words were about the benefits provided by the job's flexibility. She spoke less about the job's constraints and more about its spaces of opportunity. Mothers of young children, she told me, often fly weekends while their partners look after the kids; some fly all night and are home in time to take over from their partners before they leave for work. Other flight attendants double up with second jobs in their spare time, working in real estate, teaching, or antique dealing. In short, she was telling me that flight attendants were a group of workers with far more control over their individual space and time than I had ever imagined.

Second, while I was interviewing Ellen I also had the distinct impression that she was actually *interviewing me*. More than just questions asking about my home in England (displaying a disarming knowledge of the English soccer scene) and commenting on shared experiences of Brighton (the English south coast resort that was long Delta's choice of layover), I realized that she was figuring out if I was for real.

Over the next three and half years, I interviewed other flight attendants, often coming away with the same impression. I do not mean that flight attendants were ever aggressive, or that I was ever made to feel unwelcome. The workers I spoke to were merely acting as gatekeepers, making sure that I was sufficiently bona fide in my intentions to be welcomed into their world. Deeply protective of their profession, flight attendants seemed to be making sure I was not going to misrepresent them in the way that they have often been misrepresented, and deciding whether or not they could trust me enough to pass on other potential interviewee names. This was my first contact with this community, and I could tell from the outset that they were a close-knit group.

Ellen got the ball rolling. She gave the first of some seventy interviews I subsequently conducted with flight attendants, as well as six focus groups.[81] Given that I live in Atlanta, most participants were from Atlanta-based Delta Air Lines. United Airlines formed the second-largest group, followed by Air Tran and Atlantic Southeast Airlines (ASA). I also spoke to individuals from Continental, Song, American, Northwest, Skywest, World Airways, and US Air and a handful of corporate flight attendants. In addition to interviewing in Atlanta, I spoke to workers in Washington, D.C., San Francisco, and Los Angeles. I also had numerous conversations at the back of airplanes as I zigzagged across the country and to Europe and South America. Finally, I conducted a handful of comparative interviews with workers in the United Kingdom, as well as with representatives from the Association of Flight Attendants in Washington, D.C., and the International Transport

Workers Federation (ITF) in London. Though this book is about U.S. flight attendants, it would paint an incomplete picture without the global dimension.[82]

At the end of some of the interviews, I had the sense that I was disembarking. "Thank you," I would say, shaking my interlocutor's hand. "Thank you," they would often say back. On one occasion my interviewee repeated her thanks. "At last," she said, "someone has finally listened to our story." I hope to have done it justice.

1

Briefing
From Stewardess to Flight Attendant

Flying unsupported through space gave one a godlike impersonality. For those who could tear themselves loose from the earth there was a reward. Not in the physical release only, but in a mental freedom which swept the brain clean of cobwebs and gave one a perspective which made such tragedies as broken hearts shrink from mountains to molehills.

—Vida Hurst, *Air Stewardess*, 1934[1]

One evening in January 2005, I was driving northbound to LAX on Interstate 405 with a United flight attendant, Rebecca. Rebecca had spent most of the day worrying and venting about her job and what the future held. Would her new Denver base be an improvement on her old one in Washington? Would bankrupt United survive? And even if it did, what would life be like for its flight attendants, threatened with chaotic schedules and scrapped pension schemes? As we drove, Rebecca directed my attention out of the right-hand window. As far back as the eye could see, airplanes on approach banked and circled over the Puente Hills before forming a neat vector, one after another, coming in to Los Angeles. "Oh, my god!" exclaimed Rebecca. "Look at that! I just *love* that sight. It's like a dance in the sky."

Just as the best dancing can transport us to another dimension, for flight attendants, flying has long been a means of breaking free from the limitations of terra firma. As Barbara Dorger, a recent United retiree, suggests in her memoirs, "We traveled on a wave of energy, spending much of our time in the air—not on the earth—in a timeless kind of space. A space of serving others. A space we enjoyed."[2]

From their first hiring in 1930, women attempted to "space-out" their lives through taking to the air, even if few hung around for more than a year or two. Flight attendant imagery became increasingly important to airlines seeking to create brand identity and to differentiate themselves from their competitors. On the one hand, carriers exploited the spaces of their workers' bodies and sold "femininity"; on the other, women used the job for their own ends and, with time, capitalized on their centrality in airline marketing to reclaim their bodies from the advertising gurus. As I argue here, flight attendant history is the story of how women took the job and turned it into a full-time profession. Though they often took to the skies under strict patriarchal conditions, women flight attendants carved out a niche for themselves and ultimately challenged those restrictions. In doing so, they "spaced-out" in different ways, from being thrilled just to be airborne, to being excited by exotic locations, and then to being satisfied with being able to exert control over their movements.

Breaking Free: Women and Early Flight

Human beings have long been obsessed with flight. Nearly all civilizations have imbued it with mythical and mystical powers, the prerogative of the gods or, conversely, those with evil intent. Yet within these fantasies, flying female figures have often been disconcerting: even ancient societies reflected a gender bias suggesting women in the air could only bring trouble. In Greek mythology, for instance, notwithstanding the diminutive figure of Nike (the goddess of victory), a whole collection of nasty airborne females, such as the Furies, Harpies, and even Medusa, were primed to exact retribution on the unfortunate and hapless.[3] More recently, Christianity, from the fifth century on, provided the former nonflying—and essentially harmless—pagan "witch" with aerial powers to accentuate her diabolism, as she hurtled around on her phallic broomstick. Alternatively, priests warned of witches taking on the shape of owls or ravens, while "old crow" is a term reserved for a miserly woman, presumably no longer able to fly. For a generation of American children, fear's personification arrived in the words of a flying woman, when the Wicked Witch of the West in *The Wizard of Oz* cackled, "I'll get you, my pretty. And your little dog, too!" For a group of nineteenth-century Portuguese farmers, Satan incarnate turned up in the form of a descending woman balloonist who, having taken off from Lisbon, apparently got lost and had to make an unexpected landing. According to a report in the 1850 *Scientific American,* "some villagers fled, others fell to their knees in prayer; others gathered weapons and offered defiance to the devil."[4]

One of the originators of communications theory, Marshall McLuhan, has described how new technologies produce new forms of human emotion and feeling.[5] The airplane is certainly a case in point, opening up new vistas of freedom and escape. But women who dreamed of dancing in the sky faced a long history of prejudice. If not actually viewed as devils, they were somehow unnatural, a proposition held by many men, for instance, toward pioneering women pilots at the start of the twentieth century. Early barnstorming air shows marketed women aviators as freaks and drew large crowds in response. Following several female fatalities before World War I, the *New York Times* opined: "It would be well to exclude women from a field of activity in which their presence is unnecessary from any point of view."[6] It was fine for men to crash, but women crashing was "outside the realm of the natural," writes historian Eileen Lebow.[7]

It was not until Amelia Earhart captured public attention in the late 1920s that society began to be more accepting of women aviators. For Earhart, however, flying was a tool—one she clearly loved—enabling women to challenge gendered and biological assumptions about what they could and could not do.[8] As fellow flier Margery Brown argued, though perhaps in un-Earhart language, "Women are seeking freedom. Freedom in the skies. They have soared above temperamental tendencies of their sex which have kept them earthbound. Flying is a symbol of freedom from limitation."[9] Yet for all the efforts of women aviators, they found it hard to break into the traditional male domain of the airline cockpit (a loaded term if ever there was one). In 1934 the first documented female airline pilot, Helen Richey, lasted only a year at Central Airlines due to opposition from the all-male Airline Pilots Association (ALPA). Subsequently, no woman pilot would be employed by U.S. airlines until the 1970s.[10]

Under the 1925 Kelly Act, U.S. carriers' main responsibility was to transport mail. Passengers were a bonus, and cabin service amounted to thermos coffee and sandwiches passed by the pilot to the intrepid handful who may have been on board. Following the "Lindbergh boom" of the late twenties—when flying suddenly captured the nation after the aviator's first solo transatlantic crossing—several airlines began to copy European carriers in employing male attendants on board. Pan Am, for instance, began using male stewards in 1928 and delayed introducing women until 1944.[11]

Ellen Church and the Invention of the Profession

Despite prejudice and restrictions, some women were determined to fly, and the story of how airlines eventually came to employ them illustrates how they used any means possible to fulfill this ambition. In 1930, Ellen Church, a graduate nurse and flying enthusiast, was a regular visitor at Boeing Air Transport's (later United Airlines) office in San Francisco, where she pestered the district traffic manager, Steve Stimpson, about getting a job in aviation. Stimpson at the time wanted to foster a greater sense of care and comfort on board flights through the use of stewards.[12] Airlines in those days were less in competition with each other than they were with the railroads. Flight times were not much quicker than rail travel; moreover, airlines were up against a well-established service culture in the form of long-distance Pullman workers. In comparison to rickety, bone-shaking airplanes, rail could offer security, safety, and service in ample measures. Indeed, airlines attempted to "soften" the aircraft cabin by designing it to resemble the more familiar railcar.[13]

Ellen Church suggested to Stimpson that Boeing employ women nurses on board instead of male stewards. In turn, Stimpson approached his supervisors, and, though it initially was reluctant, Boeing eventually introduced the "Original Eight" "stewardesses"—all single nurses in their twenties—on its Chicago–San Francisco route, with a stopover in Cheyenne, Wyoming.[14]

The stewardess profession was thus invented by a woman. Like many of her contemporaries, fired up by nascent first-wave feminism and aviator heroines such as Earhart, Church wanted to fly. She would have preferred to have been a copilot but realized this was impossible at a commercial airline. She thus invented a position that would enable her to take to the air. Church was thus "savvy," according to flight attendant and historian Georgia Nielsen, "in making inroads for women within the pioneering airline industry, which manipulated masculine symbols that were so blatantly a part of aviation."[15] "Spacing-out" in this phase was directly linked to women's greater mobility in general. Middle-class women, in particular, were on the move, with the automobile especially acting as a conduit for a new spatial freedom. Flight attendants at this stage were not worried about destination. They were happy enough just to *go,* and where they went was unimportant.

However, though Church took the initiative, it was Stimpson who recognized stewardesses' full marketing power. He telegrammed the following to top management at Boeing:

> It strikes me that there would be a great psychological punch to having young women stewardesses. . . . I have in mind a couple of graduate nurses that would make exceptional stewardesses. . . . Imagine the psychology of having young women as regular members of the crew. Imagine the national publicity we would get from it, and the tremendous effect it would have on the traveling public. Also imagine the value they would be to us not only in the neater and nicer method of serving food but looking out for the passenger's welfare.[16]

An element of gimmickry therefore informed the decision to employ flight attendants, but this was overshadowed by two pillars of Stimpson's "psychological punch." First, if young "girls" were not afraid of flying, then business*men* should not be either, at a time when the traveling public still distrusted aviation safety. Second, if men *were* still afraid up there in the clouds, who better than a nurse to look after them? This appeal appeased not only male passengers but also, importantly, their fearful, landlocked wives. Nurses on board simultaneously distracted male passengers from worrying about danger and reassured them they would be in good hands should apparent danger somehow become more real.[17]

Church and her colleagues thus entered into something of a Faustian pact: they got to fly, but in the process airlines claimed proprietorship over their bodies and began to market their femininity. Thus began a trade-off that would be continually renegotiated over the next seventy-odd years, forming the basis of what Arlie Hochschild calls "emotional labor," whereby flight attendants' feelings and emotional responses become part of the onboard service.[18]

Reserving the cockpit for men and the cabin for women ensured commercial aviation's gendering at an early stage: male pilots and mechanics looked after the technological hardware of the industry, while women flight attendants looked after the software, the cabin, and the passengers. Though airlines continued to employ some male stewards, the profession became heavily feminized—both in numbers and in imagery—by the mid-1930s. As historian Suzy Kolm suggests, the stewardess provided airlines with a marketing weapon they could unleash against the railroads, one that came with a racial subtext: white, sophisticated, educated women versus black, male Pullman workers, a subtext reinforced when carriers banned tipping in the airplane cabin.[19]

However, for those women who wanted to fly, being a stewardess was better than nothing. Indeed, if anything, early stewardesses actively encouraged marketing of their femininity. It was stewardesses who most vociferously stressed the job's hostess requirements and who argued that only women could really perform these tasks properly. But though stewardesses reinforced gender stereotypes with such messages, in the process they provided strategic protection for their jobs. By emphasizing the "feminine" requirements to be a stewardess, women would not encounter opposition from men worried about losing their jobs to the other sex.[20]

The Profession's Early Days

In the early days, being a stewardess was more arduous than glamorous, as women worked in a cold, unpressurized cabin, flying at several thousand feet, where every bump would have measured high on the Richter scale. A good deal of stewardesses' time was spent assisting passengers in various stages of vomiting.[21] At United, part of their job description was to make sure seats were bolted down properly and to prevent passengers from opening the fuselage door while seeking the bathroom. For all the airlines' attempts to suggest otherwise, flying was still a haphazard experience, and stewardesses carried rail timetables with them in case a plane was grounded. If passengers did need to continue their journey by rail, stewardesses were expected to accompany them to the nearest station.[22]

Most airlines followed United and began to hire nurses as stewardesses. Nurses appealed partly because passengers often genuinely needed medical attention but also because they came from a regimented background that easily fit into airlines' quasi-military culture. Nurses had long experience in deferring to male experts in the form of doctors and therefore, so the theory went, would have no trouble in doing so with male pilots.[23] Only middle-class white women were hired. Generally between twenty-one and twenty-six years in age, weighing between 110 and 125 pounds, air hostesses (as they were then known) had to combine charm and personality with their nursing skills. For instance, Delta's first recruitment advertisements, in 1940, asked for "Eight Hostesses: Can you qualify? . . . Prefer Poise, Personality, Pulchritude." Alongside their nursing qualifications, Delta applicants had to be "knowledgeable about current affairs [and to] carry on an intelligent conversation." Keeping up with baseball, notably the Atlanta Crackers, Delta's hometown city's much-loved minor league team, was a particular advantage for potential recruits.[24]

Early stewardesses inhabited an ambivalent space. They were disposable, in the sense that if the plane was too heavy they were the first thing to be left behind (mail always took priority). Airlines also attempted to restrict their movement. At United they were not allowed to mix with pilots or passengers when off duty. At Delta, whose southern roots made it particularly protective of its young, unattached women, pilots and stewardesses stayed in separate hotels when on a layover. According to Delta's first stewardess, Birdie Bomar, "High moral and ethical standards were not only expected, but demanded."[25]

Even with such restrictions, pilots (and their wives) viewed stewardesses with suspicion. One of United's original workers, Inez Keller, recalls:

> The pilots didn't want us at all and were not enthusiastic about women as crew members. They were rugged and temperamental characters who wore guns to protect the mail. They wouldn't even speak to us during the first couple of trips. The wives of the pilots began a letter-writing campaign to Boeing, saying the stewardesses were trying to steal their husbands and requesting their removal.[26]

Some of the older pilots at Western Air Lines may have "preferred an engine fire to the presence of women aboard a flight," but copilots, who were relieved of host duties, were more welcoming.[27]

Yet women stewardesses quickly became indispensable. Despite the rigors of the real job, in which two of the Original Eight quit within four months, they approached iconic status in Depression America, with a whole new genre of novels relaying tales of bold young women restricted by their background but finding liberation in the skies.[28] Naturally, they also found love and eventually marriage, the latter of which immediately grounded them because by the mid-1930s most airlines insisted their stewardesses had to be single. Meanwhile, movies such as *Air Hostess* (1933) conveyed similar—if more dramatic—themes, and by middecade stewardesses were also beginning to appear in advertisements, not just for airlines. Photographs of stewardesses rubbing shoulders with—or at least waiting on—celebrities also cemented the job's glamorous appeal.[29]

On top of the glamour, however, society also recognized stewardesses' important safety role. During the 1930s, flying was still relatively dangerous, and by 1942 eleven stewardesses had been killed on United alone.[30] Yet, according to *Life* magazine in March 1937, despite five crashes in as many weeks in the United States, "public confidence . . . is still as great as it is in air transport due in no small measure to the air hostess whose cheery presence in the plane bolsters morale."[31] This cheery presence not only boosted morale: in a crash, stewardesses saved people's lives. By 1941, with its professional nursing background and increasing safety role, the job of stewardess had achieved a certain gravitas.

The Impact of World War II

The number of airline passengers doubled, from 3.5 million to 7 million, between 1940 and 1945.[32] Wartime required a substantial increase in the movement of people; at the same time, better airplanes and airports made flying a more feasible alternative to rail. As a consequence, the number of flight attendants also increased, from about 1,000 to more than 4,000 between 1941 and 1947.[33]

As trained nurses, existing flight attendants were logically drafted into the military, and airlines abolished nursing requirements and prohibitions on marriage for their replacements. In fact, as Birdie Bomar writes, "Air travel had progressed to the point where registered nurses were not thought to be as necessary to the welfare of passengers as they had been in the past."[34] In short, the nursing requirement was almost certainly doomed anyway, and the war merely provided airlines with a pretext for its swift eradication. Unlike the marriage ban, they did not reinforce it at war's end.[35]

Removing the nursing requirement downskilled stewardesses and undermined any claims to professional status they may have had at that point.[36] Claiming the nursing side to the job was increasingly obsolete also tacitly implied that the industry was on the way to solving health and safety issues, certainly those as mundane as airsickness. In removing the "nurse," airlines could then set about playing up the job's service side. Though carriers had already begun this process in the mid-1930s, they now did so with far greater assiduousness. As advertising in general became more sophisticated, airlines began to construct their own identity or "brand" around their flight attendants. The justification for having women on board shifted from alleviating fear to alleviating boredom, as new technology made long-distance flying increasingly viable but also increasingly uneventful. Airlines needed to reinvent their workers as entertainers, a process that began during the war and continued up to the 1970s.

Regulation in the Industry

The marketing of stewardesses was largely a product of the industry's institutional structure, which was heavily regulated at both the national and the international level. Nationally, all route awards were established by the Civil Aeronautics Board (CAB), set up in 1940 to prevent a vital strategic industry falling victim to overcompetition. The CAB supervised all interstate aviation, route awards, fares, and accident investigation. Under the later Federal Aviation Act of 1958, the Federal Aviation Agency (FAA), changed to the Federal Aviation Administration in 1967, assumed much responsibility for navigation, safety, and aeronautics. The CAB was abolished by the Airline Deregulation Act of 1978.

The airline industry in the late 1930s was also brought under the auspices of the Railway Labor Act (RLA) of 1926.[37] Though not actually part of the act, an ultimate sanction is presidential intervention (as happened in 1993 during a flight attendant strike before Thanksgiving at American Airlines). The RLA set up a clear system of collective bargaining, through the National Mediation Board, in which contracts are deemed to be active up to the point they are renegotiated. Contracts are determined at the individual carrier level (as opposed to industry-wide). Though the RLA did not provide the same boost for union organization as did the 1935 Wagner Act, it still set up clear policies for union drives, recognition, and bargaining.[38]

International aviation was institutionalized in 1944 under the Chicago Convention, called by the Allied powers to establish rights and responsibilities of individual nations with respect to their airspace and foreign flag carriers. The convention established a number of "freedoms," providing a framework for emergency assistance and route awards. "Fifth freedom" rights (also known as cabotage) subsequently proved the most controversial because they prohibited airlines from operating beyond their country of origin (as an example, Delta could not operate an internal flight between Paris and Marseilles). Since 1990, many of these restrictions have been removed.

The net effect of all these regulations was that price competition, save for a few exceptions, was generally not allowed at either the national or the international level, and airlines therefore had to find other ways of competing and differentiating themselves from their rivals. One way, logically, would be to use different airplanes. However, most carriers operated similar models, and little competitive advantage existed between them based on their aircraft fleets.[39] As an alternative, airlines increasingly marketed their stewardesses.

Branding: Flight Attendants Become a Marketing Weapon

Despite greater numbers of people flying and increasing capacity of new aircraft, airlines still feared an expanding market could become a battle over an existing market.[40] Carriers needed more subtle and sophisticated ways of differentiating themselves from their rivals and of creating a product brand and company identity. As advertising budgets grew, airlines increasingly turned to their flight attendants, who, by the 1950s, had become their most readily identifiable public persona. As historian Frieda Rozen comments:

> Public relations experts made increasing use of stewardesses in advertising and publicity during the 1950s. They called press conferences, with stewardesses there to be photographed, on every imaginable anniversary or whenever they had concocted another statistic about the number of miles stewardesses walked on a plane, the number of bottles they had heated for infant passengers, or the number who had retired because of marriage.[41]

Flight attendant imagery soon assumed a domesticated appearance that matched the social conservatism of the Eisenhower years. As the government urged women who had gone to work during the war to return home and start producing American families—enticed by cheap home loans and suburban housing developments—airlines began to offer a fused vision of both actual and potential mother and wife in the cabin.

The Flight Attendant as Mother

Babies and mothers began to feature heavily in advertising campaigns of the time. For instance, TWA ran two advertisements in the early 1950s. One bore the slogan "Where *on earth* could you find such service?" and showed an air hostess bringing a meal to a bug-eyed child, with his approving mother looking on. The copy claimed, "Guest-of-honor attention anticipates your needs, caters to every wish and satisfies your new-found appetite with a meal you'll talk about for days!" The second advertisement depicted a mother and baby disembarking, with the flight attendant about to tousle the baby's hair. "The RIGHT formula for traveling with a baby," reads the text. "We get praised to the skies by mothers traveling with small children. And kind of like it, too."[42]

Of course the salient point here lies in the subtext. Though it was true that more women—and women with children—were flying, the bottom line for any airline remained its male business passengers, and it was at this group that such advertisements were surely aimed.[43] TWA was not demonstrating feminine solidarity here: it was showing what perfect wives and mothers its flight attendants (all of whom were single) could be. This message was also aimed at potential flight attendants themselves. What better way of demonstrating your skills as a future wife than to do so as a respectable single flight attendant? This was in fact "dog whistle" advertising, where the only potential flight attendants who could "hear" what the ad was saying were also the type that airlines would want to have applying for the job. Thus flight attendants self-selected themselves even before they had begun the application process.[44]

A good example of the kind of flight attendant branding airlines developed after World War II can be found at Delta. Having hired flight attendants relatively late in the industry, in 1940 the southern-based carrier lost no time in placing them at the center of its regional-based identity. Delta's flight attendants became the embodiment of southern hospitality, an amalgam of home, family, hostess, southern belle, and ultimately implied coquetry.[45]

From the outset, Delta's flight attendants exuded southernness. One article from 1944 noted the company's "sugar voiced" new hires, whose accents were "as typical of Dixie as 'cawnpone.' "[46] With postwar expansion, these women became increasingly central to Delta's image. By the mid-1950s, the airline's in-house journal, *Delta Digest*, annual reports, and advertisements were regularly portraying those delivering meals to happy, satisfied passengers (or, more accurately, staged actors).

Delta's southern belles, marketed like debutantes at a coming-out ball, featured heavily in the airline's postwar expansion and embodied the confidence of a renascent South. "Delta brings the warmth of Southern hospitality to Washington skies," one 1955 advertisement announced, depicting a flight attendant behind a DC-7.[47] Wrapped in *Gone with the Wind*–style rhetoric, Delta's flight attendants could play Scarlett O'Hara in the cabin. Equally, United liked to promote a "midwest small-town girl" image. Writing about United's stewardesses in the introduction to Georgia Nielsen's *From Sky Girl to Flight Attendant*, industrial relations professor Alice Cook notes, "The image was precisely that of the girl next door—neat, nice, and good enough for your son to marry."[48]

As flight attendants became more central to an airline's identity, they also became subjected to greater controls upon their appearance. Carriers opened new dedicated training facilities, akin to military boot camps, where recruits were put through the mill in the knowledge that only the very best would survive.[49] Hiring regulations continued to stress figure, age, marital status, beauty, personality, perfect physical condition (including skin, legs, and hair), and willingness to retire at thirty or thirty-two (many workers had to sign agreement forms). "Good teeth, obviously," one writer noted in 1950, "are essential prerequisites."[50] Once accepted, United flight attendants, for instance, were given a checklist before boarding. It read, "Stewardess, is your . . .

- Smile friendly and sincere?
- Posture erect and poised?
- Makeup neat and natural?
- Nails manicured and polished?

- Ribbon new and trimmed?
- Gloves white and tailored?
- Uniform cleaned and pressed?
- Purse orderly and polished?
- Shoes repaired and shined?
- Insignia on?
- Hair short and styled?
- Hose seams straight?
- Slip not showing?[51]

Girdles were mandatory (indeed, they would be up to the 1970s), and supervisors would pat women on their hips to make sure they were being worn before takeoff. Pregnancy was grounds for dismissal, though airlines also persuaded women to give babies up for adoption should they want to continue flying.[52]

"Spacing-Out" in the Destination Phase

There is no doubt that airlines during the 1950s both methodically used young women's sexuality and increasingly sought to control it as a vehicle to making a profit for their shareholders. This was gendered labor on a significant scale. But at the same time, women were not passive agents. For all the talk in the 1950s of women being constrained, they fought those constraints at a wider societal level. Ironically, in taking women out of the home—even if for only a few years—and getting them to play faux mothers in the sky, the airlines were actively encouraging them to "space-out" in the destination phase and to break down traditional gendered expectations.

Again, Delta's flight attendants provide a good example. Alongside Scarlett O'Hara the putative southern belle, there is also Scarlett O'Hara the self-reliant, resourceful, take-no-prisoners southern woman.[53] On the one hand, Delta clearly marketed and sold southern womanhood. But on the other, it provided paid employment and opened up geographic vistas to a generation of small-town southern women. In 1947, for instance, the airline employed 80 flight attendants; by 1960, with the arrival of jets, there were more than 500.[54] In stressing an identity based on southern womanhood, the airline actually turned a group of southern women into paid employees—a southern belle's antithesis.[55]

And instead of thinking that the biggest town in the world was Atlanta, these women were now traveling to New York and, by the mid-1960s, to California on a regular basis.

Like other airlines, Delta replaced its nursing prerequisite with a mandatory two-year college requirement. New hires were therefore educated women, drawn from the middle class and not from the stock of southern women increasingly becoming shop girls or receptionists. Numerous interviewees told me how their alternative choices were teaching, nursing, or marriage. Becoming a flight attendant was a way out of this dilemma, the job's obvious attraction being the ability to fly and the opportunity to see beyond the small southern towns where Delta often recruited. For instance, Hazel started flying for Delta in the 1950s. She recalls:

> When I went to Delta for my interview, I was so excited and everything, and I promptly went out and got on the wrong plane. The agent got me and put me on the right flight. That was my first flight. We were the type of women, we were the type of girls, I guess, we were fresh out of college, the whole world was our oyster, but we were so innocent. You know, that was strictly back in the total family era. Mother, daddy, church, home. Entertainment at home. Stuff like that. And so that was our personality. So innocent to this brand-new new world that was exciting and glamorous and scary.

Deirdre also started flying for Delta in 1950. She offers this description:

> It's something I always wanted to do. In fact, I went to my [high school] class reunion this past Saturday, and one of the girls that was there, she wrote the "future plans" in the yearbook of every girl in our class of what they would be doing, what they would do, and she said that I would become a stewardess for Eastern airlines. So it did come to pass, and I did start flying, but I told her, I said, you were right about everything except I flew for Delta and not for Eastern.

Increasing Union Power

Women were also active in workplace organization. In 1951, the Air Line Stewardesses and Stewards Association (ALSSA) held its inaugural conference, having been formally incorporated by ALPA two years earlier.[56] In 1952, the CAB confirmed flight attendants' importance in emergency evacuation, making their presence compulsory on all flights with seating capacity for ten or more passengers. They were therefore not only becoming indispensable to company identities; they were also becoming increasingly prominent on board. Meanwhile, aircraft technology was improving, and airplanes were getting bigger. The DC-7 was the largest propeller plane yet in service; in 1958, Boeing's jet 707 made its inaugural commercial flight, closely followed by the Douglas DC-8. These four-engine jets would become the mainstay of long-distance travel until the arrival of wide-body aircraft at the end of the 1960s.

Greater flight attendant numbers, however, meant that their respective power within male-dominated trade unions also increased. As historian Dorothy Sue Cobble notes, deteriorating working conditions that arrived with the jets led more flight attendants to become involved in union action.[57] They were also quite happy to strike, if necessary, as workers at TWA threatened in 1958 and 1959.[58] The Landrum-Griffin Act of 1959 also required unions to comply with majoritarian principles in governance, leaving male union leadership vulnerable to challenge from their women colleagues.

One area, however, militated against flight attendant action and organization. The no-marriage rule and age restrictions meant that job tenure during the 1960s was about two years.[59] Here airlines were placed in a bind: it took money to train flight attendants, and the airlines therefore in theory had a vested interest in keeping them longer. But in reality, airlines acquiesced in such high labor turnover, which kept a steady flow of young women coming into the job, ready to satisfy the increasing fantasies of male passengers lured by advertising. In addition, high labor turnover prevented the buildup of a strong, cohesive leadership among union supporters. According to Cobble, "Stable female leadership was almost impossible to achieve."[60] Airlines' underlying fear, as historian Debbie Douglas suggests, was a married flight attendant as part of a two-income household: she could afford to go on strike.[61]

Sex Objects in the Sky

Civil aviation's widespread introduction of jets during the 1960s led to a massive surge in passenger growth. Between 1960 and 1970 the number of passengers increased from 62 million to 169 million.[62] Not only were long-haul jets bringing major cities and nations closer together in terms of time, but smaller jets such as the DC-9 and Boeing 727 were linking smaller communities into a national and international aviation network. This network was still highly regulated, however. Though airlines such as Delta maneuvered their way around CAB fare regulations through offers such as "Early Birds" (flights that took off so early in the morning that CAB rules did not apply), the truth was that carriers were unable to base competitive advantage on price and consequently continued to seek it through their flight attendants. The 1960s stewardess, however, was a vastly different model than the mother/wife image of the previous decade. More and more, flight attendant imagery became intertwined with overt sexualization. Paradoxically, however, a period in which sexual exploitation was at its most crude was also a period in which flight attendant mobilization and politicization were at their highest. Flight attendants found themselves actively contesting their allotted gender position, culminating in their successful abolition of discriminatory practices and the professionalization of the job itself.

The state of Texas supplied the most revolutionary stewardess images, first with the now defunct Braniff International and later with the highly successful Southwest Airlines. In 1965, Dallas-based Braniff, an ambitious airline similar in size at the time to Delta (i.e., not as big as one of the "big four"—American, Eastern, United, TWA), recruited Harding Lawrence from Continental as its new president, impressed with his desire to double the airline's size over the next five years and to overhaul its image.[63] One of his first acts was to repaint Braniff's airplanes, using garish bright and pastel shades that would make them readily identifiable.

Lawrence's most radical plans, however, concerned his fleet's interior, not exterior. At Continental he had been a driving force behind the "Proud Bird with the Golden Tail" campaign, which introduced the stewardess as sex kitten to the American public, and he wasted no time in hiring the same advertising executive for Braniff, Mary Wells. Wells, in turn, entrusted the blueprints for new uniforms to top-range designer Emilio Pucci. As she put it, "When a tired businessman gets on an airplane, we think he ought to be allowed to look at a pretty girl."[64] In fact, Wells was saying what many airline managers had probably been thinking for some time now, but even so, Braniff's overtly sexualized flight attendants raised the industry bar, with "Braniff babes" earning a new James Bond–esque nickname, "Puccis Galore."[65]

Wells called her campaign "The End of the Plain Plane," and compared with the mother/wife/nurse image of previous decades, this was no understatement.[66] Braniff's "Babes" took to the air in avant-garde designs, including plastic bubble space helmets, and in lurid colors that matched the aircraft livery. According to an airline recruitment package, "A Braniff International hostess is a beautiful person. She is alive for her interest in people for themselves. She is a daughter to the middle aged; security to the confused; a friend to everyone who boards her plane; a heroine to little girls; a source of pride and joy to her parents."[67] She may well have been all these things, but to the airline she fundamentally represented titillation in the cabin. "Does your wife know you're flying with us?" asked one Braniff print advertisement in 1967.[68] The campaign's crowning moment was the Air Strip, in which flight attendants disrobed layer by layer during the flight, beginning with the space helmet, and ending up in a short skirt. According to the print advertisement (backed by equally explicit television commercials): "When she boards our airplane she *Zip* sheds these outer garments to greet you in a raspberry suit and color co-ordinated shoes. This ensemble is too expensive to risk soiling during dinner, so at the appropriate moment she *Zip Snap Zip* changes into a lovely serving dress."[69] When Braniff's share price went from $24 to $200 between early 1965 and April 1966, other airlines attributed such success to its image makeover.[70] They too wanted a piece of the action. From 1965 on, U.S. carriers placed flight attendants' sexualization at the center of their advertising campaigns. In 1968, TWA introduced its "Foreign Accent" flights on transcontinental routes, in which flight attendants dressed up in national costumes according to the appropriate "theme." "They come in four styles with hostesses to match," the advertisement claimed. "Italian (see toga), French (see gold mini), Olde English (see wench). And the Manhattan Penthouse (see hostess pajamas). After all, hostesses should look like hostesses, right?"[71] Even moderately conservative airlines felt the need to respond to this kind of campaigning. Delta, for instance, stressed the southern carrier's "risqué but not too risqué" caution. "Dresses will be short, but not mini," *Delta Digest* reassured. New summer tones would "present a splash of color in the terminal as the stewardesses in their short but not mini length dresses go to their flight."[72]

Smaller regional carriers had most to gain in pushing flight attendant sexuality center stage. In California, for instance, Pacific Southwest Airlines (PSA) workers wore the shortest hot pants of them all. The airline's flight attendants sported buttons offering an alternative interpretation to the acronym PSA: "Pure, Sober and Available."[73] In the early seventies, however, another Texas carrier cranked up flight attendant sexualization a further notch.

Southwest Airlines is the most successful carrier in recent U.S. aviation history, regularly posting a profit while all other airlines have struggled or gone bust. Originally confined to flying the Dallas–Houston–San Antonio triangle, Southwest has brought its jocular, informal, and much-revered corporate culture to most parts of the nation.[74] Like Braniff and PSA, the airline placed its flight attendants at the heart of its brand image. According to founding president, Lamar Muse, Southwest's initial advertisement for thirty-eight hostesses received more than 1,200 applications. "They were," he wrote, "as expected, all beauties." He continued: "In their orange-knit tops and red hot-pants, together with their big white belts and knee-high boots, [our hostesses] did not go unnoticed by the public, to say the least. . . . From the beginning, our airline was known as the one on which male passengers would fight for aisle, rather than window, seats."[75] From the start, Southwest encouraged its flight attendants to bring humor into the cabin and to be less formal than the attendants on mainline carriers.[76] When I flew the airline from Chicago to Oakland in May 2005, the flight attendant told us that if we did not like the look of the person next to us, we could move around the cabin until we found someone nicer. Southwest's flight attendants fitted perfectly into the airline's brilliant brand style, based around two themes: nuts and love. Nuts were the only food Southwest served on board; nuts also encapsulated the irreverent "we break the rules" style of its front man, Herb Kelleher, and its flight attendants, with their light-hearted announcements; nuts were what some people thought of Southwest's business plan, but, hey, passengers were nuts if they didn't fly such cheap fares (because the airline originally flew only in Texas, it operated outside CAB fare restrictions).

But nuts were complemented by love—what could be better than to be madly in love? And, like nuts, love came in various guises: Southwest flew from Love Field, Dallas. In the air, flight attendants provided the love, cleverly fusing "love" in all its purity and innocence and "lover," which Southwest's stewardess iconography more than implied. Naturally, the airline's flight attendants became "Love Birds." Passengers could check in with a "quickie" (an early form of self-printed ticket). In the sky they would be given "love potions" (beverages) by the Love Birds, as they flew to Love Field. "Remember the days when nobody up there loved you?" one crew member in hot pants asked in a television commercial, as a 737 screeched overhead. "Remember?" "The Somebody Else Up There Who Loves You" campaign proved highly successful in creating a new market for passengers in Texas, stealing them from under the nose of, ironically, Braniff.

Sexual innuendo reached its zenith (or nadir) at another Sunbelt airline, Florida's National. In 1971, National launched its $9.5 million "Fly Me" campaign to mark international service from Miami to London. The whole campaign was based on innuendo implying a sexual encounter: "I'm Sandy. Now you can fly me from London to sunny Miami any day of the week. . . . I'll give you one of the quietest, smoothest and most relaxed trips you've ever had. I'll see to your every need."[77] Yet, as in the 1950s, this style of advertisement was not aimed just at passengers: it was also a recruiting tool. Just as airlines promoted the mother/wife image to potential recruits, so 1960s carriers aimed the notion of sexual freedom not just at customers but also at young, increasingly liberated women who, in turn, would be exactly the kind of worker the airlines were looking for. The arrival of the birth control pill and relaxed social norms helped produce a more sexually permissive climate, which airlines were only too happy to tap into. As one writer argues, "The airlines weren't just creating a stereotype by their advertisements; they were also hiring women who would reinforce this image."[78] An early 1960s recruiting poster for American Airlines read, "This morning, sightseeing in New York—and in about five hours I'll meet my date for dinner in San Francisco." "Marriage is fine," claimed one United recruiting advertisement. "But shouldn't you see the world first?"[79] As airlines well knew, for flight attendants during this period, destination was everything.

Coffee, Tea or Me?

The notion of flight attendant as good training for perfect wife was thus displaced by a far racier image—young women with active hormones who needed to get it all out of their system before settling down (remembering, of course, that they still could not be married). Meeting Mr. Right was always a possibility, but more fitting with the times was the suggestion that there were numerous Mr. Rights (and, indeed, a fair number of Mr. Wrongs, too) out there.

Stewardess training guidebooks reinforced this image. For instance, flight attendant Elizabeth Rich, who wrote one of the "modern" guides in the early seventies, had this to say: "Certainly there are plentiful opportunities for making whoopee—more in the circumstances surrounding an airline stewardess than in most other occupations. A stewardess's chances to meet hundreds of different people on each trip, the majority of them men, give her the edge over girls confined to an office or a school."[80] However, the biggest impetus to the popular image of footloose and available stewardesses came from the world of fiction, though dressed up as real-life documentary. *Coffee, Tea or Me? The Uninhibited Memoirs of Two Airline Stewardesses* appeared in 1967 and captured the zeitgeist of the jet age. "Here's the real low-down on the highflying stewardess scene from two audaciously outspoken young ladies who lived it and loved it," read the back cover. "Spaniards are the best lovers," the book reassured us.[81]

Supposedly the explicit confessions of Trudy Baker and Rachel Jones, two ex-Eastern fliers, *Coffee, Tea or Me?* was entirely the fictional product of writer Donald Bain. The paperback version of *Coffee, Tea or Me?* sold more than 3 million copies, and the series of titles, which included a straightforward sex manual, sold more than 5 million in total and inspired a CBS made-for-TV movie. *Coffee Tea or Me?* can be encapsulated in one excerpt: "Yes we've had them all on board—wealthy men, poor men, imaginative men, dull men, men who offer jobs, men who lavish gifts just for the fun of it and men who give little gifts with many strings attached. Yes, we meet interesting men. And good or bad, meeting men is the name of the stewardess game."[82] Though *Coffee, Tea or Me?* became the touchstone for any discussion about flight attendants in the 1960s, it was, essentially, a fabrication. For instance, in not one of the interviews I conducted with flight attendants did "meeting men" ever arise as a reason for joining the profession. This is not to say that none of my interviewees ever met men: indeed, a few of them alluded to a lifestyle of casual affairs, but nothing that was particularly unusual for people in their early twenties. I have no doubt that promiscuity existed at some level, but nothing that was beyond the realms of society at large.

Moreover, in 1973, one of the first published sociological studies of the profession found that the promiscuous lifestyle of *Coffee, Tea or Me?* was overstated. Having conducted a questionnaire study of workers at a Los Angeles–based carrier, it found that a majority (47 percent definitely, 16 percent partly) felt the profession was not a good way to begin relationships. Seventy-eight percent of respondents indicated that they had actually gotten to know no passengers at all in the previous month.[83]

Flight Attendants Fight Sexism

The *Coffee, Tea or Me?* image, enhanced by suggestive advertising and resurrected nostalgically by recent movies such as *Catch Me If You Can* and *Down with Love*, was therefore at complete odds with the profession's reality. It was an image that rankled with flight attendants themselves, who both doubted its veracity and also resented the widespread public assumption that all stewardesses were ready to jump into bed with just about anyone. Pauline, who began flying for Delta in 1964, takes up this theme:

> Back in the sixties and the seventies when we first started flying and stuff, there was a stigma about flight attendants. And when that book *Coffee, Tea or Me?* came out, that was to me a real slap in the face. I did not think that the majority of flight attendants are like that. To stigmatize us in that footloose and fancy-free way, that was just a real slap in the face to a lot of us. This job is not any different than any other job. If they're going to be footloose and fancy-free, they can be. That really hurt a lot of us.

By the 1970s, flight attendants had begun to fight these images. Fed up with having the spaces of their bodies served up for public titillation, women—encouraged by a resurgent feminist movement—began to challenge the airlines directly. In her 1974 book, *Sex Objects in the Sky*, former American Airlines flight attendant Paula Kane took aim at the airborne fantasy world created by airlines:

> The image of the stewardess has taken its place right next to the Playboy Bunny in our national psyche. Different airlines have created

different scripts for their women, from the blond bombshells of Pacific Southwest to the girls-next-door of United. But we all share the basics. We are supposed to be the fresh, wholesome girls who love men, the quiet concubines of the pilots, and the submissive partners to male sexual fantasies.[84]

The iconic Barbie Doll image created in the 1960s became a standard against which all flight attendants would be subsequently judged. In an interesting coda to National's "Fly Me, I'm Cheryl" campaign, for instance, members of the National Organization of Women (NOW) picketed the airline's New York office. Clearly understanding that the slogan implied the alternative "F" word, picketers invited National to "Go Fly Yourself." In its defense, the airline wheeled out Cheryl herself, "a twenty-two-year-old veteran," to claim that the advert had actually corrupted no one. "A few male passengers have made some questionable comments about the ad," she argued, "but those kind of fellows would have said something questionable anyway." On board, she claimed, "the pinchers still pinch, and the gentlemen are still gentlemen."[85]

That may well have been the case, but National's campaign did little to emphasize the serious nature of the job: flight attendants were on board for safety reasons and not to be pinched or ogled by pinchers or gentlemen. But, as NOW's reaction suggested, the genie was out of the bottle. In fact, at a time when sexual exploitation had never been greater, flight attendants fought back to reshape the career (as opposed to the career's image) and turn it into the full-time profession airlines had always sought to avoid.

Flight Attendants Make the Job a Full-Time Career

The CAB required stewardesses as designated safety personnel on all civil airline flights with capacity for ten or more passengers from as early as 1952, yet still carriers depicted the profession as a stopgap job and liked to remind their workers as much. "Old Maid," ran one United Airlines advertisement in the 1960s underneath a close-up photograph of a beautiful young woman who had been flying for two years without a proposal of marriage.[86] Though the turnover rate in the sixties remained at 50 to 75 percent every two years, this was partly due to the lack of long-term career prospects. Flight attendants who were not forced out by airline regulations left because they saw no future in the job. Airlines liked to think they helped the young women of America satisfy their wanderlust before settling down to marriage.[87] But flight attendants themselves had other ideas, and once legal rulings swung in their favor, they began to "space-out" in the postdestination phase, when control of their lives became more important than where they were going. From eighteen months in the late 1960s, average tenure increased to more than six years in 1975.[88]

Title VII of the 1964 Civil Rights Act provided flight attendants with the weapons to unpack sexist airline regulations, a challenge they took up readily. It prohibited discrimination in hiring, promotion, training, layoff, and discharge policies and established the Equal Employment Opportunities Commission (EEOC) to investigate cases of alleged injustice. However, an EEOC declaration of violation was not legally binding, and though flight attendants scored ready successes against age and marriage bans, airlines sometimes dragged them through the courts before acceding to EEOC judgments.

Legal progress was also hampered because the EEOC was ostensibly set up to monitor racial, not gender, discrimination and because male-dominated union hierarchies were reluctant to become involved in cases of alleged sexism.[89] But equally, some flight attendants themselves were disinclined to get involved, either perceiving no injustice or figuring they would have left the industry in a few years anyhow, so why bother with the effort? Stewardesses at the time, as Kathleen Heenan, a prominent member of Stewardess for Women's Rights (SFWR), observes, "like many other women, . . . were just beginning to be aware of their rights. They were still not accustomed to the idea they might continue working after marriage or while raising a family."[90]

In placing a feminist agenda on the legislative table, Title VII radicalized many women, not just flight attendants. Alice Cook concludes: "It is indisputable that the long struggle to lift the marriage ban, deal with pregnancy as any other disability, develop a career line for flight attendants, limit hours, and raise pay would not have succeeded had not the whole normative set of attitudes about women and work changed radically with the adoption of Title VII and the rise of the women's movement."[91] Still, movement or not, the battles had to be fought and won, and spaces had to be created. To turn the profession into a long-term career, the first things flight attendants had to eradicate were age and marriage restrictions.

Fighting Age Restrictions

"Aging" flight attendants, according to historian Dorothy Sue Cobble, were among the first workers to articulate a new definition of age discrimination in the workplace.[92] Though most left before restrictions came into effect, those flight attendants who remained found themselves ceremonially dumped on the economic scrap heap in their early thirties. With few obvious transferable skills at the time, and having become used to the job's disorienting temporal and spatial patterns, flight attendants of more than five years' service found it difficult to convert to other careers.[93] Airlines defended maximum-age policies by claiming that the physically arduous job was too much for a woman in her thirties.[94] But this spurious reasoning belied two realities: "older" women did not match the advertising fantasies airlines had begun to concoct, and a more permanent workforce could reduce labor turnover and therefore increase union effectiveness.[95]

Between 1965 and 1967, the EEOC and Congress heard union arguments about age restrictions, though chauvinism lurked in the background. When Representative James Scheuer on the House Labor Subcommittee asked the flight attendants to "stand up so we can see the dimensions of the problem," his fellow representatives collapsed in laughter. However, the committee ruled in favor of the flight attendants.[96]

The subsequent Age Discrimination Act of 1967 applied only to workers over forty, yet airlines, starting with Northwest and followed by TWA, began to abandon age restrictions. A year later, the EEOC ruled that American Airlines had been discriminatory in applying mandatory retirement to women but not to men. Though nonbinding, the ruling convinced airlines they were fighting a losing battle over age limits, which therefore were duly scrapped.[97]

Overturning the Marriage Ban

In practice, age restrictions affected only a minority of flight attendants: far more had their careers cut short by marriage bans. As Georgia Nielsen notes, the origin of the no-marriage rule is unclear. Ellen Church's Original Eight were indeed single, but United at the time did not proscribe marriage. In fact, Nielsen claims, no airline representative has ever owned up to instituting the no-marriage rule. The most plausible explanation, she suggests, was that United's president got fed up with husbands calling about their wives' whereabouts on delays.[98]

Regardless of its origin, the no-marriage rule became institutionalized from World War II on. It fit perfectly with airline branding in the 1950s and 1960s, and airlines made no attempt to modify it. They did, however, take the moral high ground in claiming that marriage was incompatible with the job. During legal hearings in the 1960s, for instance, United argued: "The rule was founded on the belief that the irregularity and uncertainty inherent in stewardesses' work schedules were in conflict with the woman's role in married life and that such a conflict would have an inevitable adverse effect upon her job performance and motivation."[99] Delta also observed—quite accurately—that stewardess work routines imposed "a more irregular pattern of living than perhaps any other job in which girls are normally employed."[100] Airlines stuck to a conservative argument, not only grooming the American housewives of tomorrow but also—in preventing them from working—keeping their homes in shape once they had married. They also argued that women would soon resent a job that took them away from husband and children on regular occasions.[101] In fact, once they were allowed to be married and mothers, flight attendants regarded their ability to escape domestic commitments as one of the main reasons for remaining in the profession. When I bumped into Kelly, who stopped flying for Delta nearly ten years ago, at a function in March 2006 and asked her if she missed the job, she replied without hesitation, "I miss being able to get away. From a husband who snores, three children, one dog and two cats."

From the mid-1960s, flight attendants began to challenge the marriage bar, pointing out that the few male stewards did not face the same restrictions. Though a 1967 court ruling argued that Delta had not been discriminatory because it hired *only* women flight attendants (the division was therefore not between men and women but between married and unmarried women—and therefore not discriminatory), flight attendant action and EEOC rulings began to undermine the ban's legitimacy. By 1967, only three of twenty-five carriers with ALSSA contracts retained marriage bars.[102] A year later, the EEOC published its opinion that marriage bans violated Title VII. Airlines subsequently dropped the ban, though a rancorous dispute raged on at United until the mid-1980s over reinstating married workers who had been forced to leave.[103] In 1971, the U.S. Court of Appeals in *Diaz v. Pan American* also struck down the female-only hiring policies of some airlines, a move that led to the widespread substitution of the name "flight attendant" for "stewardess" and the hiring of men.[104]

Getting rid of age and marriage restrictions represented the first steps in establishing the job as a full-time profession, and the importance of the Civil Rights Act for flight attendants cannot be underestimated. "It is reasonable to argue," writes historian Frieda Rozen, "that the act caused more change for flight attendants than any other occupation." This was because, she suggests, "*all* female workers in the occupation were affected."[105] The battles of the late 1960s and early 1970s represented a sea change in the profession in two interconnected ways. First, flight attendants became radicalized by the battles themselves. Rozen is particularly succinct here: "They may have come into the occupation accepting the stereotypes, proud to be pretty enough to be hired as stewardesses; but their working conditions left them free to consider new ideas, especially if those ideas were relevant to their fellow stewardesses, the people with whom they also had most social relations."[106] Second, flight attendants began to consider the job as a career, not the stopgap so favored by the airlines.[107] And, with the removal of discriminatory policies, they could now actualize this wish. However, though they could now work for as long as they liked, flight attendants themselves still initially conceptualized the job in short-run terms. Nearly all flight attendants with whom I spoke claimed to have joined the airlines with the intention of staying for one or two years at the most. Many of them stayed longer because the new full-time career allowed them to "space-out" in ways that had hitherto been unimaginable. The job became a career by increment because, having begun to fly, flight attendants became addicted to the very spaces it provided and became reluctant to give them up.

Civil Rights and African Americans

Civil rights legislation affected one other area of flight attendant hiring practices. Up to the late 1950s, nearly all workers had been white. In 1957, the Soviet newspaper *Pravda* had embarrassed the U.S. State Department by pointing out that "bigotry barred Negro girls from one of the most coveted careers open to women in this country."[108] According to Douglas, "Virtually no black women were hired until the 1964 Civil Rights Act was passed."[109] By 1970, just over 2 percent of the nation's 35,000 flight attendants were black. At Delta, despite Atlanta's progressive race relations image, only 52 of 2,500 were black, and black faces were largely absent from company promotional material.[110] Even apparently noble attempts to break down barriers come across as ham-fisted. At Southwest, Lamar Muse insisted on the airline getting its one black recruit through training: she graduated with his comment "that we were proud to have one graduate who had an extra-nice suntan."[111] Following deregulation, black representation among flight attendants increased, but only to the extent that it caught up with the norms of wider service industries. In other words, airlines were no longer able to limit the profession to whites.[112]

Flight Attendants Take Control of Unions

Flight attendants by the mid-1970s had fought their way into a more powerful position than at any time in their history. This newly confident group of workers expressed this autonomy in fighting new battles against sexism and patriarchy on two fronts: in previously male-dominated trade unions and, with less immediate results, to address weight issues.

Historically, male-dominated unions had been reluctant to go to bat for flight attendants, whose position within the unions' ranks had long been known as "the stewardess problem."[113] But the large increase in flight attendant numbers made them inevitably more powerful, with increased bargaining power. The greater number of flight attendants on board created a stronger occupational community, with its members more reliant on each other than on previously patronizing pilots.

When flight attendant Kelly Rueck was voted United flight attendants' most senior ALSSA officer in 1970, she spearheaded a campaign for greater flight attendant control within ALPA. In effect, flight attendants had formed their own union, appropriately named the Association of Flight Attendants, given an independent AFL-CIO charter in 1984. Between 1969 and 1974, the number of flight attendants represented by ALSSA doubled, from 10,000 to 20,000.[114] During the rest of the decade, flight attendants at other airlines seized control of their unions. Between 1976 and 1979, those at six carriers changed their representation.[115] In the early 1980s, no less than eleven unions represented flight attendants in the United States.[116]

Fighting Weight Restrictions

Perhaps the most high-profile workers' campaign was against weight regulations. Central to this struggle was a new body called Stewardesses for Women's Rights (SFWR), originally formed to combat sexist advertising and imagery. Like the no-marriage rule, weight regulations that were dressed up in terms of safety and concern for workers were basically about airline identity and image. As one United official told the *New York Times* in 1972, "You run a $1.5 billion business, and it boils down to whether some chicks look good in their uniform. If you have fat stewardesses, people aren't going to fly with you."[117]

At Ozark Airlines, the "Fat Seven" (as they called themselves) staged the first "weight walkout" in 1976. Claiming airline restrictions were sexist because they did not apply to men in the same way and did not take into account older women's changing bone structure, workers were quite clear what their airline's real message was. Said one: "What they're saying is that we're airborne cocktail waitresses. We have fat pilots, fat ticket agents, fat baggage clerks and fat management. Our primary concern is passenger safety and comfort, not going around looking like *Playboy* bunnies."[118] Weight remained a central issue for flight attendants through the 1970s and beyond. Indeed, it became clear that weight, rather than age or marriage, could become the main filtering device through which airlines could get rid of workers, or not hire them in the first place. Just as airlines had given ground on age and marriage, they doubled their efforts to retain control of women's weight, tightening restrictions, and increasing severity of punishment for "miscreants" in the process.[119]

Deirdre, who had originally flown for Delta in the 1950s, represents a good example of the airline's increasing obsession with weight. In 1973, she heard of the legal change saying that married women could fly at Delta and decided to reapply to be a flight attendant. She was now in her thirties, and her husband assured her that the airline would not be interested. As Deirdre recalls:

> I said you want to bet? I'm going to get that job back. So just to prove it to him I guess on a dare, I went back out there and for an interview and the girl said you're in this stack of—she had a stack [of applications] that high. And I said what is that? It's my age isn't it? And she

said it is not your age. She said it's your weight. You are twenty-two pounds overweight. This happened. So she said, I'll give you one month and you can come back, and if you have lost those twenty-two pounds —we'll talk. So, I came home and I told my husband, I've got to lose twenty-two pounds, and they've only given me a month. . . . So I combined everything, and I almost killed myself. Doing all the exercising. I have never set foot in a spa since then, I am so burned out with spas for going every day for a month. Anyway, the day came when I had my interview set up, and I wore, I remember because I couldn't weigh one ounce over 118. They said right on 118 and not one pound over. So I wore black leotards and black tights, and that's how I—and all these girls went in and all these girls in reception were all dressed up, and here I am in black leotards, tights, and a raincoat covering it up. So we went in to weigh and I weighed 117½. That was close. She said, OK you're hired. But she said, you've got to maintain this weight, if you go over it, you're out. You've got to go through training, and it was very rigid, and at that time we had to have a weight check, I believe it was once a month, but I never did go over it.

Deirdre's story illustrates that flight attendants' struggles against airline policies were not over. But she also exemplifies the strong identification workers felt toward the job. As scholar Cathleen Dooley suggests, the many flight attendants who returned to the profession after being excluded by age and marriage bans indicates their commitment to it.[120] Though they may have intended to work for only a few years, and though they may have hoped to meet Mr. Right, many women who worked as flight attendants became addicted to the space the job gave them. When the opportunity came to return to the profession, a good number willingly jumped back and put themselves through real adversity to make sure they got back in.

Changing Regulation

In 1978 the Carter administration deregulated the airline industry, phasing out the supervisory CAB.[121] Though not applicable to international aviation, the act set in motion a process leading to a more globalized international system, based on bilateral treaties between nations, "open skies" agreements, and increasing interairline cooperation and alliances. "Fifth freedom" restrictions have now been removed in numerous countries.

After 1978, airlines could essentially set their own routes and fares and for the first time compete with rivals on price alone. In the long run, deregulation led to a shakeout of excess capacity, as household names like Eastern, Braniff, TWA, and Pan Am collapsed and a big three—United, American, and Delta—consolidated at both the national and the international level. Southwest, the original low-cost carrier, maintained a uniquely successful operation, spawning numerous (almost wholly unsuccessful) imitators.[122]

The deregulated industry was hypercompetitive, and corporate executives focused on creating leaner, meaner companies. Cost reduction became the name of the game, and in such a capital-intensive industry this meant only one thing: targeting variable labor costs, over which management had a modicum of control, as opposed to fixed costs such as the price of oil.[123] Delta's chair David Garrett argued in 1983, "To meet these competitive circumstances, we must look at reducing Delta's operating expenses. . . . Much of our cost improvement will have to come from increased effectiveness of our personnel."[124]

Deregulation, played out against a backdrop of supply-side Reaganomics, essentially meant a period in which workers would be under attack: those at Continental and American found themselves particularly in the firing line. As head of Continental, Frank Lorenzo established his position as one of the most hated figures among *all* airline workers when he took the airline into Chapter 11 bankruptcy, legally tore up all labor agreements, and then rehired his staff at significantly lower rates of pay. At American, CEO Bob Crandall pushed through the introduction of B-scale salaries, with workers hired after a particular date coming in on significantly less money than their predecessors. Flight attendants on American's B scale were paid about $15,000 a year, half the salary of already existing workers.[125] Other airlines followed suit.

Having changed the profession's status in the early 1970s, flight attendants were faced with new pressures within ten years. Though A scales and B scales solidified the power of those already flying, new hires faced a worse deal, while those beginning at smaller, start-up airlines ran the risk of their carrier not being around for very long. Most of the new flight attendant jobs being created in the United States during the 1980s were part-time.[126]

Yet compared with the position of other workers in the industry, flight attendants during the early 1980s did not fare as badly as may have been expected. In terms of concessions to management, 42 percent were made by pilots, 27 percent by ground crew, and 19 percent by flight attendants (only mechanics, at 12 percent, were lower).[127] One of the reasons for the relative power of flight attendants was the competitive nature of their unions, which had emerged in the second half of the previous decade and drove far harder bargains with management.[128] However, a second round of cost cutting between 1985 and 1989 reduced flight attendant monthly earnings further, by 15 percent, while increasing the number of part-time workers.[129] "Fare wars" between U.S. carriers became a smoke screen for "wage wars."[130]

Onboard working conditions deteriorated. Most flight attendants who flew before 1978 lament what they see as the declining standards of the "flying Greyhound bus." Part of the decline is an inevitable product of flight's loss of mystique. The "hairy armpit" crowd, as some workers call "newer" passengers, would never have been seen on flights before deregulation. People used to dress up to go on a flight; now they wear anything.

Passenger demographics also became far more heterogeneous, making the job more difficult. When flight attendants dealt with only one type of passenger, they could anticipate responses far better. Now, on a flight with passengers from different classes and cultures, the capacity to offend was far greater. Each passenger had to be treated differently, something flight attendants found particularly exhausting.

Globalization

Increasing passenger heterogeneity was fueled by international code sharing, a system whereby two or more airlines sell seats on each other's flights. Indeed, globalization took deregulation onto a worldwide scale, as airlines attempted to circumvent restrictive international agreements. The globalized aviation industry took several forms. First, airlines increasingly bought one another's stock, though national regulations set limits on how much they could purchase. Delta, for instance, entered into swap agreements with SIA and Swissair in 1989, with each carrier acquiring 5 percent equity. Second, airlines entered into global code sharing and marketing alliances, the most important "breakthrough" agreement being between Northwest and KLM Royal Dutch Airlines in 1992. By 1994, more than 280 separate alliances existed between 136 airlines, 60 percent of which had been formed in the previous two years.[131] By 2000, most major world airlines were part of Oneworld, Qualifier, Skyteam, or Star Alliances. Globalization was not just about the global—it was also about global penetration of the local. Just as alliances tied airlines between major cities on different continents, so feeder networks such Delta Connection brought the global brand into the smallest of southern cities.[132]

Globalization presented flight attendants with new challenges. Alliance partners began to experiment with swapping crew on aircraft: not only would passengers turn up for a flight unaware of which airline they would be flying, they may not know which crew would be present. Delta was the most aggressive proponents of crew sharing, placing its workers on the planes of many of its code-share partners. For Delta, deepening the relationship with its global partners made sense. However, the strategy presented some problems. For a start, unions expressed fears that different crew cultures may give conflicting signals in an emergency situation. Unions also feared that the trend pointed toward the establishment of a global labor pool. United, for instance, set up numerous overseas bases, in a case of what the union regarded as job exportation.[133]

Flight attendants from different crew cultures could also clash in working arrangements on board. When Delta and Virgin Atlantic swapped cabin crew, for instance, it created much friction. Virgin Atlantic's crew, dressed in bright red to embody "Virgin Flair," were greeted by Delta international fliers, who tended to be senior crew and found themselves uncomfortable working alongside their younger, more flamboyant colleagues.[134]

Globalization also presented the problem of benchmarking, whereby wage rates would inevitably gravitate to the lowest available in the market. As the International Transport Workers Federation put it, airlines engaged in a "race to the bottom."[135] With maintenance, reservations, and other activities outsourced overseas, flight attendants feared that their jobs would go, too; if not, they would be determined by the wage rates of cheap overseas carriers. In the shipping industry, many vessels notoriously fly under "flags of convenience," operating from a major port such as Los Angeles but registered in a country with lax health and labor regulations. Airline industry unions fear a similar development.

Globalization also had a symbolic effect. As the major Asian carriers have become embedded in global alliances, their flight attendants have come to set the benchmark for how all flight attendants should look and behave. The epitome—as I have been told time and again by passengers—of the great flight attendant is the Singapore Girl. "Why can't we have flight attendants like that?" I am asked. In reality, Singapore Girls are on five-year contracts (unlike the Singapore "men") and are "retired" presumably when they get to be "Singapore women." In short, the same battles that flight attendants fought in the 1960s and 1970s have yet to be fought in other countries.[136]

A Clearly Defined Career

Throughout the relatively brief history of the flight attendant profession, it is clear that this group of workers has struggled to reshape and redefine the job. In the early days, women strategically argued that air hostessing was a job only they could perform. Airlines continually attempted to mold their flight attendants into marketable assets; flight attendants themselves attempted to mold the job into something different. The job's gendered nature was therefore never fixed in stone. With the successful intervention of the civil rights movement, flight attendants could begin to envisage the job as a career, which brought meaning and space to their lives. As Roberta Lessor argues: "When woman flight attendants began to define their work in terms of a career model they began to force others—co-workers, employers, the public, even their own families—to see them as serious careerists."[137] And as flight attendants have forged a career, many have also begun to build homes and families. Flight attendants more and more appreciated the job not for its ability to fly them to the sun but because it enabled them to manage things at home. But shuttling between work and home, as airline managers had always maintained, is never easy. For flight attendants, leaving for work is often a bittersweet experience, as I will explore in the next chapter.

2

Departure

I always feel pressure the day before a trip. I want everything in
order and I want the schedules all written down, the laundry done,
the house straightened, bills paid. I want everything in order before
I leave, so I constantly, the day before a trip, I always feel pressure.
—Lisa, United flight attendant

Like many of us, flight attendants often head off for work in
a frenzy, worrying about forgetting something, getting kids to school,
feeding the cats, and fighting bad traffic. *Unlike* most of us, however,
they are not likely to be returning home that same day, or even within a
couple of days. There is a greater sense of closure when they walk out
the door. They cannot defer things that we would put off for later, such
as clearing the breakfast plates, watering the plants, or having a reassuring chat with a moody child.

Next time you are settling into your seat on a flight, pay attention to
the flight attendant standing in front of you demonstrating safety procedures. She will have undertaken a three-stage departure ritual. About a
month earlier, she will have sat down at a computer and decided where
and when she would like to fly, a selection that may or may not have included the flight on which you are now turning off your cell phone. Airlines allocate flights according to seniority, and this attendant's presence
on your flight could be by either choice or default.

Then, this morning, or yesterday, or the day before that, she will
have gone through a whole series of routines in preparation for leaving
home. If she is a mother, she might have left a long list of directives to
be carried out in her absence. Even though she will not be thinking of
her children as she is showing you how to use your oxygen mask, she
will engage in what I call "vicarious mothering," in which the instructions she left behind help compensate for her regular absences from
home.

The final thing she will have done is to transform herself physically and mentally from Jane Doe into a flight attendant. For as long as you see her on your trip, she will be in "flight attendant mode," as workers call it, a character potentially light-years from the one you might encounter should you meet her mowing the grass one day. She might have entered this mode when she left home or maybe as late as when she greeted you at the airplane door. But you can guarantee that she, along with every other flight attendant in the skies right now, will have gone into flight attendant mode at some point in the recent past.

Bidding, the process by which flight attendants choose where they want to fly, is an exercise in which they struggle to exert control over their spatial and temporal movements. In an industry as precarious as the airlines, they walk a fine line between feeling that they have a lot of control over their lives and feeling that they have very little. The cause of this ambivalence is the seniority principle that operates at U.S. airlines and determines how much independence an individual flight attendant has. When you have good seniority, the world is your oyster; when you don't, it's a clam.

Seniority: The Holy Grail

The profession embraced the seniority principle from its earliest days, mirroring the trend in large Depression-era industrial unions that used it as a basis for layoffs. According to historian Dorothy Sue Cobble, seniority was "accepted as an equitable and rule-based alternative to arbitrary management power and as a way of protecting older workers."[1] In some cases, it rewarded jobs with limited upward mobility and, in providing an incentive to workers to stay, helped reduce labor turnover. However, airlines institutionalized rapid flight attendant turnover partly through reinforcing cultural expectations that a young woman's main purpose was to be married and partly through specific policies banning parents and workers who were married or in the early thirties. Seniority's significance kicked in only *after* flight attendants had overthrown these restrictions and transformed the job into a full-time career.

Up to the early 1970s, flight attendants had "spaced-out"—the process by which they made space a form of remuneration—chiefly through traveling to exotic destinations beyond the reach of most of their non–flight attendant peers. When they established the job as a permanent career, however, destination per se became less important. Writing in 1972, ethnographers James Spradley and David McCurdy observed that "seniority is valued, not so much for prestige or status but as a means of controlling the schedule one bids."[2] As the job became a full-time career, flight attendants changed their priorities when it came to bidding. Initially lured by the glamorous spaces to which the job gave them direct access, flight attendants became more interested in the spaces to which the job gave them *indirect* access. These could range from a therapeutic, relaxing layover to volunteering in the local school on days off. "Spacing-out" in the postdestination phase became more than just travel; it became a lifestyle.

How Seniority Works

The intricacies of the seniority system and bidding process are highly complex, and flight attendants themselves often find the rules opaque. Some even pay "bidding experts" to make their bids for them.[3] Yet the actual mechanism of the process is quite straightforward. Most airlines, once a month, issue a long roster of flights amalgamated into "lines." For instance, one line may involve a month's flying from Atlanta to Chicago on Monday, on to Los Angeles on Tuesday, and back to Atlanta on Wednesday. Another line may involve flying from New York to Washington, D.C., and back once a day, five days a week.

Flight attendants do not choose which *flight* they want to fly; they choose which *lines,* and they "bid" accordingly. Each flight in a particular line has an allotted flight time, the period when the cabin doors are closed and for which flight attendants are paid.[4] Airlines have normally stipulated minimum and maximum monthly flight hours. Delta used to cap at ninety hours per month, though this has recently been removed due to restructuring. Newer low-cost carriers tend to have few restrictions, though all airlines have to abide by federal duty hour restrictions limiting the number of continuous hours flight attendants can work and mandating rest periods between flights.

Once airlines have received all the bids for the following month, they allocate lines to flight attendants using the seniority principle. As Dave from Northwest succinctly describes, "Number One gets what they like and everybody else trickles down. And Number One is the person who joined the company first." Certain lines, such as international to Rome or transcontinental within the United States, are more competitive than others and for this reason tend to be staffed by more senior fliers. This is not, as one may suspect, because of a destination's desirability but because flight attendants like to fly the longest trips they can in one go. Flying eight eleven-hour flights a month involves much less traveling to and from the airport—for which they do not get paid—than, say, eighteen five-hour trips.

Flight attendants fall into two groups: "line holders" have enough seniority to bid successfully for a line of flights even if it is only going from Miami to Key West and back six times a day; in contrast, "reserves" are unable to bid at all and are summoned to the airport with an hour's warning to cover absent colleagues. Reserves' conditions vary across airlines: some delineate between "ready" reserve, with workers actually sitting at the airport waiting to be called, and "ordinary" reserve, where workers can be anywhere within an hour of the airport so long as they answer their cell phone. Not to do so would warrant a "no-show," three of which can lead to automatic termination.

Esther, a Delta flier since the 1970s, claims, "Seniority is the Holy Grail of flight attendants. It is what gives you control." Yet its importance to them is more complex than simply a case of Number One going first. Though each worker has a seniority number, as with any ranking system, it makes sense only in relation to all the other workers on the list. Flight attendants are continually conscious of how many colleagues are above and below them, both at an airline and also on an airplane. In similar vein, the very terms "senior" and "junior" flight attendants are relative. They connote power—derived from seniority—not age or a set number of years at the company.

These issues weigh heavily on flight attendants during bidding. Their main question is not "Where or when do I want to fly?" but "What can I hold?"—where "hold" means their ability to secure a certain line. Flight attendants constantly have to evaluate the "buying" power of their seniority against that of their colleagues, as being outbid on a line can mean you can end up flying anywhere, anytime. It is like a game of geographic bridge: if your jack is your strongest card, you only want to play it if you know the queen, king, and ace are not lurking somewhere. There is no point in a junior worker bidding for a highly popular line because she is bound to be outbid by those with superior seniority. Having failed to secure Hawaii, she could end up flying the hellish New York–Miami route for a month. Flight attendants do not know in advance who else is going to bid a certain route, though the most competitive lines are well known. So, despite the appearance of control, for all but the very senior workers, bidding is something of a gamble, and even relatively experienced workers find the period around "bid time" stressful.[5]

Seniority is not transferable between airlines. A line-holding Delta flight attendant is unlikely to leave for American because her seniority would not go with her. For this reason, during hard times more senior flight attendants will either leave the industry altogether or tough it out at their airline if they decide to stay, though junior workers at smaller carriers may switch airlines several times in the hope of eventually working for a major company, with its greater route network and higher pay.[6]

More important, a flight attendant's seniority is persistently threatened in an industry historically prone to acquisitions, mergers, bankruptcies, and liquidations.[7] One attendant I met had managed to work for three different airlines in her first two years of flying, due to acquisitions. There are no rules to protect seniority in these situations, and workers can therefore find themselves placed en masse at the bottom of the list. In the worst case, they can be furloughed, as eventually happened to TWA's 4,000 attendants after the airline was bought by American in 2001.

In cases where workers have been fed into the existing system, there can be considerable rancor among their new colleagues. At Delta, where only the top 3,000 flight attendants had their seniority protected when part of Pan Am was bought in 1991, older southern workers denote themselves as "RD"—"Real Delta"—as opposed to those coming into the company through mergers. Ex–Pan Am fliers at Delta told me they had been made to feel less than welcome by their new colleagues: RDs complained that ex–Pan Am fliers thought they were "superior" and duly dubbed those in Florida the "Miami Mafia." Meanwhile, Dave, who originally began at Republic before it merged with Northwest, recalls:

> There was a lot of bad blood. I have a "1" in front of my employee number that labels me as a Republic flight attendant. If you're a former Northwest, you have a zero in front of your employee number, so no matter where I go, no matter what I do, I'm former Republic and I'm proud of it. I don't have a problem with it, it's pretty much past now

but it was very hot because we merged right in according to date of hire and it was a horrible, horrible thing. Nobody should go through a merger like that, it was really bad.

Improving Seniority

Seniority therefore both enables and restricts. But flight attendants use numerous tactics to strengthen their position. One way is to bid multiple lines, sometimes up to 100 at a time. There are no limits, and, like playing "all lines" on a slot machine, you increase your chance of winning. In other ways flight attendants make geography work in their favor to improve the control they have over their lives. A good example here concerns commuters. Flight attendants are domiciled in numerous bases dotted across the country, often at one of their airline's hubs. United flight attendants, for instance, have bases in Chicago, Washington, Denver, and Los Angeles, among others. Just because an airline serves a particular airport does not mean that its flight attendants have a base there.

Though seniority operates across an airline's network, some flight attendant bases, the domiciles from which they begin and end their work trips, have more senior workers than others. This can be for a number of reasons, usually having to do with how long an airline has operated from a particular base, as well as the size of its operation. Generally, the greater the number of routes served, the more senior a base may be. At American, for example, Dallas is a fairly senior base, whereas New York is relatively junior. According to Kiki Ward, an American flight attendant, new hires could expect to be commanding international routes within nine months of being based in New York; if based in Dallas, it could take more than ten years.[8]

This uneven distribution has several corollaries. First, a flight attendant may elect to "commute" once a week to a more junior base, where she or he can command greater seniority. Flying free on the airline's system enables flight attendants to commute from virtually anywhere. For instance, an American flier may live in Texas but commute to New York because she is unable to get her desired trips in Dallas. She flies up to New York on standby, using free travel privileges. From New York she works her trip, eventually returning to New York before flying standby back to Texas. Most of the public is unaware of the scale of commuting among the flight attendant community. In one study, 65 percent in a sample of 113 Portland flight attendants commuted.[9] All the United fliers I spoke to in Atlanta commuted to Chicago; likewise, few of the United fliers I met in Los Angeles were based in the city. One Continental flier commuted all the way from Melbourne, Australia, to her base in Houston, Texas.

Though commuting enables flight attendants to exert greater control over their lives, it adds a further layer of complexity to the bidding process because they must work out in advance how to get to their domicile base, which is sometimes thousands of miles away. As workdays approach, they have to keep an eye on the weather, to check whether they need to leave early, especially when negotiating such storm-prone areas as Atlanta or Chicago. As far as the airline is concerned, a "no-show" is a "no-show" regardless of where the worker is commuting from, and for this reason commuters balance increased relative seniority with heightened fears of not making it to work on time. Because commuters use their travel privileges to fly for free to get to their workplace, they come behind paying passengers in terms of priority on a flight. Like any standby passenger, they run the risk of not getting on. Caron, for instance, a Delta flier since 1988, flew Paris trips from Cincinnati while living in Atlanta. "[The commute] was an extra two-hour flight," she says, "and you have the concern of whether there will be any extra seats and whether you can get there on time."

Some commuters reduce such anxiety by having temporary accommodations arranged near their base airports, usually called "crash pads." Often shared with fellow flight attendants, such accommodations provide a convenient alternative to the last-minute rush but, obviously, involve enormous added expense, especially because most workers equip them with emergency towels, linen, toiletries, and occasionally a car, just in case.

Flight attendants adopt other strategies to increase their bidding power. Airlines have always appreciated foreign language skills, and just to work for Pan Am applicants had to be proficient in at least one language other than English. With globalization and expanded route networks, and with U.S. airlines code sharing with those from overseas, foreign languages are even more useful and a quick way for flight attendants to leapfrog the rungs of the seniority ladder. This is the case with Caron. She is unable to hold London flights but can, because of her proficiency in Italian, fly to Rome, even though the Italian capital is a more competitive—and hence senior—route than the UK capital. Indeed, I have met numerous workers who could fly London but *not* Rome because they were not language qualified.

So, in an industry that, in a way, is all about geography, flight attendants exploit that geography to improve their levels of control, be it through commuting to more junior bases or becoming adept at different languages. But workers also improve their seniority by bidding for different jobs in the airplane cabin itself. For instance, one tactic is to fly in the lead position, which is not necessarily held by the most senior worker. Each trip has a lead flight attendant, though the term used varies across airlines. Delta has an "OBL" (onboard leader), and Northwest has pursers. Margaret, at Delta, deliberately bids for the "A" position—or OBL—and therefore, like Caron, improves her seniority in the process. Given the greater bidding power involved, one would imagine all flight attendants would bid to fly the lead position. In reality, many senior workers do not like the extra paperwork and avoid it like the plague. Often they find themselves being supervised on board by someone twenty years their junior. In fact, flying lead can be so unpopular that the position is "juniored down," in flight attendant parlance, to the most inexperienced worker on board, who is left with no choice but to take it.

A final way for flight attendants to strengthen their bidding power is to engage in what can be described as a "geographic swap meet" in which they effectively buy ("pick up") and sell ("drop") trips among themselves (though so far as I could see no money changes hands). Jean provides a good illustration of this practice. She started work at Delta in 1969 and retired not long after 9/11. For much of her career, she deliberately overbid the number of days she would fly. Ideally she wanted to fly twelve days a month, but so did everyone else, and she found herself down the pecking order, especially because she did not want to fly the lead position. So she bid for lines that required her to fly fifteen days a month and then "dropped" the extra three days. All she would have to do was post a memo on the bulletin board—nowadays on the company intranet exchange—and another flight attendant, perhaps short of cash that month, would inevitably "pick up" Jean's unwanted trips. This was "never a problem," she says, "especially if you've got a good trip" to give away. "You knew you would drop them. Because even the international girls wanted to pick up extra time, but they didn't want to fly another three-day international trip." Similarly, flight attendants literally "swap" or "trade" trips with each other, constructing a more convenient schedule that helps overcome lack of seniority.

There are no company regulations against this strategy. The only regulations issued by the Federal Aviation Administration—the government body in charge of airline safety—state that there must be one flight attendant on board for every fifty available seats. Airlines do not really care who these flight attendants are so long as someone is there.

In short, bidding is a complicated business in which flight attendants must continually juggle the benefits and drawbacks of seniority. As is often the case with any arcane setup, the more intricate the rules, the more loopholes there are, and I heard many tales of flight attendants "working" the system, especially around the highly complicated regulations concerning vacation time.[10] Strategies such as swaps or commuting indicate a continual attempt by flight attendants to manipulate and impose control over their lives, even when, due to seniority's limitation, such control may be more apparent than real. Indeed, as wider research has demonstrated, *thinking* you have control over your schedule can be empowering even when your *actual* control is limited.[11] I think this is the case with flight attendants, who every month do spatial battle with their employer and, it must be said, their own colleagues. But theirs is an insecure, impermanent kind of existence, as a closer look at the pros and cons of bidding reveals.

Bidding in the Balance

At first glance, bidding seems to be a good advertisement for flextime, the increasingly popular practice where workers try to balance their working hours with other commitments, especially family. Bidding appears to be a practical demonstration of "giving workers more authority and responsibility," as advocated by Ellin Galinsky of the Families and Work Institute, and indeed by President George W. Bush on the campaign trail in 2004.[12] Moreover, the female-dominated flight attendant profession is unusual in that women in general are about 50 percent less likely to be on a flexible work schedule than men.[13] Just as women flight attendants challenge gendered patterns by working farther from home than their partners, here they also exert more control over scheduling than do most other women workers.

But consider this exchange I had with Margaret, a Delta flier since the early 1970s. I had met her once before, and as I sat in the kitchen of her home in the northern Atlanta suburbs, I asked her what she had been up to recently:

Margaret: [Laughs] Like I remember. . . . I've been flying. This month Zurich. I did one Stuttgart. Last month I think I had Paris and I swapped those around because I don't like Paris.

DW: Oh, really?

Margaret: No. [Laughs] Well I don't like the flight over. . . . I don't remember what I flew the month before that. . . . Next month I have Zurich again. I'm trying to swap. I don't like Zurich. I don't like where we stay. And there is nothing around there. I mean you've got to get the tram into town.

DW: Oh, really? But presumably you must have bid Zurich in the first place.

Margaret: I missed bids for this month.

DW: Oh, how come?

Margaret: Well, I always bid the A position first, the onboard lead. And then the B position, which is the galley position. And I don't know what I did. I must have changed something and I had three Bs before I ever did the As. I don't know how *that* happened, but I missed bids.

DW: So, you got lumped with Zurich?

Margaret: Yeah. But it's high time. You know, it's worth nineteen [hours] forty [minutes]. You know?

DW: Oh, yeah, that's good going.

Margaret: Yeah, so I try to go for the high-time trips because I usually [then don't have to pick up other trips]. I picked up last month, and I've got about eighty-two hours this month and I probably won't. Next month I'll have to because I've got vacation. And I've dropped one trip. I'm only losing like fifteen minutes because we get nineteen fifteen for our vacation. So I guess it's worth nineteen thirty next month. I don't know why it's a little bit less next month. But, anyway, I'll have to pick something up.

In language that is impenetrable to the outsider, Margaret is saying here that, when coupled with her vacation, her bids for the next month will leave her short. Yet despite the missed bids and muddled explanations, it seems that it is not just flextime on offer here: it is also flex*space*. Flight attendants do not decide just when they want to work but also *where*. Here they differ from other flextime workers: the spatial choices flight attendants make are intrinsic to the job itself, not part of a program that, say, encourages "working from home" once a week. As Margaret explained, between pouring me cups of coffee, she could choose not only between several European cities but also between different airplane positions.

This sense of control is crucial. Flight attendants regard being able to set their schedules, and the flexibility that comes with it, as a prized asset. "It's ideal," says Pauline, a recent Delta retiree. "Most people working on the ground can't do that." Indeed they cannot, and few of Margaret's contemporaries coming of age in Tennessee in the early 1970s could match the control she displays over the spaces of her life. Moreover, control and seniority increase with time served at an airline and therefore always provide an incentive for flight attendants to stay in the industry. Here is Shelly, who joined United in 1977, relaying an emblematic tale at a focus group in Atlanta in late 2002:

> I started flying and was going to fly for about a year. . . . But flexibility gives you, it's just sort of addictive. I chose to go back to school and get a master's degree. I do a lot of volunteering. I think the choice is really neat that you have so much time off, and the way you can schedule your time, and the longer you fly, the better your schedules get and the more flexibility you get and the more trades you get. So that's the best part, and you can do so much else outside of your life.

Some flight attendants even have second careers as a fallback, as scholar Carol Pollard found, teaching or selling real estate as a safety net in case the airline industry hits one of its periodic slumps.[14]

Flight attendants exert control over not just where and when they work but also, implicitly, when they do not work. In waxing lyrical about the job's flexibility, they are usually talking about their control over time off, not over time on. It is a fundamental tenet of capitalism that workers sell their labor power in exchange for the ability to do and buy things in their own time. But flight attendants seem to be doing something that is qualitatively different: they are exchanging their labor power for space and for control of their lives. They are willing to put up with the job's unpredictability because of its externalities, a trade-off that, according to Pauline, "is worth a few dollars, in my opinion." Thus, when flight attendants sit down to make their bids, the unspoken question behind, "What can I hold?" is often, "Where do I need to be this month, while at home?" "I'm fixing to bid," says Shelly: "What days do I need off? What are we doing this month?"

Yet here is the crux. When it comes to bidding, only the most senior fliers can be entirely certain that their bids will be successful, and hence the whole process takes on the form of a giant roulette wheel in which they place next month's time and space as chips on the table. Even if Margaret had not "missed bids this month," she may have found herself flying a trip she did not want. Beneath a veneer of control and praise for the job's flexibility, flight attendants exhibit a good deal of insecurity that comes to the fore in the bidding process.

Obsessing over Time

Without being too flippant, one can say that addiction can lead to obsession. For flight attendants, continually thinking about where they will be at some future date can be arduous; most large organizations pay big money to human relations departments to do this kind of work. And yet, given the nature of the industry, where bad weather or mechanical delays can throw a well-oiled machine into chaos, even the most senior flight attendants are aware that the control they have can disappear at any moment.

As a result, flight attendants do not tend to think of the long term. There is no point. This attitude partly emerges in the way that every flight attendant I interviewed who started working more than twenty years ago is still in the job not because of some grand design but because it just "happened." Sociologist Roberta Lessor refers to the job as a "career by increment," where flight attendants build a long-term career through a series of very short-term decisions to stay.[15]

Moreover, the bidding process itself exacerbates a condition whereby flight attendants' concerns are immediate, continually projecting into a short-term future. As Margaret puts it, "I never know what day it is. Our lives are based on a month's schedule, and everything is based around that." Claudette, another Delta flier, says: "You get your schedule, plan six weeks in advance. And then you fill in all the rest of the blocks on your calendar. And you go, OK, I've got the next four weeks planned. There's not going to be much deviation in there." Because of the job's peculiar temporal and spatial disorientation, flight attendants consume time in "chunks" and also, bizarrely, before it has even happened. They conceive their trips more than anything as segments of time.[16] In living their lives by constantly projecting into the short-term future, flight attendants seem to anticipate time before it has actually arrived. Carole, a Delta flier, observes: "My husband says, 'You know I figured you out after twenty-six years.' He said the other day, 'You lived your thirty-one years looking at a clock. Look at the clock. Look at the clock. Constantly telling whomever you're with you've got how many minutes.'" It is a paradoxical mix, in other words, in which flight attendants relish the apparent control and freedom on offer, and yet at the same time micromanage to the point of obsession. The more control they have, the more they seem to need to control; it is not for nothing that many flight attendants have confessed to me to being "control freaks."

It's Hell: Being on Reserve

At the bottom of the pile, reserve flight attendants have no control at all and can only look on enviably at a world of swaps and bids and lines. They are effectively a temporary, short-term labor force. Carriers need a readily available group of workers standing by at short notice in case a scheduled flight attendant calls in sick or is delayed on another flight. Being on reserve, flight attendants tell me, is akin to being in hell. "You never knew where you were going to be and you never knew when they were to call you," recalls Kelly. In the days before beepers and mobile phones, reserve flight attendants would literally spend their days waiting around at the end of a telephone in case they were called. Even now, with new technology, they talk of mowing the grass while keeping one eye on the beeper. Then, having raced to the airport to report for duty, there is always a chance that the person originally designated for the flight will turn up at the last minute, leaving the reserve with no choice but to return home again.

Reserve, which is akin to the kind of apprenticeship schemes used widely in industry, contains elements of the rites of passage associated with such programs. Sometimes the butt of practical jokes played by pilots and other crew, reserves at worst face outright hostility from senior workers.[17] "Surviving" reserve and becoming a line holder is a demonstration of commitment to the career. But reserves can encounter a soul-destroying experience never faced by an apprentice: having got off reserve, workers can easily find themselves back on it. Maya, flying for Western before it merged with Delta in the mid-1980s, sums up how reserves are prone to the vicissitudes of the industry:

> I got off reserve in four months because of the small base [I was at]. Then I got transferred to L.A. and got immediately put back on reserve. I was on reserve there a year. Then we got furloughed, and I moved to Salt Lake City. I was off reserve in Salt Lake because it was a small base. I was there for a year commuting—I lived there for a year, then I went to L.A. and was back on reserve for about another year.

On, off; on, off. It is a precarious setup. During an industry downturn, as happened after 9/11, airlines tend to close flight attendant bases and transfer those workers elsewhere. In 2003, for instance, Delta closed its base in Portland, Oregon, leaving West Coast workers with grueling new commutes to get to work. But it also led to an influx of senior flight attendants into bases in New York and Atlanta, forcing more junior flight attendants down the food chain, and some line holders suddenly found themselves back on reserve. Workers who had spent five years on reserve and had just reached the Holy Grail of line holding had the prize snatched away from them again at a second's notice.

This was the case with Donna, at Delta, who had just gained what she felt was a modicum of control over her life in becoming a very junior line holder when she was dumped back on reserve. Now, her world is light-years away from that of more senior flight attendants plotting their time off. She describes it as follows:

> I go on duty at midnight, so, Monday, at midnight. . . . Like tomorrow actually, I'm relaxed today because I already know my trip and I have standby tomorrow from 4 P.M. to 8 P.M. Standby is where you stay at the airport for four hours in the lounge, and if they need you, they call you up. But they usually assign that early in the morning. . . . But any reserve can get the airport standby. Usually they assign those early in the morning, so I checked this morning before I came to meet you. Now I can plan my day, now that I know what I'm doing. I'm OK if I know what I'm doing, but most of the time because I'm ready reserve they

don't assign me something. So, you don't know what time to go to bed. I don't know if I should wash my hair before I go to bed, or if I'll have time to wash it in the morning. So, I can't sleep, I can't sleep when I'm on a trip. It's probably my personality, you know, but I can't sleep, and I wake up a lot looking at the clock. You just don't know what you need to do. Do I need to pack? Do I have time to pack some food to take with me? It gets old, you know?

For Donna, the worst time of day is in the late afternoon. She lives about twenty miles from the airport and worries that she will not make her sign-in through the Atlanta rush-hour traffic should she be summoned. Her "solution" is to drive down to a mall near the airport, spending her time waiting by browsing the stores, bag packed in the trunk (most reserves have their bag permanently packed), just in case she gets a call on her cell phone. If there is no call, she goes home again.

Tenuous Control

Seniority's benefits are therefore not fixed in stone, and in a volatile industry they can be taken away alarmingly fast. In the United Kingdom, it is interesting to note that cabin crew generally do not use a seniority system and are allocated trips with very little worker input.[18] In interviews, American flight attendants, even in a turbulent industry, still registered a greater sense of control than their British counterparts. Sarah, with seventeen years service at a UK charter carrier, still feels she has "very little" control over her schedule. A U.S. worker with similar seniority would almost certainly not make this statement. Nevertheless, workers who have constructed their routines around the assumptions afforded by their seniority can have these routines thrown off by a base closure, merger, or layoffs. Even a short-term rush of popularity for a particular holiday— most notably Halloween, for which parents want to supervise trick-or-treating—can displace junior fliers down the ladder rungs.

Bidding is an exercise in the intersection between geographic place and control. Flight attendants play one place against each other, swapping Paris for Zurich, commuting from Atlanta to Chicago, in an attempt to get a greater degree of control over their own spatial movements. Then, having figured out where they are going, all they have to do is to figure out how to get out of the house.

The Play or the Field Trip: Bidding with Families

Senator Conrad Burns of Montana made the headlines in October 2005 after Northwest Airlines flight attendants alleged he insulted a worker expressing fears about the carrier's downsizing plans. Kari Johnke-Henzler told the Associated Press that she heard Burns suggest fellow flight attendant Karen McKelvaney stay home and be a mother, should she lose her job. "I am a mother," retorted Johnke-Henzler, "and I need to support my family."[19]

Having dependent-care duties is particularly at odds with the profession's public image. Passengers assume—and airlines reassure them—that flight attendants are there to care for *them,* and few appreciate that once their jobs are done, many attendants go home and care all over again for their families. As in other service jobs with a high level of public contact time, "permanent" caring can be exhausting.[20]

When aging parents are thrown into the equation, roughly half of flight attendants care for dependents, and this figure excludes those with adult children.[21] Senator Burns's alleged comments, with their binary logic implying an either-or choice between work and family, come from an era when flight attendants lasted a couple of years before settling down to motherhood, and when homemaking and pursuing a career were regarded as antithetical for women in general.[22]

Even when they were banned from doing so, many flight attendants wanted to work *and* have families; accordingly, they returned to the profession once legislation made this possible. However, like millions of other workers—men and women—they have found, and continue to find, balancing home and work commitments difficult.[23] Their disorienting lifestyles make the balancing act particularly tricky.[24] While many workers find just getting out of the front door a major achievement, flight attendants bear the added burden of having no fixed idea of when they will return. Airline scheduling operations are notoriously fickle. They are dependent on weather and also on the smooth running of the whole route network. A mechanical delay on one flight affects not only connecting flights but also all the flights for which that particular aircraft was assigned. To maximize revenues, airlines have to keep their planes in the air as much as possible, and thus there is very little slack in the system. As a result, all flight attendants probably have missed an important occasion because of delays. They *hope* to be home on, say Friday, but they are never 100 percent sure.

Flight attendant parents structure bids around their children. Some fly as little as possible, preferring long, high-time routes that ensure the most days off a month. But these are senior routes with limited availability. An alternative is "day turnarounds"—flights that are out and back in the same day—but these tend to be even more senior. The other strategy is to fly when least needed at home.[25] Some fly weekends, when partners are around and expensive child care is therefore unnecessary.[26] Those without partners rely on extended family members or sometimes ex-partners. Caron is separated from her son Philip's father but still shares child care duties with him. "I fly Friday to Sunday as it fits into Phillip's dad's work routine," she says.

> I get the dog cared for. Philip is at school three days a week, and I carpool. Sometimes I go back to bed after that or I go to work out, since that is time for me. The girl across the street often plays with Philip, so I get time to get ready for me. I iron, pack. His dad knows what time I am dropping him off. He and I have a very good working relationship regarding Philip. He loves going to his dad's house. It works. Philip knows when I'm leaving. I would feel guilty more at leaving Philip if he didn't love his dad so much. And it is a great working environment with his dad. He looks forward to being with him. The rules are relaxed at dad's house. Philip's in a loving safe environment.

There is a lot of shuttling around here, but it seems to work, and the communication channels are open. Caron, because of her language skills, can also fly senior high-time trips, minimizing her absences.

Those with less seniority, or less choice in the system, may have to make alternative arrangements. Flying night turnarounds—out and back in the same night—is one of the more radical solutions to child care responsibilities. Angie, who flies for Air Tran, which does not have long high-time routes, leaves her one-year-old daughter with her parents, who live near the Atlanta airport, and flies two nights consecutively. She then flies one further all-nighter over the weekend, leaving her daughter at home with her husband. Ann, at Northwest for twenty-seven years, flew night turnarounds when her two sons were growing up, tag-team parenting with her partner over child care.[27] Kirsty, still flying at Delta after nearly thirty years, did the same when her son and daughter were younger. "You'd go late at night," she tells me: "We got a hotel room for a short period of time. So we'd still be able to get a short little nap in, but some of them just had black chairs in the office, the lounge. Sleep in the black lounge chairs. I'd be home for the kids and do their activities."

Rather than "layovers," some workers lightheartedly call such flights "leanovers" because they spend such a short time in the hotel they almost end up sleeping while standing up. But joking aside, flying all night and then looking after the kids can be exhausting. Such parenting patterns are not unusual among shift workers, as sociologist Angela Hattery has discovered, with exhaustion and lack of sleep being the most-cited drawbacks.[28] Throw jet lag and disorientation into the mix and it is easy to see how flight attendant parents face particular dangers of fatigue. They put themselves through a hellish routine in order to minimize the job's impact on children and, importantly, themselves. Such punishing scheduling allows them to be around their children when "needed," validating, as Hattery puts it, their status as "good mothers" despite their absences from home.[29] According to Carole, also at Delta: "I was a puppet on a string after my daughter came along. I would have done anything, if it meant sacrificing something for her. I flew 8:00 at night until 6:00 in the morning. Slept on a couch so that I could do a field day. Yeah, stupid stuff like that."

But sometimes, even a hellish routine is not enough, and parents find themselves in an invidious situation when it comes to bidding. Take Kathleen, for instance, mother of two daughters, who describes this situation:

> There would be school plays that I would try to get to and I would miss them. At United you have to jump through hoops to get some kind of control, and you have to prioritize. I would get my bids and would sit down and say, "What in the next month is *the* most important?" I would prioritize right down, but what about with two kids? I would be constantly juggling between the two kids. This was the most stressful part of the job: scheduling. And feeling guilty that I was not home for my girls. With the kids I had to make choices. Was it going to be the play or the field trip that I would come to? I burdened them a lot with choices that I shouldn't have at such a young age.

Patricia, also with United, recalls: "I missed football games and tennis games. I tried to make sure I was there for proms so I could at least see how they looked before, but there was always something major going on, and there was no way that I could work around everything. So, I tried to pick and choose those things that were truly, truly important and make sure I was there for them." Meanwhile, Linda, whose children were already teenagers when she joined American, suggests:

> You never know. You could have a mechanical [repair problem] and not leave a city for two days maybe, and yet you were supposed to be home two days ago but there you're sitting. You don't have any control over that. And I think that would be very difficult with [young] children. Even with my kids my youngest one was in college when I started flying, and just to get home for certain things like for her high school graduation, I mean it was a big deal to work that around because I was a new flight attendant, for just something one night.

Flight attendants with very good seniority have great empathy with parents lower down the ladder. Eileen, the most senior worker I interviewed, did not have "to be as creative about child care, maybe because I did have seniority." She contrasted the amount of time off she had with "some of these people [who] have three or four kids and go away for three days and you have to have some kind of incredible calendar with everything written on it." Numerous flight attendants expressed bewilderment at how reserves juggle the job with parenthood. "I don't know how they do it," was a common refrain.

They do it in a number of ways: parents on reserve, or single parents in *all* cases, must have a reliable backup system. This normally involves extended family (in Caron's case, her child's father) or friends. Even with cell phones, contact is not necessarily straightforward in an emergency, and parents need to know that their child is in good hands. Suzie, for instance, who flies for ASA and has recently separated from her husband, had "no idea where [her] child was," for twenty-four hours on 9/11. "I knew he was taken care of. But I didn't know where he was." Clearly friends and family are more useful here than paid child care. For reserves and single mothers the latter gets expensive. Equally, child care workers themselves need regular schedules, not the kind of thing one associates with flight attendants. Some flight attendants I met do use paid child care, but these invariably are more senior workers who could control their schedules better.

Flight attendants with children do cope. However, scholars Alyce Desrosiers and Arthur Emlen make the obvious but necessary point that the "airline industry effectively 'selects out' those parents who cannot manage work and family."[30] Of my interviewees, only one gave up the job because she could not balance the two, which she freely admits. In other words, those who can't cope don't stay flight attendants.[31]

For parents, it becomes something of a relief actually to go to work. Flight attendants fit into a pattern in which work becomes a respite for women seeking to get away from the time-frenzied families around them.[32] But even though they want to get away, these women are still "vicarious mothers," preparing extensively in advance for their absences.

Preparations and Post-It Notes

Flight attendants talk about departure routines and rituals, designed to smooth the transition from home to work. Yet, despite these time- and emotion-saving devices, many flight attendants seem to head to work with a mixture of dread and relief. States of preparedness vary. Commuters watch the weather in their home and base cities, in case they need to leave early. Those on reserve have a bag packed, ready to go in case the airline summons them and they need to get to the airport quickly. Of all the problems this presents, one of the most glaring is what to pack in the bag. Reserves have no advance warning of where they are going or how long they will be gone; given that it could be anywhere from the Caribbean to the Canadian Rockies, they need to be prepared for all eventualities.

Those who know where they are going may have a more set routine. Giselle, recently retired from American, is fairly typical. She says:

> It's like a checklist. The night before I would hang my uniform up, I would make sure my belt was on my skirt, I'd make sure my hose were in my shoes, I would make sure that my cockpit keys were attached to my skirt, take my flight bag out, make sure my manual never, ever came out of my bag. Most flight attendants don't ever take it out and then, you know, you pack the night before.

Flight attendants have a mental checklist of things they need. The flight manual, for instance, is a rule book full of up-to-date regulations that flight attendants must always carry with them. They fear mislaying it, and two retirees I interviewed recalled having had nightmares in which they had lost it. They also want to prepare for unforeseen eventualities, planning for the short-term future. Linda continues:

> You want to pack that extra little food because a lot of us don't eat [on the plane]. You always have a little ziplock bag of your raw vegetables and you'd always take a bunch of fruit and I'd always take those little cans of chicken and tuna, pop them open. That's one thing about this job, you're always planning ahead, I think, and you have to get your clothes ready for your layover, or if you've got to take an extra flight, you know, if you're on a three- or four-day trip.

Vicarious Mothering

Flight attendants with families have the most intricate preparations. Mothers, especially, often express a need to compensate for their absence by leaving the house in a functioning and ordered state. "I go to the store, buy food for my husband, clean the house, you know. I think all the girls do that," comments Roseanne, a Delta flier since the late 1970s. "I'd have Tuesday off," recalls Amy, who flew night turnarounds for Delta: "Of course, you don't sleep, you make all the beds and you do the laundry and you sweep and you go to the grocery store and then you get your uniform ready for Wednesday morning, same thing."

Flight attendants conform to what feminist philosopher Sara Ruddick describes as a sometimes "frustrated desire for the activity of caring" on the part of parents forced to be away from their children regardless of the reason.[33] Flight attendant mothers, especially, implicitly assumed (and perhaps secretly hoped) their families could not cope without them. Even in their absence, they could vicariously mother their family through preparing meals in advance, leaving lists of things to do and post-it note reminders all over the house. Maggie, recently retired from Delta, exhibited the most extreme form of vicarious mothering I came across in my interviews: "There's nothing I didn't prepare. I would arrange every carpool. Now at this point, I've got four kids. . . . My husband would take them where he had to go, but he did not make any decisions. He did not make a decision as a parent while I was gone. Everything was decided before I left." According to Maggie, her husband was incapable of doing anything that was not written down on her list. He was "great" at following directions, but throw in something that required initiative and he would be befuddled. "I made sure that they had the school uniforms laid out," she continues. "I was in charge of every single thing on their agenda except executing their arrival and pick-up. That was the only thing I didn't do because I was gone, I couldn't do that. But I could do everything but that."

It is striking how involved Maggie was. Though she claimed, unlike other mothers, not to feel guilt at leaving her children, there does seem to be an element of overcompensation at work here. Not only did she not seem to trust her husband to do things, she also did not seem to trust her kids much either. Either way, clearly getting away from this frenzied household must have been something of a relief. No wonder Maggie claimed the hardest part of her job after she became a mother was "getting out the door."

Workers at other airlines and with children of different ages tell similar stories of advance preparation. For instance, at Air Tran, Angie, who leaves her infant daughter at her parents' home while she flies, goes into "panic mode" even though she knows "what's coming up and [she] has to go to work." Therefore, "getting out of the house is a big deal." Because Angie will be at her parents' house for three days, she has to live out of a suitcase, and she has to remember to pack stuff for herself and her daughter. Her flight bag remains virtually unpacked the whole time as she "rotates things in and out of it." Meanwhile, she is mystified at what her husband does for dinner in her absence: "I guess he doesn't eat for a couple of days . . . when he's there by himself he's like, 'there's nothing to eat.' I'm like, that's really sad. . . . I guess he just looks in the fridge and he doesn't see the potential. He just starves himself for a couple of days."

About half the parents I talked to spoke of preparing meals in advance. For some, it was a question of what their family otherwise would eat. "He would take the kids to McDonald's twice a day," recalls Kirsty. For others, it was another attempt to maintain the role of wife and/or mother, a strategy that could lead to resentment. "I used to cook all the meals!" recalls Shelly, at United:

> I mean I used to make meals for them to throw in the oven, and I would say, "OK, this is in the freezer." I think a lot of people do that. I was finding that I was scurrying around to get all that stuff and get it made and sort of losing good fun, relaxed quality time, and I thought,

"You know? They could deal with this." As long as I make sure there's enough food in the house. And that's what I would do. I would make sure there was enough food in the house, and then if they ate, they ate it. [Before] you would have this little resentment thing that could come up. If you had said, OK, here is stuff for spaghetti on Friday night and this thing on Saturday night and then you come home on Sunday night and it hasn't been eaten.

Denise, at Delta, echoes these comments:

Well first of all I used to prepare all of these meals. Put them in the re-frigerator. I mean, I think that's a supermom or flight attendant mom mentality sometimes. You've got to make sure everybody had some-thing to eat. You've got meals, all the laundry has to be done. That's the way I was. I mean everything had to be done when I left that house. When I came home I would prepare a meal, and as years went by, I re-alized I am knocking myself out for nothing. Sometimes they wouldn't even touch the meals. . . . I started resenting that.

By their own admission, many flight attendants are people who like things to be ordered and organized in a certain way. But there is more going on here than just logistics. Flight attendant mothers, it seems, de-spite transcending gendered expectations in being the ones working far from home, often try desperately to conform to these expectations even if only during their absence. It is as if they jump through hoops to square the family they live "with," in anthropologist John Gillis's terms, with the one they live "by," meshing their "real" chaotic family with an idealized notion of how a "normal" family "should" be.[34] By leaving notes all over the place and lists of instructions, it is as if the mother is still *actually there,* present mentally if not physically, casting a domestic spell over the rest of her "normal" family, when deep down she feels the family could not be more abnormal.

To highlight the gender point being made here, what happens to pi-lots, the overwhelming majority of whom are male? Pilots face equally disruptive schedules. The FAA allows them to fly up to 100 hours per month, often more than their flight attendant colleagues and with a greater sense of responsibility, too. Pilots also bid for their schedules. They feel the pressure of economic cutbacks sharply, and many feel downgraded due to the post-9/11 recession in the industry.[35] Many also have families, and research—albeit on coastguard pilots—suggests that stress at home can impact performance in the cockpit.[36] Other analyses have identified long periods away from home as a potential stressor for pilots.[37]

Pilots, like any parents, worry about their families, especially during difficult periods. But they do not seem to get involved in day-to-day minutiae the way flight attendant mothers do. "Vicarious fathering" is not a term I would associate with pilots. In fact, several of the mothers I interviewed were married to pilots, and they made quite clear who did the organizing in the house. According to Sarah, at Delta: "[My husband is] an 'It's got to be written down' person. He can't remember the stuff written down, and I remember everything. If my husband is coming home that day, I'll start the list, the list going of who goes where, who goes to gymnastics, who goes to cheerleading, what time. . . . Post-it notes all over the place."

Mary Ann, recently retired from Delta and with one son, also has a pilot for a husband and suggests the house would fall apart in her absence:

> With the preparations, I needed to make sure everything was done at home. Much more than the men did. They just don't prepare like a woman does. [My husband] made sure the cars had been serviced and there was air in the tires and that the bills had been paid and that sort of thing. But domestically, I really had a sense of feeling it necessary to have the house in order before I left. I always wanted the house in order. I wanted to make sure that I had everything lined up. I would leave a list of "Steven [her son] has to be here at this certain time," and "Don't forget to pick up that," that sort of thing.

There is no doubt that flight attendants like to typecast pilots, even when they are their husbands. "Pilots look at parts, while we as flight attendants tend to look at the whole picture," a flight attendant instructor informed a training group I attended in Long Beach, California.[38] Equally, many pilots come from a military background cemented by hierarchy and division of labor. But the key point is not necessarily that pilots do not do the housework but that flight attendant mothers *like to depict* them as not doing it. In doing so they reaffirm their own worth as mothers, reestablishing their gendered position within the family at the same time as their job, with all its traveling, undermines it.

At the same time, flight attendant mothers are not unique in making all these preparations. As journalist Cindy Goodman points out, increasing numbers of businesswomen find themselves "embarking on the draining process of organizing family affairs so that they can be away from home."[39] But flight attendants differ from other businesswomen in two chief respects: first, they have a different level of control over their lives. Businesswomen are far higher up the ladder in terms of where and when they want to go, probably travel at shorter notice, and do not spend half a transatlantic flight on their feet. By contrast, a flight attendant's sense of control is derived solely through seniority, a link that is often highly precarious. Second, there is a qualitative difference in the sheer monotony of displacement between flight attendants and businesswomen. Going away, for businesswomen, is part of their job; for flight attendants it *is* their job, and the constant, routine nature of their displacement is altogether more wearing. In interviews, flight attendants use the word "leaving" with a regularity that suggests it plays on their mind constantly. "You're always going away, always leaving," Kathleen, a United flier tells me. "I've spent all my life leaving," says Patricia, also at United. Having recently retired, she now does not want to go anywhere at all. "I just want to stay home," she smiles.

Flight attendants are perennially saying good-bye to their loved ones, which can be a wrenching experience, no matter how many times they do it.[40] Before entering the flight attendant world, they have to make an often irreconcilable peace with their home world. Though separation anxiety affects many partners in relationships, the tensions involved here are most glaring for parents.

Bad Mommy

In Arlie Hochschild's book *The Time Bind,* the sociologist talks of the daily scene of pathos to be found at the "waving window," where children line up to wave to their parents as they leave them at day care.[41] Flight attendants face an altogether more extreme situation. They may be flying to another continent, they are often going to be gone for a few days, and there is no certainty that they will be back when they hope to be. Parents of small children talk of guilt at parting, and plenty of tears. "I'm angry," says Andrea, a Delta flier with two children. "I have to put my life on hold. It stops."

Kelly flew with Delta for eight years from the late 1980s and found leaving her young children a traumatic experience: "Dropping off my daughter broke my heart. The whole feeling would build up during the week, and I would leave her in the playpen. It was a really depressing scene. I would drive to the airport and not be able to see out of the windscreen I was crying so much." Eventually she found juggling job and family too wearing and quit. Her seniority was never particularly high, and having been transferred to Atlanta from Washington, D.C., she found herself even farther down the rungs. "I could be on reserve, with a forty-five-minute call from the airport, with a child," she explains.

Caron, despite her excellent relationship with her son's father, says of her child:

> He used to cry and say, "I want you to stay," and I would think I'm a bad mommy. I would read books on it, and they would say that they would still love you when you come back. "I'm always coming back," I would say. I used to get upset as well. In the beginning it was very difficult. Your heart is breaking, and I would think how can people get used to it? Your mom is getting on a plane and going to a foreign country.

"I would be crying all the way to the airport," echoes Stacey, another Delta flier, also with an infant son. "I had a bad feeling when he cried for me on leaving him." The word "guilt" lurks beneath the surface with most flight attendant parents. "I felt guilty!" exclaims Kathleen: "I felt guilty at leaving them and not coming back, and they have no concept of time. 'I'll be home tomorrow night' means nothing to a child. And then I would promise to come home that night, and the plane would be delayed and I wouldn't get home."

Working moms feeling guilty is not exactly uncommon. Fueled by sporadic moral panics about the "end of childhood," mothers worry about the damage they are doing to their children by going to work. Flight attendants sometimes get reminders of such dangers from the unlikeliest of sources. Deidre, who started flying for Delta in the 1950s and then flew again in the 1970s, was stunned when a friend of her young daughter announced from the back of the car, "When I grow up and get married and everything, I would never leave my children to work." In Denise's case, it was her own daughter who became critical:

> My daughter would pop that on me every now and then. She would say, "Why do you have to leave? Why can't you?" . . . [This was when she was] oh, probably eight, nine-ish, ten-ish type and I would explain to her that this was my job and that I liked my job, and one thing I've always told my children is make sure you get into a job that you really like. . . . My mother was another one that at times said, "Denise, I just can't believe that you can be gone that long." I said, "Well, Momma, I've got people that are taking care of my kids that I trust. Their dad is there all the time."

Three points emerge here in relation to guilt. First, guilt at being absent is exacerbated by the length of time flight attendants are gone. There are degrees of scale, in short, and a mom working all hours at the office downtown will not have the same kind of guilt as one flying to another continent for three days every week. Those flight attendants who stressed no guilt at all, such as Maggie, flew night turnarounds and so were absent mainly when their kids were asleep. Again, the flight attendant experience is one of extremity, not uniqueness.

Second, many flight attendants admit that guilt is their way of rationalizing the fact that they are missing out on mothering, not that they are seriously worrying about long-term damage to their child. "It probably bothered me a lot more than it did them," says Margaret. "That's all they have known." Moreover, some flight attendants try to assuage their own discomfort by claiming their absences make their child more self-sufficient. As Eileen puts it:

> If you've ever witnessed a parent trying to leave a child at school for the first time and that child has never been away from their mother, it's just painful to watch what that does to the child. I wanted him to be independent. I didn't want him hanging onto my leg when I took him to kindergarten. By the time he was four, he was going four days a week to a preschool at our church.

Suzie, who flies for regional airline ASA, endorses this view: "You know the first day of school I saw kids that were just hanging onto their mom's legs for dear life, and I was like, 'Oh, no!' You know I was crying the first day of school, and [her son] wasn't. He was like, 'Bye mom!' You know, 'See ya.'" Interestingly, on one of the few occasions when I spoke to a flight attendant and her adult daughter at the same time, the daughter directly challenged her mother's talk of guilt. "You made leaving a big thing," she said, suggesting that her mother had felt guilty. "I didn't care. I was here alone a lot, and I was OK with it. It made me independent."

The third point to emerge from Denise's response relates to her comment "I liked my job." If she did feel guilty at going away, such feelings were tempered by the returns she got from being able to "space-out." For moms, in particular, the job allows them to command and control their spatial movements far better than many other working moms. Indeed, many argue the very nature of the job provides a win-win situation. For a start, it provides therapeutic space for moms to just get away from everything. As Shelly argues: "[Layovers] are their own time, and a lot of people with little kids love it. But people say, 'Well, how can you leave your three-year-old?' You know, what mom with a three-year-old that's running around after them all the time wouldn't like it?"

"There would be so much going on before a trip that I can't really remember it," says Sandra, who flew for Delta from the 1970s onward. "I had a routine of getting my act together and getting out of here. With a sense of relief of getting out of the house. This was one of the perks. Layovers were your own time."

Many flight attendants talk of getting away as their source of sanity. "When the kids were babies, I really saw [my trip] as my R&R," argues Lisa, also at Delta: "It was a refreshing time when the kids were babies because when you're at home it's, 'Why do worms yawn?' and 'Why do I have to take a nap?' It was just you were always on. When the kids were little, then layovers sort of became fun times for me. I felt like a great selfish teenager in Paris just walking around by myself." Other workers also talk of sanity. Here is Danielle, from ASA:

I felt terribly guilty when my son was younger, and that's because I'd done a complete turnaround. I got divorced. I now have my own image whereas before I was Jack's wife, Jimmy's mother, and that's all I did. That was my whole existence. Even though I was flying, I was doing everything, it seems like, for them. But I'd continue to do it, which meant I wasn't that guilty I guess. But I had to do it, I had to get away. I really needed to get away, especially from the ex-husband. So it was my little piece of sanity.

So, on the one hand, flight attendants get their sanity from getting away. But "spacing-out" is not just about being able to control time away from home; it is also about having greater command *at* home. While the job provided spaces for recreational recuperation in Paris, it also provided three- and four-day blocks of time at home, allowing far more contact time with their children than other working moms could have. "I am at home more often than many people are with ground jobs," says Sofia, a Delta flier since 1977 and with an infant son. "This is an ideal job for raising a child." Molly, who works for United and is an AFA union representative, agrees. "In this job, time off with children is very important," she says. "In a good way, it is an incredible lifestyle. Women have more time with their children than nine-to-five working mothers." Kathleen, also at United, comments: "I could have stopped flying and moved. I could have gone into teaching. I kept flying as I felt I was home a lot more than I was away. I had more time with my girls than a working mother on eight-to-five. I had more quality time with the kids. When I was home, I had quality time. Three days a week I was there when they got home from school."

So the bottom line for many flight attendants is that, even though they may feel guilty, they continue to do the job because it enables them to create space away from home and, for some, more time and space *at* home. Yet things are never that simple. Despite their rationalizations, flight attendants—like all parents—still worry about being away from their loved ones. In a recent survey, 90 percent of working women expressed worry about their families when on work trips.[42] When you are leaving for three days on such a regular basis, it becomes very important to do so in the right frame of mind.

"Good-bye and I Love You"

Though, statistically, flying is safer than ever, flight attendants are well versed in a culture of safety. At the Long Beach training session I attended, numerous slides were shown of crashes and crash situations as a means of demonstrating the best emergency practices. The flight attendants recognized all the crashes by flight number, airline, and location. They knew what had caused the crash. Some even knew how many people had been killed.

Flight attendants are trained to consider the worst, and that it might well happen, unlike your average commuters setting out on the freeway, even though they are actually in far greater danger. Since 9/11, though flight attendants express feelings of greater security, they are still aware that—having seen two airliners deliberately crashed into the World Trade Center—anything is possible.

It is in this context that flight attendants find parting from loved ones particularly painful. Not only may they not be coming back that evening, many flight attendants acknowledge fatalistically that, should the gods turn against them, they may not be coming back at all. Because of that, they seek closure when walking out the door. As Dave, at Northwest observes:

> I personally feel, especially after the events of 9/11, my emotions better be in the basket because if I don't say "I love you," if the plane goes down, or something happens. . . . We've already discussed how I'm going to be feeling, who I'm going to be thinking about . . . because I don't want anyone to feel guilt or that I felt fear or anything else. Emotionally every night it's got to be OK. Especially after the events of 9/11, I didn't realize how much this job touches you in those terms.

"You make sure you say good-bye and I love you every time you leave," says Esther, at Delta. Her husband, also a flight attendant, concurs. "We try to resolve conflicts before a trip," he says. "Usually they don't last more than a few days. We always say good-bye. I love you, kiss. Especially [our son]. Even if he is asleep. You have to be halfway civil when you leave, just in case." Yet resolving conflicts is not necessarily easy. As Heather Healy, director of the AFA's Employee Assistance Program, observes: "It is very difficult to deal with conflict on a flight attendant schedule. You can't complete a fight. Under a mental health model you are told that there is fair fighting and you complete a fight. How do you complete a fight when it is five minutes before you walk out the door? You are going to work with that fight held in suspension for five days."[43] As if reaffirming Healy's point, here is Clare, from Continental:

It's very difficult. Leaving it unsettled. And that's not good with me. Knowing that, with anything, whenever you leave . . . we may not come back. Of course, that's the reality of things. I've never been that type of person. I don't like to leave things unsettled. If I have had an argument or we're not in tune together, I feel miserable of how I left. I don't want to remember that if something were to happen. And I think it's with anything, we want to leave it where we're feeling good about things. Closure, so to speak.

"When I stopped flying my husband was glad," says Sandra. She continues:

"I'm sick of worrying about you," he said. And the kids too. Gemma [her daughter] was glad I retired. I have become more concerned with safety, and I have a sense of relief that I don't have to worry about it, even though I wasn't sure that I was concerned. My husband now says to me, "I'm so glad you're home." We've always tried to do our own thing. The job is good for the relationship in that you're gone and then you are back. But there are issues and misunderstandings, and sometimes I would leave in an angry mood, but I always called before I got on the plane. And I would say, "I hate this," and he would say, "I hate when you go like this."

Getting out the door is no mean feat, either logistically or emotionally. Flight attendants are often running late, driving too fast, worried about missing sign-in, worried about responsibilities left behind.

Flight Attendant Mode

In her study of flight attendant subcultures, anthropologist Joan Volpe talks of "cultural boundaries" in which people move from a dominant to subordinate culture. This could be as simple as a baseball fan attending a game involving his or her favorite team. At some point, that person shifts from being an "ordinary" member of the public to being a Yankees fanatic. Flight attendants, Volpe argues, undergo this transition in the buildup to a flight. Sleep patterns, in particular, become disturbed. Flight attendants stress about oversleeping, missing the flight, or causing some kind of trauma to their fellow crew members. They often worry about losing their flight manual. They also worry about the type of crew they may be working with, and the type of passengers they are likely to meet on the flight. But, as Volpe argues, "the final transition seems to have little connection with these external concerns and takes the form of an internal state of preparedness to mark the total separation from the dominant culture."[44] At some point between getting out the door and greeting the first passenger, flight attendants metamorphose into often completely different characters. Having gone through the turmoil of bidding and securing their trips, preparing and caring at home, and worrying about making call-in, they enter the final phase of leaving, when they go into "flight-attendant mode."

Many service occupations involving face time with the public require some form of shift in persona, part of what Hochschild calls "emotional labor," whereby the emotional relationship between worker and "customer" and performance delivery becomes part of the job. Though Hochschild wrote extensively on flight attendants, who are trained to adopt a "nice" persona, she also analyzed bill collectors, trained to be "nasty" in order to collect payment.[45] Both "good cop" and "bad cop" involve an act, and it is no accident that flight attendants sometimes talk about acting. Paula, an ASA flier for eight years, fixes me with a wry smile as she explains:

> We, basically, are the best actors and actresses in the world. Because even if you know your life is crumbling and going to pot at home, you still have to come do a job. And you've got to have that smile, and you've got to have that good attitude and "what can I do to help you" when it's more like "I need the help and you need to help me." So we're the best at, you know, acting. We should get Academy Awards every month.

Flight attendants conceive of work as "showtime" and talk about "putting on their game face." "I get in the car to go to the airport and put my flight attendant face on," says Andrea. "My emotion stops at the airplane door. Put on your happy face." "You get on that airplane, and you put on a different face," echoes Dave. "You've got your uniform on, and you're ready to go, and you've got a different face, because now you're on."

Flight attendant mode represents closure—albeit temporarily—on life outside the job and therefore seals the departure process. Sometimes people snap into it; other times it is more protracted, as Rebecca, at United suggests:

> I get in flight attendant mode the night before when I'm packing because you're focusing on what you have to do the next day, when you have to get up and all that stuff, writing it down. Then there's the second phase of putting on the uniform. . . . Again, it gets you deeper in the mode depending too on how far away you have to drive. That's where it starts for me, when I put on the uniform because then I'm focusing, I'm not thinking about partying or what I have to do at home. I'm only thinking about my trip and where am I going, how long am I going, what am I going to do when I get there, what do I need, all that stuff even all the way up until I step onto the aircraft. Then everything else gets cut off, going in for the briefing and all that, and all the things you have to take care of in the domicile, blah, blah, all that gets pushed away when the first person comes on the aircraft and it's just *solely* the airplane.

Flight attendant mode, as Hochschild suggests, protects workers from passengers. Workers are taught to think irate customers are not angry at them personally. As she quotes one flight attendant trainer: "If a passenger snaps at you and you didn't do anything wrong, just remember it's not you he's snapping at. It's your uniform. It's your role as a Delta flight attendant. Don't take it personally."[46]

But, equally, flight attendant mode also protects workers from their own feelings about what they have just left behind at home. As Rebecca continues:

> I think part of it also is getting rid of anything. If I've had an argument or something like that with my husband, part of that getting into the flight attendant mode is you're pushing all that stuff behind because you can't be thinking about the argument you had as you're greeting people. And you just don't. It's gone by then. You're not thinking about what's going on in your family life when you finally get to that final mode when you're greeting people. Otherwise you can't put on a smile and greet people. I can't, anyway. I can't sit there and go, "Hi!" and really feel it. Not that you always feel it anyway.

Clare echoes these sentiments:

You're sort of looking back and saying good-bye and dragging your bags, and then once I get through security I seem to just turn into a different person. Flight attendant mode. You just switch everything off in order for you to go. Like if I were to go and continue to feel sorry for myself, how good am I going to be for anyone else? I guess sometimes you have to take yourself out of yourself to deal with things. It's like leaving yourself behind in some respects. . . . And to go off and say OK, this is going to be what I do next. This is an adventure. And you become someone else in order to face it.

"Becoming someone else" is another common refrain I heard on numerous occasions. Hazel, who has flown for United since the 1970s, talks about role switching when making the transition between work and home: "I usually do commute to work in my uniform, and to me, once I put my uniform on, there is that persona, you know, I become that person and I stay that person until I get home, at which time I become me." Several times, flight attendants went so far as to tell me that they often felt like two people, in itself hardly an unusual claim, especially among workers doing emotional labor.[47] But the bifurcated personality flight attendants require is exacerbated by the spatial displacement of the job. The geographic extremities involved mean that when flight attendants "space-out," they not only switch characters but also switch location. Their two characters are physically removed from each other, often by thousands of miles, as they enter a lifestyle that is completely distinct from that at home.

It is worth pushing this point a little further. Being "two people" is different from acting, resembling more the kind of schizoid condition and multiple identities analyzed by some theorists of postmodernism.[48] The compression of time and space to the point of instantaneity, they argue, renders people catatonic and unable to forge anything approaching an "authentic" identity. Being more than one person is merely the spirit of the age we live in, as we switch from one character to another as easily as we change a style of jeans. With flight attendants, however, that identity switching comes about not through the compression of time and space but through its *reverse*. It is because of the very distances involved, the sense of physical dislocation, and the almost complete removal of one world from the other that flight attendants become "different people" as they describe themselves, both on board the airplane and when away from home.

Flight attendant mode is the final stage of the departure process. As Jenny, a former PSA—and now corporate—flier, puts it, "You get on the plane, you clear your mind, you're there to do your job and you can focus on what's going on." The thing flight attendants focus on more than anything else, as the next chapter argues, is safety. As a doctor could not perform an operation if he or she were emotionally connected to the patient, so flight attendants divorce themselves from their "home" characters to enable them to concentrate on what to do should something go wrong. By the time the flight attendant standing in front of you demonstrates how to use the oxygen mask, home is the furthest thing from her mind. Says one worker:

> I have an outer appearance of calm and reserve. I look relaxed, professional and ready to serve the passengers' needs. I am all those things, but what they don't see are my antennae which are always raised for something out of the ordinary. You always have to be ready for an emergency—something with another crew member, passenger has an epileptic attack, emergency landing. I could go on and on.[49]

3

Safety Checks

Safety is always our first concern. On takeoff we're supposed to be thinking exits, crash position, who's where. We're supposed to be going through our mind, in case this is a bad takeoff. We're not thinking about "What am I going to have for dinner tonight? Is that guy going to call me?"

—Kelly, former Delta flight attendant

On July 30, 1992, Trans World Airlines (TWA) Flight 843, a fully laden Lockheed L1011, lumbered down the runway at New York's JFK airport bound for San Francisco with fire from a ruptured fuel tank melting its rear windows.[1] Alerted by a stall warning in the cockpit, Captain William Kinkead aborted takeoff at the very last moment—the plane was airborne for a matter of seconds—and veered off the rapidly disappearing runway.[2] By the time the L1011 had lurched to a halt in a field, its nose wheel had collapsed, and flames were licking the main cabin.

While passengers in business and first class evacuated relatively calmly, those in the back of the plane found themselves facing a terrifying prospect. The rear exits were inoperable, one of the wing exits had blown on deployment, and flight attendants had to prevent passengers using the second one because it was surrounded by fire. The only way out was via the forward exits. Yet in the confusion and smoke, flight attendants at either ends of the plane had no idea what was going on in front of or behind them.

Karen Lacey, an off-duty TWA flight attendant commuting home and sitting in the main cabin, began yelling, "MOVE, RUN, GO FORWARD, GET OUT NOW!" In crash situations, some passengers freeze, and later reports credited Lacey with saving many lives by literally grabbing hold of people and dragging them into the aisle. Those stuck in smoke at the back of the cabin claimed that Lacey's voice led them to safety, as they realized that moving forward was the only way to get out of the airplane, and that it was safe to do so. Having slid down the chutes (in a scene resembling a Marx Brothers movie, workers grappled with a man intent on keeping his prize antler hat, which could have ripped the slide apart), passengers literally ran for their lives. Flight attendants on the ground warned them that the L1011 could explode. Within three minutes of stopping, the aircraft was completely engulfed by flames that took firefighters forty-five minutes to extinguish. No one left on board could possibly have survived: but no one *was* on board. Nineteen flight attendants (including seven who were off duty) and three cockpit crew had got 273 passengers, and themselves, off the plane in ninety seconds, using only two escape chutes. The most serious injury, sustained by a passenger, was a fractured leg.[3]

Flight 843's evacuation passed into the "hall of fame" of such incidents and is often cited among flight attendants as an example of excellent emergency procedure. Yet those workers involved subsequently underwent an experience indicating a contradictory relationship between flight attendant attitudes toward safety and the attitudes held by their airlines. The National Transportation Safety Board (NTSB) report on the incident noted that off-duty flight attendants such as Karen Lacey played a major part in the evacuation, assuming responsibility when others were incapacitated.[4] The NTSB report concluded Flight 843 was lucky in having these off-duty workers on board, yet such workers stepped up to the plate, much as off-duty emergency personnel have often done.

Despite the NTSB's praise, flight attendants on Flight 843 found their knowledge amounted to little when American Airlines bought TWA in 2001. TWA had a better safety record than American; the latter's thirty-eight accidents in nine years resulted in the airline being placed under special FAA scrutiny in 1999. Having crew around who had carried out a renowned real-life evacuation might have counted for something. It didn't, and American furloughed Flight 843's remaining heroines and heroes, along with its other former TWA flight attendants, in 2003.[5]

Flight Attendants as Safety Workers

The speed with which women such as Karen Lacey snap into flight attendant mode, the character they adopt as part of their job, illustrates how safety conscious flight attendants are. Even when they are not on an airplane, safety and anticipating the unexpected are rarely far from their minds, with occasionally amusing results. Several times when lunching with flight attendants, I caught them working out the escape route from the restaurant, just on the off chance we needed it. Kelly chuckles when telling me about her nightly bedtime routine: "Before I go to bed, I say, 'Are the exits clear?' just in my head. And what I mean is, I don't want stuff on the stairways, I don't want stuff in the path from the kids' door, from the kids' bed to the hallway to the stairs, out. There should be nothing on the ground, and I do that every night. I still want [things to be clear], just in case. It will always be in my life."

Yet this image of flight attendant safety consciousness is not matched by their airlines. If you believed numerous advertisements, safety is the very *last* thing a flight attendant is thinking about. She is thinking about *serving* you, not saving you. As far as airlines seem to be concerned, safety in the sky is a pilot's preserve, with flight attendants playing, at best, an appendage role.[6] Most carriers' institutional structure reinforces this distinction: pilots fall under the umbrella of flight operations and accordingly report to this department; flight attendants, on the other hand, report to in-flight services, which is part of marketing. At the same time, up until the mid-1990s, the FAA was both the industry watchdog and its chief promoter, and workers long complained that this dual role amounted to a conflict of interest and that the FAA was reluctant to take action against airlines over safety matters. Unlike predominantly male railroad workers, predominantly female flight attendants are not under the auspices of the Occupational Safety and Health Administration (OSHA), which many believe would offer them better protection against injury on the job. Equally, until 9/11's aftermath, flight attendants were the only airline workers with safety duties not to be required to have federal certification.

The net result is that flight attendants often feel undervalued and underappreciated when it comes to safety.[7] They are quite adamant about why they are on board: ask any flight attendant this question, and she or he will answer, "Safety."[8] It is *never* a laughing matter for them, even amid the jokes and wacky anecdotes of popular flight attendant memoirs. "Your safety is of utmost importance to us," claim former American Airlines flight attendants Corylee Spiro and Elizabeth Harwell in *Cabin Pressure.* "We've been trained so thoroughly that emergency procedures are second nature to us—but they're not to you."[9] In another light-hearted flight attendant "memoir," Joann Kuzma Deveny claims passenger ignorance of safety rules is the number one way to "make a flight attendant fly off the handle." [10]

Safety, Seniority, and the "Space-Out"

Flight attendants consistently stress safety for reasons that date back to the substantial gains they made in the early 1970s. In transforming the job from a stopgap position held by adventurous college graduates to a full-time career, they redefined themselves as safety professionals first and foremost. Though it was always important, safety consciousness took on a new gravitas as part of a wider women's movement seeking greater status among occupations associated with protection. Hitherto, gender stereotypes painted men as "protectors" and women as being "protected," and women's equal-opportunity aspirations were illustrated by their desire to join such potentially dangerous professions as the police, firefighting, and the military.

As women stayed longer as flight attendants, through overturning restrictions on age, marriage, and parenting, safety became a core part of their occupational identity. Thinking of themselves as safety workers first and foremost gave women flight attendants a sense of pride, self-esteem, and membership within a group in which colleagues were responsible for each other's welfare. The growth in trade union participation in the 1970s was one demonstration of this new thinking, as was the developing awareness of specifically feminist health matters.[11]

But flight attendants also began to emphasize safety because it was in their strategic interest to do so. For a group of mainly unskilled service workers, being a safety professional became their best card when it came to bargaining with management. A labor force composed of experienced permanent safety experts has more traction than one composed of inexperienced recent college graduates who only hang around for eighteenth months. From a labor perspective, safety is a wedge issue, one that workers can stress, knowing full well that, especially in post-disaster situations, the public will back them. After 9/11, for instance, the Association of Flight Attendants saw its opportunity to obtain federal certification for flight attendants, a goal cherished since the 1950s. As Pat Friend, AFA president, told me, "We . . . shamelessly have taken advantage out of this opportunity to push it through."[12]

Though they do not say as much, flight attendant demands for greater recognition as safety workers is a manifestation of their sense of control over the job, and the concomitant spaces it provides. On the one hand, constructing your own image of your profession, as opposed to having someone do it for you, is in itself empowering. On the other, the control that flight attendants find so compelling is predicated on them being full-time safety workers and not "flying waitresses."

Their logic is quite straightforward: from the 1970s, the key component to "spacing-out" in the postdestination phase was the growth in seniority's importance, allowing flight attendants to control their geographic movements according to their needs; the key component to seniority's growing importance was the developing notion of the job as a full-time career, allowing "time served" to really matter; and the key component to making the job a full-time career was flight attendants' self-transformation from Barbie Doll into safety professional, emphasizing a new occupational identity in the process.

I am not suggesting that flight attendants are acting here in a purely utilitarian manner. Time and again in crash situations, as the experience of TWA Flight 843 illustrates, flight attendants save lives. But at the same time, they would not be the first group of workers to play their strongest card in negotiating their position in relation to capital. And if they have had to shout loud to be heard, it is because they have had substantial gender prejudices to overcome, which their employers have done little to redress.

A culture still dominated by the "nostalgic flight attendant," seen in films such as *View from the Top*, undermines flight attendants' attempts to impose themselves as safety professionals so that even passengers often do not take them seriously. After all, if they are merely flying waitresses, why listen to them on safety matters? Women in authority positions have always had more difficulty than men in asserting themselves. But women flight attendants have faced the extra problem of overcoming trivial images, and a lack of corrective ones, put forth by their own airlines. They have to battle wider gendered stereotypes consigning women to acting hysterically in a crisis, or to being overtly neurotic and not able to separate the harmless from the harmful.

Yet the truth is that any compromise on safety tends to affect flight attendants before any other airline employee, as the events of 9/11 tragically showed, when they were the first to be killed. Because of their direct contact with the public, flight attendants are finely attuned to things going wrong. Though overall pilots are in charge of airplane safety, shut off in the cockpit they can be oblivious to potentially hazardous developments in the passenger section. Flight attendants argue they complement pilot safety responsibilities, not act as some kind of optional extra, especially because problems endangering an airplane are as likely to emerge from the cabin as from the cockpit. These can range from kitchen fires and turbulence to the increasing threat of air rage and passenger disruption.

Flight attendants often find themselves arguing in a void. They have had to fight for their place within the context of a popular image that is diametrically opposed to their claim to be safety workers. And their insistence on keeping safety issues in the public view has to be set against an airline culture historically bent on keeping them out of sight and out of mind.

Safety: The Problem with No Name

Airlines originally deployed flight attendants partly for safety reasons. In the days before pressurized cabins, when passengers regularly fell ill, "it made everyone flying feel a little more secure, knowing there was professional nursing assistance immediately available," according to Birdie Bomar, Delta's first stewardess.[13] Alongside hands-on, practical assistance, the presence of "ordinary" women in the skies sent a message that flying was routine and boringly safe.

With the development of airplane technology, especially pressurized cabins, the "nursing" side of the profession's image became obsolete. During World War II, airlines scrapped the requirement that flight attendants be registered nurses and, unlike with restrictions on marriage, parenthood, and age, did not reimpose such prerequisites. Carriers began to use their flight attendants' attractiveness, not their safety knowledge, in their branding. Although in 1952 the Civil Aeronautics Board (CAB) made flight attendants' presence on board mandatory for safety reasons, carriers continued to downplay the connection. As late as 1970, American Airlines objected to union proposals including the term "safety" among stewardesses' designated duties.[14] Even today, you will look in vain for any mention of a relationship between flight attendants and safety in airline advertising.

The bottom line is that airlines do not like talking about safety.

Rather like theater actors who do not like referring to Shakespeare's "Scottish play" by its proper title, *Macbeth,* airlines seem to view safety as an unmentionable factor in aviation. In his book *Cleared for Take-Off,* writer and industry expert Stephen Barlay notes how even carriers with good safety records, such as Hong Kong's Cathay Pacific, refuse to discuss the matter.[15] Airlines never boast about their safety records in advertisements because rather than attracting nervous fliers, they are likely to put them off flying altogether. Like Dustin Hoffman's character in *Rain Man,* people with a fear of flying are not going to be won over by one carrier's "better" safety record. Safety is a given, not a bonus, and suggesting your airline is less dangerous than all the others, carriers believe, risks backfiring and provoking a reduction in total passenger numbers. As a corollary, airlines never depict their flight attendants as safety workers, preferring to draw attention to "attributes" such as looks, charm, and service skills. In airline thinking, "This gorgeous twenty-three-year-old may pull you from a burning wreck" somehow does not have the right ring to it. Union campaigns seeking to highlight flight attendants' safety role know this only too well.

Public Perception

The public's experience of flight attendant safety roles is generally limited to apocalyptic crash situations, in which workers do, in fact, pull people from burning wrecks and often subsequently receive awards and recognition. Aircraft crash investigation reports the world over are filled with praise for cabin crew saving lives in such situations. Yet there is a double irony here. On the one hand, very few flight attendants are ever involved in a full-scale evacuation. In this they differ from, say, firefighters in that they are safety workers who only very rarely deploy their full expertise.[16] None of my interviewees have been involved in a real-life full-scale evacuation, though a few have been involved in preparing for one, and most know of colleagues killed in air crashes. Like the military, bunkered down, ready to launch first-strike nuclear missiles, flight attendants are meticulously prepared for something that hopefully will never happen. In this context, their jobs are 99.9 percent routine and 0.1 percent potential sheer terror. They have to be permanently ready for that 0.1 percent.

On the other hand, that 99.9 percent routine contains a sizable safety component that the public either does not see or does not appreciate. It does not see it because workers hide their emotion by deploying flight attendant mode. They are trained to disguise any hint of a safety problem and to act as though everything were normal. Maya, who began flying for Western in the late 1970s, makes this point:

> I'll smile because that's what I'm paid to do and they want to see a pleasant face. If we hit some bad, bad turbulence in the beginning, that used to frighten me, but I couldn't let passengers know that I was intimidated or anything, so I would keep a very strong strength look on my face because it never fails, I would always get major glances when we get real bad turbulence. So those are things that I would act.

In general, the public is oblivious to flight attendants "incorporating a world view of watchfulness and readiness," as anthropologist Joan Volpe describes it.[17] But it also does not appreciate the routine nature of flight attendant safety. If it did, passengers would pay more attention during safety briefings and not think of the flight attendant insisting that extra piece of carry-on luggage should have been checked as merely being overofficious. But, other than in a full-scale emergency, passengers tend to ignore flight attendant safety advice, and in an industry that has not exactly placed it front and center, one can hardly blame them.

Flight attendants occupy a curious space, therefore, in which they want to stress their job as safety workers and are yet continually undermined by passengers who do not take them seriously or airlines that choose to downplay their importance. This disjuncture between how flight attendants see their role and how everyone else sees it is compounded by two factors. First, there is often a gender element at work, with women flight attendants either not listened to or lacking the confidence to exert themselves. When it comes to air rage incidents, in particular, women have difficulty asserting themselves when faced by passengers whose mental construction of a flight attendant's job revolves almost exclusively around service. Second, flight attendants need to continue to emphasize their safety role to maintain their bargaining position within an industry that is already subjecting them to a "squeeze-in," depriving them of those remunerative spaces they find so attractive. Embedding safety means deepening flight attendants' overall sense of control over their lives and, for that reason, often becomes a site of negotiation and struggle. When it comes to communication with the cockpit, air rage, dangerous airplanes or operators, and the pressing problems of fatigue and ill health, flight attendants have had to consistently assert their position as safety workers.

Bumps in the Cabin: Pilot–Flight Attendant Miscommunication

Pilots and flight attendants have always had frosty relationships. Onboard nurses in the 1930s were never made particularly welcome by their male colleagues. In turn, by the 1970s, the larger presence of women on board wide-body aircraft often left pilots feeling outnumbered. In interviews, many flight attendants have few good words for their higher-earning colleagues, perennially regarding them as "cheap" —never paying their share on layovers—and often chauvinist. Though there are some women pilots, the overwhelming majority are men, many of whom hail from a military background tending to reinforce gender hierarchies.

Pilots and flight attendants are also trained very differently. Pilots are taught to exude calmness and to be virtually devoid of emotion; flight attendants are trained to exude warmth and enthusiasm, even if they do not actually feel it. In this scenario, a pilot monosyllabically requesting a crew meal from a flight attendant can come across as rude and brusque, with the two groups of workers using the same words but speaking different languages.

Turbulence

Miscommunication over a beverage is one thing; a communication breakdown over a safety issue is entirely different. Take turbulence, for instance. Though they hide it well behind their flight attendant mode mask, many flight attendants dread turbulence, and with good reason.[18] During 1992, flight attendants at one major carrier experienced 206 turbulence-related injuries, including broken bones, crushed ankles, and back injuries. According to the FAA, turbulence is the leading cause of serious injuries to passengers and flight attendants in nonfatal air carrier operations.[19] Flight attendants represent only 4 percent of aircraft occupants, yet they account for more than half the number of serious injuries and fatalities.[20] Indeed, Bureau of Labor Statistics figures on flight attendant injuries—of which turbulence is only one cause—suggest that the worker injury rate is higher than for construction or mining.[21] Fly for long enough, flight attendants reason, and you are going to get hurt.

Turbulence in itself is hazardous, but its danger is compounded by the fact that, unless it is bad, flight attendants are expected to work through it.[22] On U.S. airlines, the decision to suspend service is in the hands of the captain, who, at the front of the plane, can be completely unaware of beverage carts sliding around at the back. At least one airline flight attendant manual, that for Alaska Airlines, emphasizes how the experience of turbulence can vary greatly according to position on the airplane. Yet, as Canadian flight attendant Nattanya Andersen writes sardonically, in her book *Broken Wings*: "When turbulence hits and they have nothing to hang on to, flight attendants might experience the doubtful joy of weightlessness, and risk breaking bones or having their faces slashed open when they come crashing down on seats or trolleys. Presumably the captain knows when it is safe for them to perform their duties."[23] Besides the fact that pilots may be ignorant of how bad turbulence is in the back of the airplane, airlines expect flight attendants to complete their service duties, so as not to disappoint customers. For flight attendants, turbulence represents a potentially dangerous beverage or meal service, where the risk of getting hit by flying objects or overturned carts is not inconsiderable, or a *suspended* service, leaving them feeling guilty about their passengers. "When we would have turbulence and you only did half the cabin, we felt terrible," Lisa, a Delta flier told me. Some flight attendant injuries stem from the pressure they feel at not getting the service finished.

Regular travelers nowadays may have noticed the cockpit commanding flight attendants to suspend cabin service on some airlines during turbulence. But it does not happen every time the seatbelt sign comes on, which sends mixed messages to passengers who want to know why it is not safe for them to be standing up but OK for flight attendants to be doing so. This confusion in itself can undermine flight attendant authority. But flight attendants standing up when even a hint of turbulence is in the air are in danger. Just before Christmas 1996, an Alaska Airlines Boeing 737 hit two severe bursts of clear air turbulence (CAT) while cruising at 35,000 feet, leaving all three flight attendants injured, two of whom were hospitalized with fractures. Though the seatbelt sign was on, workers were not strapped in because up to that point the pilots had considered the turbulence merely "light chop."[24]

"I Didn't Want to Bother the Captain"

Beyond immediate physical dangers and mixed messages, questions over turbulence are indicative of communication problems between the flight deck and flight attendants. Most women flight attendants are reluctant to second-guess pilots in safety matters, even if they feel unsafe.[25] When things go wrong in the cabin, pilots can underestimate their seriousness, flying on regardless. For example, on one U.S. flight in the early 1990s, flight attendants reported to the cockpit that they were unable to breathe properly and requested that the captain land the aircraft. The captain refused, telling them that the cabin pressurization controls were faulty and were being administered manually and that they would carry on flying for another two hours to their destination. The fact that the whole flight attendant contingent suffered the same symptoms suggests that something was seriously wrong with the air supply in the cabin, but the pilots, ensconced in the cockpit, with a different air hookup, had no idea of the scale of the problem.[26]

In return, flight attendants may underplay a situation's gravity for fear of looking overly anxious in front of male pilots. In 1981, the FAA introduced the "sterile cockpit" period, restricting flight attendant contact with the cockpit to emergencies when a flight is below 10,000 feet. The problem is that flight attendants are sometimes reluctant to make such a call, a judgment that led to disaster in 1989, when twenty-four people were killed when an Air Ontario Fokker F28 crashed during takeoff. Flight attendants had noticed ice formation on the wings—the cause of the crash—but felt they should not disturb the cockpit to relay such information during a "sterile" period. In other words, in a culture that does not take flight attendants' safety role seriously, flight attendants themselves are uncertain about asserting themselves. In one of the most important studies of the matter to date, aviation safety experts Rebecca Chute and Earl Wiener comment:

> Flight attendants, many already intimidated by the authority and mystique of the flight deck, are expected to determine which situations are essential to the safe conduct of a flight. Rather than take a chance on being wrong and thereby breaking the law or embarrassing themselves, and perhaps subjecting themselves to a reprimand from the captain, they opt not to communicate valuable, safety-related information to the pilots.[27]

One particular problem has been the shift from three- to two-person cockpit crews as airlines bought newer aircraft and in the process abolished the old position of flight engineer, who had hitherto acted as an informal conduit between the front and back of the plane.[28] Though airlines such as Southwest and Delta set up programs to foster a greater sense of inclusiveness between pilots and cabin crew, the events of 9/11 have exacerbated the division once again.[29] Air marshals now flying anonymously on U.S. flights have made it clear that their remit is to protect the cockpit and little else, a point brought home jarringly in one worker's recollection of her first encounter with them:

> I worked the flight to Chicago and the air marshals were there. The first lot were fine, but the second lot said that they wanted us to know that if there's a situation where you're taken hostage and are approaching the cockpit door, "We will have to shoot you." One of the flight attendants said, sarcastically, "Thank you. Thank you so much." But I just said to them, "You don't give a shit about us."[30]

Or consider this comment from another worker:

> You know, you're stuck in a tube with somebody at 40,000 feet and we've got a lack of oxygen. You know, the pilots are [at] one end and we're at another. There's a tremendous amount of friction. What goes on, for example, on the 777 the pilots are told not to have as much fresh oxygen in the back because it does curb fuel cost. And when I fly I'm constantly talking, "We need air, we need air, we need air." And one flight, screw it, every flight attendant on the trip, we all took a bottle of oxygen with us.

Since 9/11, paradoxically, flight attendants feel more expendable, even as they are asked by their airlines to pay more attention to passenger behavior. They still feel as though their role in airplane safety plays second fiddle to that of pilots, although, as in the case of the shoe bomber Richard Reid, who tried to blow himself—and the airplane—up on an American Airlines flight over the Atlantic, it was the flight attendants, not pilots, who prevented a disaster. Moreover, obsession with terrorism has overtaken the more quotidian problem of air rage, to which flight attendants find themselves increasingly subjected. Here they not only feel their airlines are reluctant to back them up; they also feel that in undermining their safety authority, messages conveyed by airlines make air rage more likely in the first place.

Air Rage

Since deregulation in 1978, unruly onboard behavior and sometimes physical assault against staff have become an increasing industry problem. Intriguingly, one of the most disruptive groups have been the first-class passengers, more and more annoyed at what they see as declining standards, as opposed to new, inexperienced travelers unused to flying.[31]

Since the 1990s the problem has worsened. In some of the more notorious incidents, passengers have defecated on the serving cart, defecated on people's books, urinated in the aisle, and committed physical assaults on other passengers, flight attendants, or both. Between 1990 and 2000, "unruly passenger cases" opened and closed by the FAA rose from under fifty to more than 200 per year.[32] Admittedly, more people were flying, but even so, these figures are likely to underestimate the scale of the problem. According to Andrew Thomas, author of *Air Rage,* the number of such incidents could be as many as 10,000 per year in the United States alone.[33] Numerous theories abound over the cause of the increase. Reduced leg room, smoking bans, alcohol abuse, and a general decline in behavioral standards have all been cited.[34]

Women Workers and Air Rage

Just as gender plays a role in women flight attendants' struggles to assert themselves as safety workers in dealings with (mainly male) pilots, so air rage often contains a gendered theme. At the International Conference on Disruptive Airline Passengers in 1997, psychiatrist Jerrold Post outlined three passenger traits that could lead to abusive behavior. First, some passengers have a sense of entitlement or "significant narcissistic features." They board an airplane expecting to be able to do and get whatever they want. Second, some passengers, especially business executives, react badly to being made to feel subordinate to flight attendants. Even mild requests from cabin crew, such as asking someone to turn off a laptop, can trigger an outburst from such passengers, especially if they regard the flight attendant as below them in social ranking. Finally, some passengers experience a sense of loss of control that may be manifested in a fear of flying. Placing one's life in the hands of a group of strangers can be anxiety provoking.[35]

In all three cases, women flight attendants are particularly likely to be on the receiving end of disruptive behavior, and at times they ask their male flight attendant colleagues to step in during confrontational situations. As one male worker admitted, "I'm a big guy," and passengers provoke little fear in him. Certainly women workers fear air rage more than their male counterparts: in one study of Australian crew, 47 percent of women pursers (lead flight attendants) who had been on the receiving end of an incident worried about it being repeated compared with 33 percent of male pursers.[36] Similarly, a study of women cabin crew at Alitalia, the Italian state airline, found that passenger harassment was the strongest among a series of work-related risk factors associated with poor health and psychological distress.[37]

Two things seem to be going on here. In *The Managed Heart*, Hochschild discusses how women workers in public service jobs receive less basic deference than men in the same job because of gendered attitudes regarding social status. Flight attendants, she argues, suffer from an "absence of a social shield against the displaced anger and frustration of passengers."[38] A combination of status reaffirmation—passengers needing to feel "above" such workers *and* passengers resenting being told what to do—and outright misogyny makes air rage more likely against women than men.

But, second, women flight attendants find themselves up against images put forth by their own airlines. When passengers view them as service workers, and not safety representatives, they resent being told what to do even when, as the dangers of turbulence illustrate, it may prevent them from being injured. It is hard for passengers to square the woman demanding they sit down when the seat belt sign is on with the one boasting about how she had "auditioned" for her job. In other words, there is a big difference between why passengers think flight attendants are on board and why flight attendants think they are. Passengers may appreciate their presence in an evacuation but view the regular enforcement of safety minutiae—tray tables put away, seat backs upright—as somehow nothing to do with safety, as though flight attendants are just making things up to appear useful. "Why should they care if I have my seat back during take off?" my neighbor moaned to me as we taxied on a Boeing 767 bound from Atlanta to Madrid. When I pointed out that it was not actually for his benefit but for that of the man behind him, who may struggle to get out of his seat in an emergency if the chair in front is reclined, my fellow passenger looked at me as if I had just asked him the square root of 567. Because airlines never equate safety with flight attendants in their advertisements, passengers do not make the connection either. One remedy, as writer Louise Taylor suggests, could be "corrective advertising [which] could help a great deal with issues of authority and respect in the cabin."[39] But, as she admits, that is unlikely to happen in an industry that tries to keep safety off the agenda altogether.

When airlines train flight attendants to treat the unruly passenger as "a child" and to "kill" such passengers "with kindness," flight attendants feel ill equipped to deal with such violent—and dangerous in terms of airplane safety—situations.[40] "In the confined environment of a crowded aircraft at 30,000 feet in the air, cabin crew simply cannot walk away from threatening or violent situations," according to the International Transport Workers Federation.[41] Carriers seem unprepared to deal with the problem: an ITF survey of sixty-four international airlines found fewer than half (42 percent) provided restraint equipment for use on disruptive passengers in the cabin.[42] Even after 9/11, the self-defense classes for which flight attendant unions have been clamoring have not been forthcoming.

Flight Attendants Lack Support

Flight attendants also worry that the FAA and their airlines will not support them. A good example here involved a passenger who pulled a pocketknife on flight attendants and then invaded an Alaska Airlines cockpit during a flight in 1999. The passenger suffered from a delirious condition known as encephalitis, though the chilling parallels with 9/11 are clear. Flight attendant Ginny Cavins wrote Congress to plead for knives to be banned on airplanes and for cockpit doors to be fortified. "We need your help," she argued. "Changes must be made. It could be you or your loved one onboard a flight, next time an air rage or even a hijacking incident occurs."[43] An investigative report in *USA Today* concluded: "Airlines considered costly changes to the doors and the FAA urged a 'zero tolerance' approach to handling unruly passengers. But for all the talk, the agency seldom punished passengers and never ordered airlines to address many of the weaknesses terrorists exploited on Sept. 11."[44] Another flight attendant on that trip commented: "What happened to us should've been big enough for the government to step in and do something about it . . . but to the FAA, it was just another episode that got put in a file somewhere."[45]

Though the FAA sent out an advisory for "zero tolerance" of unruly onboard behavior in 1996, penalties against such passengers were hardly draconian, with regulators preferring warning letters to fining passengers. According to Pat Friend, "the truth is they didn't act. And they acted as though they didn't care."[46]

The FAA does not keep a database of air rage incidents, in itself an indication of its low priority. Plus, there is a lack of international standardization across the industry. If one airline tolerates unruly behavior, it sets the tone for all others. By the late 1990s, some airlines and unions had codified a system of warnings in which passengers would be given written notification that their behavior was unacceptable. KLM and British Airways were in the forefront here, with BA using soccer-style yellow "caution" cards on flights.[47] Still the ITF pressed for stronger action:

> When profit margins are tight or the pressure is on, it is all too easy for the company—or the individual—to pass the buck to the next one down the line for them to exercise responsibility for matters of safety. This is particularly the case with disruptive passengers. Passenger handling increasingly involves a chain of separate companies, and it is important that they each play their part.[48]

Angela Dahlberg, an air rage expert, places the phenomenon within what she calls the "central paradox" of safety and service on airlines.[49] Flight attendants, on the one hand, are trained to think of the company's image and customer satisfaction. On the other hand, they should be thinking of safety above all. Women flight attendants, in particular, struggle to square the circle here. They feel undervalued by both airlines and passengers, particularly irksome when safety is so important to them and their identity within the job. Though airlines pay lip service to recognizing attendants' safety contribution, they do not acknowledge this in advertising. And when flight attendants do point out safety problems, they often find they are not listened to at all.

Is Anyone Going to Listen to Us? Flight Attendants and Safety Concerns

In the early 1990s, American Airlines began operating Fokker F-100 short-range aircraft. With a passenger load of ninety-seven, Fokker manufactured the F-100 with an optional rear door exit. However, American chose not to purchase this variety and instead operated it with two forward and four over-wing exits. Two flight attendants were used on the F-100 with jump seats at the very front and very back of the plane. The problem for the rear flight attendant was that if the front worker was incapacitated, the rear worker would have had trouble getting forward to operate the emergency exits. And, as American waived the extra safety feature, there was no way out of the back. In 1992, American's flight attendant union, the Association of Professional Flight Attendants (APFA), conducted a survey in which workers wrote in the following comments:

> I am *terrified* of sitting in the rear of the plane (#2 position). Will I get fired if I refuse to fly it?
> Why does the FAA allow an aircraft to have no aft exit?
> This aircraft is an insult to our intelligence.
> If we were in an emergency situation, I feel I would not have the means to get pax [passengers] out safely and effectively.
> The aircraft is a fire trap for the #2 flight attendant. It's a violation of safety standards not to have an aft exit.
> This aircraft is a hazard. I refuse to bid it because it scares me.
> Get rid of these absolute death traps.[50]

The FAA took no action to allay these concerns. However, the June 1999 Little Rock crash of American Airlines Flight 1420, an MD80, which killed ten passengers and the pilot, exposed how potentially dangerous the F-100 was. In a violent thunderstorm, the MD80 ran off the runway and collided with a lighting structure. The airplane split apart, and fire broke out, working its way from the middle toward the tail section. Though the tail cone exit had not deployed, flight attendants were able to open it manually and led passengers to safety. In all, 131 passengers survived. However, as Lonnie Glover, APFA safety spokesperson, pointed out to me, "Had it been an F-100 you can only imagine the outcome."[51] With no rear exit, and the fire past the over-wing window exits, at least eighty passengers in the back section would have been trapped and almost certainly killed. Still, American operated the F-100 beyond 9/11 and has only recently retired the jet, though not due to flight attendant pressure. In this situation, it is easy to see why flight attendants feel their safety expertise is ignored.

ValuJet

A more infamous example was ValuJet Flight 592, a DC-9 that crashed into the Florida Everglades in May 1996. ValuJet was the industry darling, having turned a profit in only its second month of operations in 1993 and seen its share price increase to $27.50 from an initial public offering of $6.25.[52] Its low fares and market strategy placed ValuJet at the forefront of the emerging "second wave" of low-cost carriers leading the industry recovery from the first Gulf War recession.[53] On May 11, 1996, ValuJet's image collapsed as one of its DC-9s caught fire due to hazardous materials in the cargo hold and plunged into the Everglades swamp, killing all 105 passengers, three flight attendants, and two pilots (including the first woman airline pilot to be killed in the United States).

Media scrutiny and the subsequent investigation focused on the airline's consistently shaky safety record. The Department of Transportation's inspector general, Mary Schiavo, had labeled the airline unsafe in a *Newsweek* article only days before the event. She also criticized the FAA for allowing ValuJet to continue to fly. After the crash, the FAA revoked the airline's safety license, while the subsequent NTSB investigation laid blame on a subcontracting operations system increasingly endemic among low-cost carriers. ValuJet eventually bought Air Tran and rebranded itself under that airline's banner.

However, what also emerged from the crash investigations was the extent to which flight attendants had led the safety critique of ValuJet, and yet been largely ignored. As many as fifty ValuJet flight attendants resigned after the crash, out of fear for the airline's safety, while several of them went onto ABC's *Nightline* to voice their concerns.

ValuJet had seemed intent on preventing flight attendant unionization, with the safety expertise that such a move would have brought to the table. Its flight attendants, having voted for union recognition before the crash, eventually won their first contract at Air Tran in 1998.

But keeping costs low was the highest priority. In fact, ValuJet regularly fired flight attendants who complained about working conditions or showed support for AFA. Many flight attendants were receiving less than $1,000 a month, with no sick or holiday pay. If flights were canceled, workers would not be paid, which created a clear conflict of interests.

ValuJet's most flagrant safety violation occurred when an off-duty pilot took the seat of a five-year-old child, whose parents were told—over a flight attendant's objections—to hold the child in their laps during the flight, a clear infringement of FAA regulations. The flight attendant subsequently called the FAA emergency hotline to report the incident, which the FAA largely ignored, passing the buck back to ValuJet. ValuJet fired the flight attendant seven days after the worker reported the violation.[54]

The AFA targeted ValuJet's safety record before and, even more so, after the Florida crash. Pat Friend, AFA president, speaking at House Subcommittee on Aviation hearings into whistle-blower protection in the industry, said that ValuJet's staff turnover rate, with about 15 flight attendants fired per month, would be the equivalent of between 600 and 1,000 flight attendants leaving at an airline the size of United.[55] Susan Clayton, AFA's local president, testified:

> When flight attendants were repeatedly injured by faulty cockpit doors, AFA complained to management. Shoddy repairs did little to solve the problem, leaving some flight attendants with permanent injuries. Another flight attendant came to me after she witnessed major safety violations. I had to tell her that if she spoke out, she would have little protection. When she did come forward, the company's response was to send her to a psychiatrist. She was later forced to quit because of her safety concerns, and the company repeatedly denied the incidents had occurred. There was no law to protect her. I had a flight attendant friend who quit because she said she knew it was time to quit when she looked out the door when they were 20-something thousand feet in the air and she could see the blue sky because the door seals weren't intact.[56]

Clayton claimed that up to 60 percent of ValuJet's flight attendants were concerned about safety prior to the Florida crash. At one point during the hearings she was asked whether she had taken these concerns to management. "Yes, I did," she replied, "[To President] Lewis Jordan." On being asked what the management response was, she said, "Well, I just felt like the attitude that I got from them was 'We'll look into it, but you're not really a mechanic or a pilot.' I've never claimed to be. 'We'll get back to you.'"[57]

In his book *The Culture of Fear,* Barry Glassner talks of the obsessive media overreaction to the ValuJet crash, with *USA Today* running more than seventy pieces in the two weeks after the incident, and argues quite plausibly that in putting people off flying the media pushed them onto roads that were in fact far more dangerous. But he also makes an important point when talking about the AFA's spokeswoman, appearing on *Nightline,* linking ValuJet's safety record to its poor treatment of flight attendants:

> While her reasoning may be specious (an airline certainly may treat its workers poorly and at the same time fly its customers safely), who can fault her for capitalizing on the crash to draw attention to the plight of her members? ValuJet's flight attendants were paid far less than their counterparts at major airlines, and their duties also included cleaning the cabin between flights. Yet what were the odds on *Nightline* devoting a program to the working conditions of low-level airline employees?[58]

It is because a crash is one of the only times the public considers flight attendants' safety role—a vital part of their identity within the job, and the key to their retaining control over their spaces inside and outside of it—that workers will seize on the window of opportunity to upgrade their status, before the public once more begins to think of them as flying waitresses. In the aftermath of the ValuJet crash, flight attendant unions succeeded in getting Congress to attend to two long-cherished aims: to split the "dual mission" of the FAA, where the body was responsible for safety *and* the promotion of the industry; and whistleblower protection, to prevent airlines taking action against flight attendants who report safety concerns.

Flight attendants are therefore in a continual struggle to entrench their position at the airlines, thereby creating the kind of job security that enables them to exert control over the movements of their lives. Stressing safety is the best way to achieve this, be it concern about turbulence, air rage, or warnings of dangerous operators or aircraft. But they still feel that airlines do not listen to them: hence their need to cap-italize on crash situations and refocus public attention on flight atten-dants as safety workers, not flying waitresses. There is a chain of causa-tion here, albeit an indirect one. However, a far more direct link can be made between flight attendants' concerns about fatigue, and health in general, and their ability to "space-out." There is no point in creating time and space for yourself when you are too exhausted to actually do anything.

Worn Out: Flight Attendant Health

Fatigue is a particularly acute problem for flight attendants, especially when they are working in a pressurized cabin, subjected to abnormal g-forces on every takeoff and landing. Throw in long days and jet lag, and it is easy to see how flight attendants can become more tired than, say, ordinary shift workers.[59] Flying across times zones on a regular ba-sis is disorienting and exhausting. "You never get over it," Angela, who started flying for Delta in 1969, tells me. "It took me two years to figure out how to do it on international," says Molly, at United. "My final so-lution was turning the clock round and not looking at it. On the crew bus in Europe people would always be saying 'Did you sleep?' or 'How did you sleep?' In Paris I sat up all night and watched the sun come up over the buildings. This wasn't a glamorous job."

Healthwise, jet lag is a serious problem for flight attendants.[60] Older workers have particular trouble adjusting to it, presenting a conundrum on U.S. airlines in that it is normally senior flight attendants who work high-time, transmeridian flights. Those working economy sections suffer particularly from jet lag–induced fatigue.[61] All flight attendants crossing time zones find their sleep restless and easily disturbed on layovers.[62]

However, high-time flights are the most popular, which suggests tiredness is a price that flight attendants are willing to pay in return for being able to "space-out." "To have no jet lag you have to work extra days or harder trips," says Carolyn, from Delta. Derek, also at Delta, dismisses jet lag as part of the job: "It's like being an athlete and playing with pain, it's just something you've got to do. I chose to fly and be on those flights, so, you know, it's the consequence of flying it."

Still, flight attendants get confused over where they are, especially those flying out and back in the same night. Jill, from Air Tran, for instance, says this:

> We get disoriented. Oh, definitely. Especially what we call a standup, which is that one where we get in at midnight and we go back out and we check back in at 5:00 or 6:00 in the morning. I mean, you're not going to sleep in three or four hours, or get enough sleep. And if you do those, like, three in a row, I couldn't tell you which way I'm headed, which direction, what city I'm going to. Am I going to Atlanta or coming back? Personally I think that they are unsafe. I really do. I don't do those anymore, that was way back when I started. I really think they need to dispense of those. You can get disoriented. And another thing that disorients you is the day of the week because of your schedule. When you're first starting, you fly all days of the week and it's never the same. Every trip goes to a different city, and I would have to ask another flight attendant, what is today?

Her Air Tran colleague Angie also gets disoriented. She flies stand-ups because doing so allows her to spend the most time with her infant daughter. I met her early one morning after a flight, and as we sat in the atrium at Atlanta's Hartsfield Jackson Airport, she smiled and said: "Like last night, that was pretty good for a stand-up. We call them stand-ups because it's five hours rest. I think I went to sleep at 11:30 and I got up at 4:30, so that's a good five-hour stint there. And, usually on my stand-ups we're talking about three to four hours of sleep. So, I have to take a nap when I'm at home, but I don't always get to."

Fatigue is clearly a problem for many flight attendants, especially for mothers who attempt to slot straight back into family routines on return. However, industry arguments over work hours tend to polarize along traditional gendered lines in which (mainly male) pilots, with their safety focus, have been in need of protection since 1972 but flight attendants, whose safety contribution is regarded as more anomalous, have struggled to get any protection at all. Despite numerous promises during the 1970s and 1980s, congressional hearings in the 1990s, and a House bill in 1991 that failed under pressure of presidential veto, the only action taken on flight attendant hours since 1958—despite revolutionary technological and institutional changes in the industry—was an FAA notice issued in 1993 mandating rest periods, and not hours worked.[63]

Flight attendants thus must have a minimum rest period of nine hours following any duty period of more than fourteen hours. The latter is calculated from fifteen minutes after the engines are turned off to one hour before scheduled takeoff. The rest period can be reduced to eight hours if an airline schedules a rest period of ten hours the next time around.

Yet fatigue will not go away. The difficulties start in the FAA definition of "rest period" as all off-duty time. According to the APFA, this is "misleading because much more must be done during this period than sleep."[64] Flight attendants will often only get five or six hours of sleep on layovers, if they arrive late and take off early the following morning (within the regulations). Regulations remain both vague and complex, and flight attendants themselves are often unsure of them. The FAA argues that it is up to an operator, not a flight attendant, to ensure that rest requirements are met. The onus is upon a flight attendant to declare if she or he is fatigued, yet most are reluctant to do this for fear that it will lead to a mark on their record.

Wendy, an Employee Assistance Program representative at Air Tran, describes the continuing problem of fatigue:

> You know the length of days, and these flight attendants just get worn out. I mean they are tired. They can't get in at 10:00 at night, fall into bed, and start again the next morning. They get ill. Then they start getting snappy with each other. I mean, I'm not saying that happens all the time, but when you get tired and you get frayed, then those sorts of things pop up. There is a safety issue there.

A series of factors compound this problem. For a start, carriers are increasingly utilizing the "minimum" eight-hour rest period as a standard practice, as opposed to an emergency requirement. As one union official admitted to me, "That part of the regulations bit us in the butt." On international flights, in particular, increasing the numbers of flight attendants on duty above the legal minimum (one per fifty seats) allows a carrier to increase the length of duty days, as rest periods can be built into the flight (though how restful these are is unclear). Delays throw flight attendant scheduling off. It is often up to the attendants to contact crew scheduling if they feel they are in danger of becoming illegal (i.e., exceeding duty hour levels). As computers have been increasingly used in working out bid lines, trip pairings for flights have moved up closer to the fourteen-hour maximum.[65]

Other Health Issues

If fatigue is a problem, then so, too, are a number of more specific health-related matters. As passengers and the media alike are increasingly aware, the airplane cabin is not the healthiest environment on the planet. The rise in stories concerning sometimes-fatal conditions such as deep-vein thrombosis and SARS is the tip of an iceberg that extends to poor air quality (through pilots reducing cabin oxygen levels), dry skin, radiation exposure, and problems with pressurization.

Gender plays a part here, too, in the sense that some of the most common complaints from flight attendants are specific to women. Foot, leg, and back problems have been exacerbated by shoe regulations that forced women flight attendants to wear heels. Given that during a ten-hour international flight, workers can take more than 10,000 steps, averaging 17 a minute, it is no surprise that such issues crop up.[66] Pauline, who started flying for Delta in the 1960s, says:

> When you're up on your feet, I started way back when you couldn't have alternate shoes. You had to wear high heels, three-inch high heels. Ridiculous. Three-inch heels boarding, during the flight, you had to wear a hat. Times have really changed. But very hard on your legs. Hard on your back. And you can imagine when you are having to go up and down the aisle pushing/pulling the cart, which weighed 250 pounds and most of the airplane sits at like a forty-degree angle because the engine is in the back.

Airline footwear regulations play a part here, but flying conditions themselves affect women when it comes to nonmusculoskeletal problems. A 2002 study among AFA members in California found a female breast cancer incidence rate more than 30 percent higher than among the general population and a malignant melanoma rate twice what was predicted.[67] Women flight attendants also have fertility problems, and time zone changes can wreak havoc with menstruation.[68] Though early research suggested pregnant flight attendants faced little danger in continuing to fly through the first trimester, later studies found spontaneous abortion to be more common among flight attendants who continued flying than among those who had pregnancies outside a time span of active flying.[69]

Despite such health problems, as well as physical injury caused by turbulence, flight attendants remain outside the jurisdiction of the OSHA, set up in 1970, and under the auspices of the distrusted FAA, which workers have long viewed as too industry-friendly.[70] They have campaigned for many years for the OSHA supervision they believe would give them better protection against the many injuries and ill-nesses they suffer each year.[71] Though a memorandum of understanding was issued between OSHA and the FAA in 2000, little has been done since, leaving flight attendants, according to AFA, "without any mean-ingful health and safety protections."[72] In fall 2005, AFA-CWA filed suit in district court against the secretary of labor and FAA for "failure to ensure the health and safety of flight attendants and other employees working in the airline industry."[73]

Continuing Safety Issues

After 9/11, flight attendants capitalized on the new, though short-lived, public concern for their safety to point out the inconsistency of being classed as "safety-sensitive" in drug testing procedures but not when it came to FAA certification. They were the only "safety-sensitive" group in the industry not to require it, with safety training left to individual airlines. Even though training courses were subject to FAA approval, standards varied—especially during recurrent refresher courses—a point made by the NTSB in the early 1990s.[74]

In late 2003, as part of the FAA Reauthorization Bill, Congress ap-proved the introduction of flight attendant certification. For the AFA, certification represented recognition that flight attendants were safety professionals, period. But it also increased the portability of their skills during a period of potential industry upheaval. Before certification, in-dividual airlines kept records of safety training, which were not trans-ferable if a flight attendant moved or was laid off. With certification, the AFA hopes records will be kept in a central database to which airlines can refer when checking proof of competence in new recruits coming in from other carriers. Of course, carriers had long resisted transferability of skills because this tends to raise wage rates, a point of which flight attendant unions seemed only too aware.[75]

But despite industry certification, flight attendants still find them-selves in a battle. Their personal health and safety are still not covered by the OSHA. Many, especially in the economic downturn, feel their airlines do not really care about them, and the spaces they once carved out for themselves in the job are being increasingly eroded. The new-found respect they won as safety professionals after 9/11 has already declined. The recent movie *Flightplan* depicts flight attendants as uncaring automatons—"It's OK to hate the passengers" one worker says to another—while the twist in the plot has one of them as a terrorist, in extraordinarily bad taste following 9/11.

At the same time, the public still does not seem to grasp flight attendants' position as safety workers. In a recent book review, novelist J. G. Ballard had this to say about safety briefings: "Before take-off the cabin crew perform a strange folkloric rite that involves synchronised arm movements and warnings of fire and our possible immersion in water, all presumably part of an appeasement ritual whose origins lie back in the prehistory of the propeller age. The ceremony . . . has no meaning for us but is kept alive by the airlines to foster a sense of tradition."[76] *A sense of tradition?* Actually, the preflight safety announcement is a critical part of airplane safety whose purpose is to remind passengers that flight attendants are in charge, as well as focusing workers' minds on the job. Numerous accident investigation reports have credited the safety demonstration with saving lives in an emergency.[77]

Thus, despite achieving their aim of gaining safety certification, flight attendants are still up against images that challenge their status. And removing the gravitas from their profession is the first step in removing its sense of permanence. Flying on Independence Air from Washington Dulles to Atlanta in June 2005, I was alarmed to find the safety demonstration being conducted not by the lone flight attendant but by the recorded voice of a comedian, Dennis Miller. The entire dialogue was a series of jokes—"We have fully functioning seatbelts, what other airline gives you that?"—that seemed to deny that flying is in any way dangerous and to suggest that the worker in front of you really was there just to serve the drinks.

In using such announcements the airline claimed to be responding to FAA guidelines suggesting airlines be "innovative" and "make safety information briefing as interesting as possible." CEO Kerry Skeen claimed Independence Air had "come up with an approach that's not only innovative and fun, but will create more awareness of the safety information being presented."[78] Southwest, for instance, with its superb safety record, has always had a reputation for impromptu jokes during the safety demonstration. I have laughed along with most other passengers when flying that airline. Equally, many airlines use videos instead of flight attendants to get across the message. But the problem in the case of Independence Air seemed to me to be the position of the flight attendant, who stood at the front throughout with the worn smile of someone who had heard the jokes one too many times. Unlike Southwest, or with videos that invariably use flight attendant models, the Independence Air demonstration seemed to decouple the flight attendant from safety procedures entirely.[79] When the airline recruits its flight attendants with the tagline "Want to deliver Tender Loving Service in the skies?" it seems, as the next chapter explores, that we have come full circle, to flight attendants being entertainment figures and not safety professionals.[80]

4

In-Flight Entertainment?

Let's keep our fingers crossed for some turbulence. . . . What better
way to start a vacation than being in a confined space with a couple of giggly Hooters Girls? I can't wait.
　　　　　　　　　　　—Hooters Air passenger Henry Coleman[1]

The only airline in the world that truly relies on the attractiveness
of cabin staff is of course Hooters Air. But I have flown them before and although you have two nice little Hooters girls playing
games during the flight you are actually served by a lumbering
granny employed by Pace Airlines.
　　　　　　　　　　　　　　　—Internet discussion forum[2]

　　　Midway through a short hop on Hooters Air from Atlanta
to Myrtle Beach, one of those "nice little Hooters Girls" rose from the
front seat and took the microphone. Clad in tight orange shorts and a
white tank top emblazoned with "Delightfully tacky yet unrefined"
across the back, she began to probe passengers with trivia questions.
Unfortunately, the microphone did not work properly, and from my
backseat position I heard only a few garbled inquiries about when
Hooters opened its first restaurant (the airline is part of the famously
garish restaurant chain) and the date of its first flight. Though she was
often inaudible, the Hooters Girl rewarded first correct answers with
various Hooters memorabilia and freebies. Ironically, the technical
glitches disappeared just in time for the final question: "OK, here we go
. . . does anyone remember my name?"
　　I actually did remember Brigitte's name because she had introduced
herself before takeoff. But, in an increasingly uncomfortable silence, I
was not sure if the question might not have been rhetorical. Eventually
a man raised his hand and answered correctly, and Brigitte gave him his
prize. "That went too fast," she complained. "Now I've nothing to do."
　　Two Hooters Girls were in action when I continued from Myrtle

Beach to Baltimore. This time, after "What are our names?" they asked, "Where is the 2005 Miss Bikini-USA contest located?" To my surprise, someone knew it was Fort Lauderdale, which was Alison's cue to reveal that she was, on top of being a Hooters Girl, Miss Bikini Maryland. A generous round of applause ensued.

I do not mean to disparage Hooters Girls, who, as sociologist Meika Loe reminds us, work hard for their living.[3] We all have bills to pay, and at $13.50 an hour a Hooters Girl—the airborne ones are plucked from the restaurants—is a good step up from minimum wage.[4] Brigitte, having risen early in Atlanta to work the Myrtle Beach flight, ran straight to the plane bound for Las Vegas—a tiring day in anyone's book.

There is no accurate way to gauge the airline's success because, as a private company, Hooters does not have to publish its earnings. However, in two years it has expanded the number of airports served from two (Atlanta and Myrtle Beach) to fifteen. Small regional airports such as Scranton welcome the arrival of Hooters Air, providing it with subsidies by way of short-term revenue guarantees and free marketing of its flights.[5] Business groups in South Carolina have been lobbying the airline to run charter flights to London.[6]

According to President Mark Peterson, Hooters is not "trying to measure up" to Southwest, JetBlue, or other low-cost carriers. "We are small," he insists, "a niche player."[7] Despite such modesty, however, Hooters is a standard-bearer for an industry that continues to exploit and control women's bodies in the name of selling tickets. The Hooters Girl featured in airline advertisements is a direct nostalgic link—albeit supposedly laden with irony—back to the kind of 1960s imagery U.S. flight attendants had fought so hard to abolish. Taken from a global perspective, however, placing women's bodies at the heart of an airline's identity never actually went away, as the case of Singapore Girl, Singapore International Airlines' marketing phenomenon clearly illustrates.

I have been arguing that flight attendants have a special relationship with space and that the "space-out," in its various phases, is one of the job's main attractions. In the postdestination phase, especially, women's ability to control where they will be and when becomes a key reason for staying in the profession. As described in the previous chapter, however, that control is predicated upon the job's image as a safety professional as opposed to a stopgap position. Nostalgic images rekindling the *Coffee, Tea or Me* era do flight attendants no favors, depicting a period of temporary jobs and not a full-time profession.

Body Controls

In fighting restrictive employment practices in the 1960s and early 1970s, flight attendants developed a political consciousness that resonated with wider changes in the feminist movement. Where once women struggled over equal opportunity and access, steeped in the kind of liberal feminism advocated by writers such as Betty Friedan, by the early 1970s flight attendants were challenging notions of "femininity" itself. In an important development, women increasingly insisted that being female did not equate to being feminine.[8] One is a biological description; the other is a social construction that largely served patriarchal capitalism. As feminist thought radicalized, for writers such as Shulamith Firestone and Mary Daly, breaking femininity's grip was the main issue, and this could be done only through women regaining control over their own bodies.[9] It is in this context that the 1973 *Roe vs. Wade* Supreme Court decision legalizing abortion was truly radical.

Taking control of one's body is perhaps easier said than done, though. Figuring out how patriarchy, capitalism, or both control and exploit women's bodies has become a major area of academic research.[10] The French philosopher Michel Foucault looms over much of this work. In his classic book *Discipline and Punishment,* Foucault explored the relationship between discipline and the human body, using an analysis of prisons and, in particular, the Panopticon, the futuristic prison designed by the English utilitarian thinker Jeremy Bentham. In the Panopticon, discipline was enforced not through physical punishment but through surveillance, with prisoners fully aware that they were being constantly watched and modifying their behavior accordingly. For Foucault, the major effect was "to induce in the inmate a state of conscious and permanent visibility that assures the automatic functioning of power."[11] Individuals under constant surveillance become highly aware of their bodily movements and, in effect, perform in ways that they think authority will approve.

Naomi Wolf's book *The Beauty Myth* pursues a similar line of reasoning. As women have made great strides from a legal and institutional perspective, winning the vote, entering paid employment in large numbers, and challenging sexist legislation, they have also become, Wolf argues, increasingly obsessed with an unattainable ideal of beauty and femininity. Citing the case of *Vogue* magazine's greater focus on women's bodies, as opposed to fashion, from the late 1960s, Wolf outlines how the media created a "problem"—namely, how to be a perfect woman—where none previously existed. A cultural backlash is at work, she argues, in which women become the enforcers of their own bodily enslavement due to the need to conform to cultural norms.[12]

Flight attendants provide an almost perfect subject for these arguments. As sociologist Melissa Tyler has written, bodily discipline has never been far from flight attendants' lives, be it weight watching, correct appearance and grooming, or, drawing on the work of sociologist Erving Goffman, display and performance according to strict company procedures. "To secure employment as a flight attendant," Tyler (with Philip Hancock) writes, "a woman must achieve and maintain a particular state of embodiment, prescribed primarily according to an instrumentally-imposed concept of a feminine body and practiced largely according to constraint, containment and concealment."[13] Airlines have infamously sought to control the spaces of flight attendants' bodies. But it has never been a one-way fight, even though carriers often have the upper hand. As feminist critics of Foucault have argued, constant surveillance can become not only a means of imposing societal norms about femininity but also a consciousness-raising exercise leading to a greater sense of one's identity and political agency.[14] In flight attendants' cases, "the perfect body" in advertising became a unifying target that turned an inchoate sense of grievance into a highly organized activist campaign.

Flight attendants have attempted and continue to attempt to reclaim their bodily spaces, both through redefining their role as safety workers, as opposed to sex objects, and through challenging and subverting the idealized flight attendant norm. As Jean, a very senior Delta flier says, "I started thinking it was a line when guys would say, 'You're not like I thought a flight attendant would be.' What did you think a flight attendant would be?" In other words, flight attendants attempt to construct multiple images of themselves, not conform to a nonexistent "Barbie Doll" norm. In so doing, they have fought to reclaim *their* space, not conform to a fictitious bodily space of airline fantasies.

Image Wars: Selling Sex

Between 1960 and 1970, passenger numbers on U.S. airlines skyrocketed. But they did so within a tight regulatory framework, forcing airlines to compete on service, not on price. As chapter 1 describes, airlines in the 1960s increasingly placed conflated images of stewardesses and sex at the heart of their brand image. Braniff International was perhaps most extreme, with its Air Strip, in which an onboard worker removed her outer garments piece by piece, but most airlines adopted subtle, and not so subtle, facsimiles. Even conservative Delta was moved to ask, "Why do people say Delta's the best thing that ever happened to air travel?—You're looking at 4 good reasons!" under a picture of four of its flight attendants crossing the apron.

In the 1970s, however, overt sexualization in the United States began to exhaust itself. For a start, constructing airline identity around the figure of a smiling young woman only worked if passengers thought the smile was genuine. Doris Lessing was one of several authors who took aim at the "smiling, smiling, smiling" stewardesses who seemed incapable of appreciating the "monstrousness" of the situation in which they found themselves.[15] In an era that spawned *The Stepford Wives* and other monuments to lost identity, flight attendants seemed to embody not so much company sincerity but company *in*sincerity.[16] Medical research at the time argued that these smiling women verged on the android: "Stewardesses seldom find in their profession the evolution of the great existential problems that arise for women in their 20s and their 30s: love, fulfillment, well-balanced work adjustment, occupational prospects for the future."[17]

In fact, it was these supposedly maladjusted workers who challenged sexist imagery to ensure they *had* occupational prospects for the future, by overturning marriage bans and age limits in the late 1960s. As more women in the profession worked into their thirties, or were married, advertising that presented flight attendants as young sex objects seemed increasingly incongruous. Perhaps the airlines themselves recognized this: in 1974 Southern Airlines—responsible for some of the era's more racy images—released a spoof television advertisement depicting an orgy in first class. As flight attendant historian Katie Barry suggests, Southern—despite a good dose of hypocrisy—"announced that the theme of sex had become so predictable and widespread in airline advertising as to be a target of satire."[18]

Workers found both the advertising and the imagery that spun off it derogatory and simply inaccurate. When I ask Rosanne, a Delta flier, about the *Coffee, Tea or Me* image, based around the notorious book of the late 1960s, she says:

That's one of the things that is such a fallacy. . . . Flight attendants usually are not interested in passengers and hitting on passengers. Very
rarely, that I know of. . . . But even back in the seventies—I'm trying to
think if I ever met any passengers. I don't think I did. I met one and he
was a nut case. It was like his wife called me up and said, "Why are you
going out with my husband?" And I said, "I just talk to him." You
know, on a flight, that was it. More of us just partied amongst the flight
attendants rather than got involved with the stuff on the airplane, the
Coffee, Tea or Me stuff. Because I always thought that was stupid.

I get a similar response from Claudette, also at Delta, when I ask her
about the sexual imagery surrounding the profession:

It makes you feel like they don't know what they're talking about. I
could sit here and tell you hundreds of stories of stuff we used to do
that we would all be fired for today. Some of the crazy stuff we used to
do. But to be a sex goddess? Most airlines, other than PSA, pretty much
hired all-American-type girls. I kind of sit back and go, in a way it's
kind of funny to kind of laugh at yourself and see how a producer or a
screenwriter thinks what we do.

But at the time many flight attendants objected strongest to the suggestion that it was the airlines, rather than themselves, that controlled their
sexual behavior. Given the more relaxed social and sexual mores of the
time, it would be surprising if an element of promiscuity did not enter
the profession. Women at this time were taking control of their bodies,
and exercising choice in sexual partners was part of this development.
Some flight attendants I spoke with openly admitted to having casual
encounters when they started flying in the 1970s. But this is beside the
point. The argument here is not whether flight attendants slept around:
it is that sleeping around became a marketable product, a commodity
owned and advertised by the airlines. Barbara, a San Francisco–based
attendant, put it succinctly: "What I think really pissed people off is
that we are on our own . . . that we *could* have sexual affairs if we
wanted to. That's the issue. *That we have a choice.*"[19] "In the jet age,"
writes historian Suzy Kolm, "serving as a flight attendant could considerably expand a woman's sexual choices. . . . the enhanced control
women sometimes gained through the sexy images of the occupation
was not what many women resented—they resented the insinuation

[that] they were available to any and all men."[20] "We like flirtations when we have the freedom of choice," wrote one flight attendant, "but do not like to believe that just because we are Hostesses we must endure the reputation of professional flirts."[21]

The argument flight attendants articulated was akin to that of a prostitute claiming to have been raped: just because she engages in sex for a living, it does not mean that she should be subjected to such an ordeal. Even if flight attendants chose to sleep around, it did not mean that they were open to advances from every fantasy-fueled male passenger. Indeed, they bitterly resented the assumption that airlines did not take complaints about sexual harassment seriously or, perhaps even worse, dismissed it as "part of the job."[22] In her book *Sex Objects in the Sky* (1974), Paula Kane, a former flight attendant and organizer for Stewardesses for Women's Rights, talks of her friend Jan's contrasting experiences working as a flight attendant and working in a bar:

> In a bar [says Jan] the customers seemed to consider us more in the public domain than passengers do a stewardess, perhaps because there wasn't such a mythic aura about barmaids. But the owners of the bar were far more protective and respectful than the airlines. If a man hassled a barmaid he was out on his ear, but if he hassled a stewardess the airlines apologized to him and disciplined her.[23]

So it was not sex but the marketing of sex that women resented. Increasingly, flight attendants rejected the imagery that surrounded the profession. As Lisa, a Delta flier puts it: "[There was] that horrible book *Coffee, Tea or Me?* That was a horrible book. I could look at it and see the flippant sense of humor in it, and it was during the sixties, when the sexual revolution was really taking off. But it did create an atmosphere there for a while. And then that 'Fly Me' campaign came along."

"Fly Me" and Stewardesses for Women's Rights

The "Fly Me" campaign, launched by National Airlines in 1971 to the tune of $9.5 million, crystallized flight attendant objections to being continually portrayed as sex objects and not as safety workers. It also led to their increasing politicization as battles over bodily space and image shaped a new identity and consciousness among these workers.

National, based in Florida, had already established a reputation for risqué advertising, with a bizarre penchant for representing women as cats: one 1965 television advertisement contained a purring female cat boasting about the airline's flight attendants, "If they'll do that for a woman, dahling, just imagine what they'll do for a man."[24] The brainchild of the F. William Free advertising agency, "Fly Me" attempted to give the airline a single, manageable and controllable personality.[25] Though the agency for a while began naming the actual airplanes (i.e., you really *were* flying Cheryl), this was something of a smoke screen. As one former National worker told me, "Before every flight boarded, we had to go to the gate, say our name, then say 'Fly Me.' It was very upsetting for me, but I loved my job and did what had to be done."

With a catchy theme song, Barbie-style stewardess dolls for sale, and other paraphernalia, National reveled in—and benefited from—the publicity surrounding its women workers and its little "F" word, which everyone knew stood for another word beginning with the same letter.[26] Its 1973 annual report announced the company's highest ever revenues.[27]

On the face of it, the "Fly Me" campaign—whereby Cheryl or Karen or Margie invited passengers to "Fly me all the way across the Atlantic" —can be lumped into the same sexist cauldron as Braniff's Air Strip and TWA's hostess flights. But a lot had changed between 1965 and 1971, not the least of which was flight attendant successes in overturning restrictive employment practices on marriage and age. Having been involved in these battles, flight attendants were far more conscious of their position and far more prepared to fight. They also were well aware of the message they were being asked to convey to the public.

SFWR, formed in 1972, gave them a new outlet. With its origins in the feminist movement—its first national coordinator was a former Eastern flight attendant, twenty-seven-year-old University of Maryland women studies student Sandra Jarrell—SFWR initially disdained trade unions, with their male-dominated leadership. "Instead of building cross-gender coalitions with working-class men," historian Dorothy Sue Cobble writes, "SFWR turned to closer partnerships with middle-class women, including airline women in managerial and supervisory positions." SFWR took the lead against "sexploitation," though the flight attendant unions—especially once they had been taken over by flight attendants themselves—later joined them in this task.[28]

SFWR created a "countercommercial" to National's "Fly Me," with an actress posing as a stewardess dismissing popular myths surrounding the profession. Broadcast on a feminist public affairs show in December 1975, the advertisement contained the following message: "I am a highly trained professional with a serious job to do. Should an emergency situation arise, I urgently need the respect, confidence and cooperation of all my passengers. . . . Fantasies are fine—in their place—let's be honest, the 'sexpot stewardess' image is unsafe at any altitude! Think about it."[29] SFWR joined the National Organization of Women (NOW) to demonstrate at F. William Free's offices in New York and picket ticket offices in the city as well as in Washington, D.C. Free disingenuously claimed not to have appreciated the offensive nature of the advertisements and then promptly released a version with a semiclad woman promising, "I'm going to fly you like you've never been flown before." SFWR and NOW complained to the National Association of Broadcasters and the Federal Trade Commission, and Free was forced to tone down the adverts by getting a series of other workers, not just flight attendants, to front the slogan.

"Stewardesses for Women's Rights put a very public face on a broader movement in which stewardesses *en masse* rejected business as usual," concludes historian Katie Barry. "Female flight attendants of the 1970s—working during the heyday of the women's movement—had grown numerous enough, were staying on the job long enough, and were becoming angry enough with how they were being stereotyped to push for sweeping changes."[30] In fact, National had to face up to a delicious irony. By giving its flight attendants such prominence, it also gave them license to exert their new importance. Those women fronting the "Fly Me" campaign took matters into their own hands in 1975 by twice going on strike, the second time for more than a hundred days, which seriously eroded the company's profits.[31]

In a way, the "Fly Me" campaign, rather than being the apex of sexist advertising of the *Coffee, Tea or Me* type, was its last hurrah. Industry developments and wider social changes rendered such imagery obsolete. After deregulation in 1978, carriers could compete strictly on price and no longer had to worry about "outsexing" their rivals. The women's movement had also helped reframe the notion of what was acceptable in advertising. But also, and more important, flight attendants themselves, because of their success in converting the job into a full-time career, increasingly looked nothing like the twenty-two-year-old college graduates beloved by airline advertising. As the average age of workers increased, the old sexist advertising looked more and more out of place.

This does not mean that airlines gave up trying to control their workers' bodies. If they could no longer advertise them so brazenly, they increased surveillance of weight and appearance. Moreover, sexist advertising did not disappear from American skies, only from American airlines. Overseas carriers continued to pedal such images while landing at U.S. airports—often as part of airline alliances with U.S. counterparts—every day of the week. Most damagingly, in a global industry, foreign flight attendants—especially those from Singapore International Airlines—became the benchmark against which the aging workers at U.S. airlines were increasingly judged.

"Asian Charm"

At the global level, stewardess marketing reached its apogee in the creation of Singapore Girl in 1972 by the fledgling SIA. The brainchild of advertising agent Ian Batey, Singapore Girl is one of the most famous advertising icons of the late twentieth century. Batey himself recalls the thinking behind "her" creation:

> Physically, she has the attractive, natural looks of most young Asian women, and her trim figure is ideal for the distinctive *sarong kebaya* uniform. Character-wise, she mirrors her Asian heritage—natural femininity, natural grace and warmth, and a natural, gentle way with people. For all of us working on the flight stewardess' persona—both the ad agency and the SIA marketing team—this young woman represented the essence, the soul of the airline's unique style of service, and we all got to work, enthusiastically and patiently, to build her into a very special global symbol, an icon for the airline.[32]

One of the remarkable things about Singapore Girl is that "she" has remained essentially unchanged since 1972, despite SIA being one of the most dynamic and adventurous airlines in terms of new fleet acquisition.[33] As any advertising expert will tell you, changing a brand image can be fraught with difficulties (think of the problems Coca-Cola had with its "Classic" versions), and SIA has singularly avoided meddling with Singapore Girl, even as the Pacific Rim has become one of the most competitive areas in aviation over the last fifteen years. Longevity is the key here. As one industry analyst puts it, Singapore Girl represents "a long-running example of positioning based on a theme designed to add tangibility to the essentially intangible attribute of high-quality service."[34] There is no question that SIA has been enormously successful and throughout its life span has been one of the key industry players. It has never posted a yearly loss and in 2004 was the world's most profitable carrier, with a market capitalization second only to Southwest's.[35] It regularly wins high praise and awards for its customer service.[36]

According to one senior SIA executive, "What we wanted was an icon to represent Asian graciousness, kindness, gentleness, care—just what the passenger needs."[37] Singapore Girl has been consistently successful at this. In 1979, *Fortune* commented, "Singapore Airlines thrives on Oriental charm, mainly the charm of its cabin hostesses."[38] More than twenty years later, one industry analyst could write, "It was the bevy of beautiful young flight attendants, immaculately groomed, outfitted in colorful figure-hugging sarong dresses that turned heads everywhere they went."[39] According to Batey, "These young women are naturally attractive Asians," he claims, "with an inbuilt natural grace, charm and femininity that comes from being Asian."[40]

As critic Edward Said has argued, the very notion of the "Oriental" is a construct of the Western mind, and Singapore Girl represents a particular Western notion of Asian femininity.[41] The airline's main target has always been premium-paying business and first-class passengers, overwhelmingly Western males, and it rarely upgrades people from economy for fear of diluting its brand. SIA's front-of-the-plane passengers contribute 70 percent of revenue while occupying only 30 percent of the airplane space.[42]

Yet Singapore Girl, the icon, hardly helps the real women working as cabin crew on SIA flights. For example, the airline prides itself on always using its actual "stewardesses" in advertisements, as opposed to actresses. "What you see in the advertising is a genuine, unabridged reflection of the inflight service personality," Batey writes.[43] Conflating "real" people with the "fictional" icon allows the Girls' image to seem more authentic, SIA seems to believe.

However, what is striking about SIA's advertisements is that it is almost impossible to date them. No matter the year, the Singapore Girls always have on the same sarong uniform and are often presented in soft focus. Though they are real workers, they seem literally ageless, begging the question, Where are all the Singapore Women? This is no moot point, because it is not particularly easy to build up a career as a woman flight attendant at SIA. Women cabin crew sign up to a maximum of three renewable five-year contracts. In contrast, their male counterparts, who in fact make up about 40 percent of cabin crew, are on permanent contracts up to retirement age. In its ads SIA resembles the science fiction movie *Logan's Run,* in which people over thirty are terminated.

Moreover, rather than the Singapore Girls reflecting the icon, the icon reflects the Girls, and crucially the only Girls allowed to join in are those who will not let down the image. To ensure this, SIA polices its women flight attendants' bodies at both the applicant stage and after they commence work. Applicants must have a body "in proportion. If they get fat, their uniform won't fit," claims Glory Henriette, the carrier's public relations manager. Though the uniforms are tailor-made, the company would not provide them for women with "disproportionate" bodies. "They cannot do anything that will downgrade the Singapore Girl image. They have to work out to keep in shape," Henriette says.[44] According to one graduate of SIA's training program: "They teach you how to walk, how to eat and how to carry yourself. . . . They even teach you what kind of bra to wear. Soft ones don't look good, so they recommend padded ones. Some might say it's a bit regimented, like in the military."[45] Women recruits must take a swimming pool test—male recruits are excused—ostensibly to check that they can swim but more accurately, admits cabin personnel manager Lu Thai, so management could "check out" women's figures and physical appearance.[46] Then, having joined the ranks of Singapore Girls, women sign a contract in which they agree not to have a child. Pregnancy means termination. The five-year contract means that the moment a woman begins to show signs of age, to not be "slim and attractive with a good complexion"—as stipulated by the airline—and thus no longer conforms to the mythical advertising icon, she can be got rid of.[47]

In short, SIA operates the kind of flight attendant policies more akin to U.S. airlines before civil rights legislation. The average turnover rate for women crew is four and a half years. Though they are well remunerated, earning three times what a Singapore secretary would earn, and the cost of training is high, most Girls never really make the transition to "Singapore Women." According to one airline spokesperson, "The constant turnover means passengers always see young beautiful girls. It helps our in-flight image."[48]

The Global Consequences of Singapore Girl

Singapore Girls present their counterparts at other airlines with two problems. First, when Singapore Girls are regarded by industry analysts and business traveler associations as the top of the tree, other flight attendants find themselves under pressure to become more like them. In the increasingly competitive East Asian market, for instance, both Thai International and Cathay Pacific have attempted to rebrand their flight attendants in direct response to SIA. In 1997, Thai reduced the maximum retirement age for women crew to forty-five. According to the airline's president, Thai's crew were "too old, too unsmiling and not pretty enough."[49] Unlike its male cabin crew, Thai's female flight attendants do not receive pensions. In 1996, Hong Kong's Cathay Pacific similarly rebranded its flight attendants to stress Asian charm, going head-to-head with SIA.[50]

Fortunately, no other airlines have matched Air China's prerequisite that cabin crew be virgins (a policy it applied to men as well as women). The airline seeks references from teachers about young applicants' dating habits, in the belief that those with little dating experience work harder and tend not to get involved with passengers.[51]

Yet Philippines Airlines insist that its female cabin crew be single (a policy that *does not* apply to men on this occasion). Malaysian Airlines System (MAS) limits the number of children its flight attendants can have to two and forces women cabin crew to retire at forty-five. At least the airline's corporate services manager did not mince words on the matter, though he tried to justify the policy through reference to safety: "Let's face reality. Customers prefer to be served by young, demure and pretty stewardesses, especially Asian ladies. We need frontliners who are mentally and physically alert, young, pretty and quick to respond to emergencies, as safety and security of passengers is our priority."[52] In not a single crash investigation report in aviation history has the age of flight attendants been cited as a factor in determining passenger survival rates.

Meanwhile, the rising stars of the global industry, Emirates Air and Qatar Airways, see SIA as a role model not just with its small, pro-business nation-state behind it but also in its flight attendant hiring policies. Both require potential recruits to submit full-length photographs with their applications, unheard of on U.S. carriers. Additionally, Emirates Air offers only three-year renewable contracts to new cabin crew.[53]

The second problem Singapore Girl raises for U.S. flight attendants in particular is that though they have fought some of the discriminatory practices found in overseas airlines when they were prevalent at their own carriers, in a world of globalization and airline alliances, U.S. carriers condone such practices by default. For instance, SIA is a member of Star Alliance, the code-sharing international grouping that includes United and US Air. United frequent-flier club members can earn miles on SIA, where they will no doubt be "entertained" by Singapore Girls whose hiring conditions would be challenged in court in their own country. This reflects back onto workers at U.S. airlines, with customers wondering why American flight attendants cannot be more like Singapore Girls.

Flight attendants therefore may not just be undercut in terms of pay and conditions, as critics of globalization contend.[54] They may also find themselves "outglamorized" by overseas workers. SIA cleverly uses the *sarong kebaya* as a filter for women it does not consider suitable on board; in similar ways, uniform revamps at U.S. airlines have left older women feeling uncomfortable and more likely to leave the job. The continuous stress on aspects of the job other than safety renders the experience of older American flight attendants redundant and, by default, challenges the security of the job as a full-time profession.

Antisexism Campaigns

Asian flight attendant imagery therefore affects all flight attendants—Asian or not. But many Asian workers recognize this and have been vociferous in challenging their airlines' sexist policies. For instance, an ITF forum in Bangkok in 1997 revealed the other side of the "oriental mystique." Thai International crew reported that they were being threatened with lost wages if they failed to lose weight, while a familiar catalog of incidents involving male-passenger harassment emerged. One Thai cabin crew member complained when she heard two Chinese businessmen (not realizing she spoke Chinese) discussing how much they would pay to sleep with her. She responded by dropping a hot beverage on them and was dismissed.[55] The level of anger shocked London-based ITF officials. As one said, "We were surprised at how widespread it was but also how vocal people were. They knew their rights."[56] They not only knew their rights; they also knew how to exert them. Workers at Cathay Pacific, for instance, used seductiveness and the very qualities for which they were hired, to undermine managers' sense of control during the early 1990s, when on strike against the airline.[57]

In 1997, the ITF launched its first global antisexism campaign. In a tactic reminiscent of the SFWR, the campaign incorporated satire, with a spoof flight attendant in uniform who on closer inspection turned out to be a blow-up sex doll. "If an airline treats its employees like this," the poster asked, "what must it think of its passengers?" Despite ITF's fears that such imagery would go down poorly in Catholic countries, it struck a chord particularly in Latin America, where cabin crew have struggled to have their safety concerns taken seriously.[58]

In the United States, AFA gave prominence to the antisexism campaign in its house journal, *Flightlog*. While recognizing that different cultural norms existed in other parts of the world, Pat Friend, AFA president, asserted:

> We cannot impose our values on others, but AFA members have protections in their contracts which we will help them enforce. AFA will help every worker who wants to assert her rights and defeat sexism in the workplace. Our participation in the ITF campaign is a worldwide call for respect for female flight attendants on the job. It demonstrates our willingness to stand against practices which we believe are wrong.[59]

In allowing sexist advertising and discriminatory policies to exist in some parts of a global industry, airlines make it harder for all flight attendants to assert themselves. This can have direct implications in emergency situations as workers lack the respect to give and enforce orders. It also gives license to unruly behavior and potential air rage, as passengers either do not credit flight attendants with their safety responsibilities or else equate them with the advertising still prevalent in the West—

even if not being disseminated by most Western carriers—suggesting flight attendants are there just for entertainment purposes.

Eradicating sexist imagery was an important step for flight attendants seeking to impose professional status upon their job. But they were continually undermined by images emanating from abroad, presenting flight attendants as stopgap service personnel, not full-time safety workers. With the rise of Hooters Air, and other references to the "nostalgic flight attendant," U.S. flight attendants are being undermined on the home front, too.

Hooters Air: Putting the "Fun" Back into Flying

Hooters Air, with its Hooters Girls parading the cabin, further weakens the gains flight attendants have made. For starters, there is the emphasis on "fun." Since 9/11, numerous airlines, especially low-cost carriers such as Song and Independence Air, have seemed to suggest that the antidote to fears about terrorism is to revamp the airplane cabin as a venue for entertainment. According to its Web site, Hooters promises "a great experience that enlivens the senses and puts the fun back in flying!"[60] At the company's Myrtle Beach base, staff sport T-shirts proclaiming "Hooters Air. Getting there is half the fun," with the word "half" crossed out. The company's chief executive, Robert Brooks, claimed not "to have any airline expertise," but clearly positioned the carrier as an alternative to struggling mainline outfits such as Delta and United.[61] The implication here is that older, established carriers just are not entertaining enough.

But why aren't they fun? At Hooters, fun's personification comes in the form of a woman: not any kind of woman but a young, bubbly, large-breasted, vivacious Hooters Girl. The suggestion here is that all other women, by default, are *not* fun (or "un-fun," in Orwellian terms). The brand here sends a subtle message, as only the best branding can: in using the slogan "delightfully tacky," Hooters can claim its Girls are, in fact, nothing *more* than fun, an ironic, postmodern send-up of a world of dour, rampant political correctness. "If you don't like Hooters Air" (i.e., "if you can't take the joke"), as says Mark Peterson, "don't fly it."[62] But any joke here is at the expense of the older flight attendant whose main battle over the years has been to replace her public image as entertainment figure with that of safety professional. In the process, as the Hooters logic runs, what these women actually did was take the fun out of flying. Regardless of their safety expertise, *they are to blame for Americans not feeling good about being in the air.* And so, here is a Hooters Girl to represent everything—most of all, fun—that modern flight attendants supposedly lack.

Oddly, Hooters' own flight attendants—the "lumbering grannies"—become implicated in this message. They are clearly in charge on the airplane, handing out beverages, performing safety briefings, and even determining whether the Girls can play or not. But it is a blurred picture: a Hooters Girl—not a flight attendant—adorns the onboard safety card, which in a crisis might have people yelling for the untrained Brigitte. Moreover, one flight attendant told me cheerfully of how "the girls" could "pitch in" and help out if things got hectic. "Pitching in" from non-safety-qualified workers should not be happening in any circumstances: something as apparently mundane as a wrongly placed coffee pot can become lethal in turbulence or during an emergency.[63]

However, with its Girls embodying fun, Hooters is effectively saying that *its* flight attendants are as boring and dull—in their sober outfits—as all the other flight attendants out there. Fun refers to how things used to be, before the cabin crew all got too old. As a reminder, here are some serious real flight attendants on board to go through the tedious safety stuff: juxtapose *them* with the twenty-two-year-old in the skimpy vest. On my flights, when the Hooters Girls were in action, the real flight attendants seemed to hide—crouching down at the back to restock drink cabinets.

The Hooters Girl is the low-class flip side of Singapore Girl, where Asian "charm" and "beauty" become embodied in SIA's successful marketing creation. From diametrically opposed ends of the industry, both carriers send the message out loud and clear: there is no space for older women in our airline identity. It is the "beauty myth" in the air. "Fun" or "high-class" flying becomes once again reified in the concept of the perfect body, one that never ages, and one that certainly does not put on weight.

A Tale of the Scales: Weight Controls in the Industry

The most controversial and consistently draconian form of bodily control exerted by airlines has been weight restrictions. Though flight attendants forced carriers to abandon the humiliating practice of regular "weigh-ins" in the 1990s, weight restrictions still apply at U.S. airlines. Continental, for instance, insists on "height and weight proportionate to maintain professional appearance."[64] Southwest states, "Weight must be of such proportion to height that a neat appearance is maintained and physical ability to perform all job functions is not hindered."[65]

Airline weight restrictions should be seen in the context of flight attendant successes in removing restrictive employment policies, thereby making the job a full-time profession. As workers took control of their spatial movements, airlines sought to claw back control through tighter regulations over weight and appearance. Though airlines had used "weight charts," calculating the "correct" proportion between height and weight since the 1950s, it was not until flight attendants reshaped their profession in the early 1970s that airlines began to really crack down.

The central question was one of gender and age. Airlines hitherto had not had to deal with "older" women flight attendants because most left after eighteen months, and those who stayed were forced to leave in their early thirties. Therefore, the airlines had not had to face the issue of women putting on weight as a natural outcome of getting older. As they lost control of some aspects of hiring and retention policies, carriers became doubly determined to strengthen bodily controls in areas where they retained leverage. As scholar Cathleen Dooley argues, "Airlines continued to market flight attendants' bodies, and in fact focused more on physical appearance because they could no longer control the marital status and age of flight attendants."[66]

From being sporadically enforced, weight supervision became more systematic, as the case of Braniff illustrates. In 1974, the Texas carrier claimed its goal was to create a weight program that could be "consistently and fairly administered so that the image of all Braniff flight attendants can be upgraded to the level it should be."[67] It had changed its weight policy two years earlier, replacing a graduated series of punishments, in which "overweight" flight attendants would be given time to lose weight while still working, with a more draconian one that immediately suspended them from duty. Hiring a new "hostess counselor," Lynn Townsley, to help flight attendants with "grooming problems," Braniff pressured its flight attendants to conform to strict new standards. Townsley clearly conceived the "problem" of being overweight as emotional in origin. Flight attendants who failed to meet the company's standards did so not because those standards were absurdly rigorous but because they suffered from personal problems, stress, and a lack of self-worth. She cited several success stories: in one case, a woman had dropped twenty pounds in a month because of "the importance of positive thinking while dieting." In another, a woman achieved "marvelous results" through a cabbage diet. As Dooley notes, Townsley painted Braniff as a "benevolent patriarch who simply needed to help delinquent women attain a standard that was desirable not just for the company but 'obviously' for the women themselves."[68] Airlines dubbed "overweight" flight attendants "noncompliants." In other words, this was someone who was not fitting into the company plan; airlines easily translated this into rebellion and/or psychological problems, rendering a flight attendant unfit for duty.

For some workers the "weigh-in" was an experience that can only be described as horrendous, at which their employment record, experience, and expertise counted for nothing compared with their ability to hit their "official" recorded weight. Flight attendants would take laxatives or diuretics, starve for three days to lose weight, or be unable eat for nerves.[69] Of all the stories I heard, this flight attendant's was the most disturbing, and worth repeating in full:[70]

My husband resented the weight checks because it created problems for us because it affected the food I'd make at home. Whether we'd go out to eat, where we would eat, and sometimes just turning down social evenings because I didn't want to deal with the food. When you're dieting all the time, you're angry, first of all, that the restrictions are put on you, you're angry that you can't keep the weight off, and you're short-tempered because you're not eating. We've spent a fortune on diet programs over the years. The flight attendants, there are many of them that couldn't even drive to the airport they were so weak after taking diet pills and diuretics, and more than one husband and boyfriend have had to drive them to the front door so they could go in for a weight check, come right back out, and I know of one flight attendant that said that she would be so weak she'd have to lie down in the back of the car to get home.

I have my own personal story on that. In St. Louis, I had taken so many diuretics, but being a nurse [previous to joining the airline], I had a lot of medications that were left over. Back when I was in nursing the drug detail man handed all of it out like candy. I had friends in nursing, and I was giving myself Lacix shots, which is a powerful diuretic, so that I could make weight check. One Friday afternoon I had just made my weight check and knowing that my potassium level was very low from all the diuretics, I had gone back upstairs and was standing in the line at the snack bar to buy a quart of orange juice, and the last thing I remember was talking to this nice businessman from Des Moines and the next thing I remembered was waking up on the floor with people surrounding me, and a TWA pilot fortunately came to my rescue.

I ended up being taken to the emergency room, and the doctor after the examination and after talking and they're starting IVs on me and everything and they had found out that I was a nurse because they wanted to know what I had taken, and I told them how I happened to have it. I remember the doctor came over to me and said, OK. How important is this job to you? I said it's very important. He said is it important enough to lose your life because you came damn near close to dying? He said you of all people know how diuretics work. He said you have a cardiac arrhythmia. He said you were extremely dehydrated. He said you're just very lucky that you didn't kill yourself.

We were weighed like a side of beef once a month, and that does something to your self-respect. You begin to lose the image of who you are. Worse than that, you develop terrible eating patterns, you build up all this resentment and anger about it, and when they finally had to do away with the weight checks by law, the whole industry ended up with a whole great number of women that didn't know how to eat properly. Even if they had all the knowledge in the world about how to eat properly, they were so angry about the years of deprivation that they just rebelled and said I'll do what I damn well want to now. So, it was a lose-lose situation for the airlines, and a lose-lose situation for the flight attendants.

Airlines were well aware that flight attendants resorted to desperate measures to make their official weight, but they fought tooth and nail to keep weight checks in place. Weight checks were finally abandoned as recently as 1994, following court action against US Air, at which the carrier was forced to admit that stereotype-driven aspirations for thinness had nothing to do with protecting passenger safety and providing service.

A Moving Target: Why Did Weight Checks
Continue for So Long?

It is fair to say that flight attendants made much slower progress in eradicating weight checks than they did in abolishing other restrictive employment practices. On the one hand, carriers had learned from their defeats over marriage and age bans and fought the issue not on discriminatory practice but on questions of appearance. By bringing weight programs under the overall banner of appearance control, airlines could argue that weight was merely a part of a flight attendant's image, which in turn was crucial to an airline's marketability. Rather than becoming embroiled in arguments over equal opportunity, airlines reasoned that courts would be far less likely to intervene if the central debate concerned a worker's image in relation to airline profitability. In this, they were generally correct. It was not until 1987 that the courts deemed unequal weight policies for male and female flight attendants illegal, though not weight policies themselves.[71] Equally, though under the 1978 Pregnancy Discrimination Act pregnant workers could no longer be dismissed, the courts generally left it up to the airlines to decide whether, and when, a pregnant worker could actually fly.[72]

On the other hand, though, weight checks lasted so long partly because flight attendants did not mobilize against them in the same way they did against sexist imagery, such as National's "Fly Me" campaign. Their objections to the *Coffee, Tea or Me* imagery in advertising were often on the ground of accuracy—they felt nothing in common with the images portrayed and believed they sent misleading messages, particularly to male passengers. When it came to weight checks, though, flight attendants took on some of the guilt lying at the heart of what Wolf calls the "beauty myth." At a time of increasing obsession over thinness, dieting, and the "perfect body," it would be surprising if flight attendants should buck the trend, especially when they were in such public view. In countless grievance briefs, Dooley states:

> Flight attendants, as [mainly] middle class, white women, had internalized the concept of thinness as beauty, and also accepted that the dominant notion of beauty was one that they could and should fulfill. As a result, they did not challenge its power over them to the degree that might have been expected from a group of workers who had achieved legal successes over other manifestations of sex discrimination.

Testimony by flight attendants in grievance hearings reveals that the women were deeply embarrassed by their inability to meet this beauty standard.[73]

Roberta Lessor suggests that lurking beneath some women's ambivalence toward weight restrictions was the fear that they actually needed supervision. One union leader she interviewed claims, "Well I don't know about not having *any* weight limitations. Some women, who just don't care that much, would really get to be a mess."[74] When I ask Denise about the weight restrictions being removed at Delta, she replies: "I do think that in a way I think that's kind of bad. I always fought my weight, but I kind of like knowing that somebody had my thumb on me that I had to watch how heavy I got . . . it kind of put the pressure on me and in a way I kind of liked it."

Self-Surveillance and Professionalism

In their study of weight restrictions in the UK airline industry, sociologists Melissa Tyler and Pamela Abbott conclude that flight attendants often internalize company perspectives through the adoption of "panoptic management." Here, as Foucault argued in relation to Bentham's Panopticon prison, surveillance is pivotal. "The significant element in the disciplinary 'gaze,'" write Tyler and Abbott, "is that those who are subject to discipline internalize the very possibility of their being watched and so behave in accordance with this possibility."[75] In other words, flight attendants police themselves, carrying out self-surveillance and monitoring fellow workers at the same time.

But what, or who, exactly, are they policing themselves for? While some may be following the company line, more, I would argue, carry out self-surveillance of their own femininity for none other than *themselves* as an expression of their professionalism. When older workers complain about colleagues, they often do so about younger workers they feel let down standards not of the company but of the profession. "All the great flight attendants left last year," says Sandra, a senior international Delta flier. "The new faces are different. They've come in from domestic to international, bringing their dirty little domestic ways with them." Out of concern for their profession, flight attendants sometimes worry as much about appearance as do the airlines.

Seen from the perspective of flight attendants wanting to maintain professional status, there is perhaps less inconsistency between their vehement opposition to sexist advertising and their more ambivalent opposition to gendered weight policies. Both reflected a deep-seated attachment to the job, especially when it gained the gravitas essential to "spacing-out" in the postdestination phase. Challenging stereotypes and reinforcing their own notions of professionalism, flight attendants demonstrated commitment and community, two qualities that, as the next chapter illustrates, can be found in abundance once up in the air.

Above: In the 1930s, flight attendants, like these United women, were registered nurses. In prepressurized cabins, workers had to brave the elements, and thus provided perfect models for manufacturers of heavy coats. *Source*: *New Yorker*, 1939.

Right: By the 1940s, flight attendants were being used to endorse a range of products. *Source*: *Life*, 1946.

Left: Like most airlines in the 1950s, United often depicted its flight attendants as mothers supplying food. This advertisement also tapped into United's pioneering role in the profession. *Source*: *Time*, 1955.

Below: With its southern roots, Delta inevitably fused "home" and "hospitality" to create a strong flight attendant image. *Source*: *Time*, 1956.

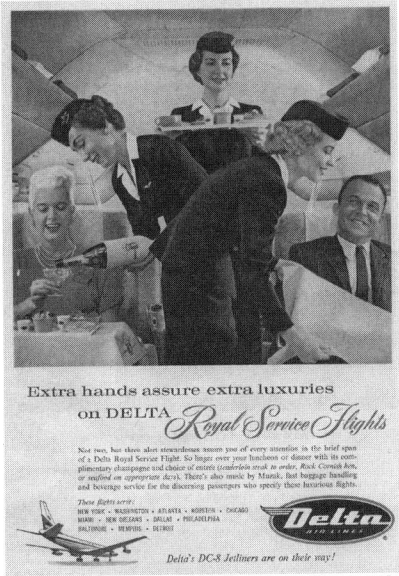

Extra hands assure extra luxuries
on DELTA *Royal Service Flights*

Not two, but three alert stewardesses assure you of every attention in the brief span of a Delta Royal Service Flight. So linger over your luncheon or dinner with its complimentary champagne and choice of entrée (tenderloin steak to order, Rock Cornish hen, or seafood on appropriate days). There's also music by Muzak, fast baggage handling and beverage service for the discerning passengers who specify these luxurious flights.

These flights serve:
NEW YORK • WASHINGTON • ATLANTA • HOUSTON • CHICAGO
MIAMI • NEW ORLEANS • DALLAS • PHILADELPHIA
BALTIMORE • MEMPHIS • DETROIT

Delta's DC-8 Jetliners are on their way!

Left: With competition over fares largely restricted, airlines competed on service. Delta built a strong reputation on its flight attendants' hospitality. *Source*: *Time*, 1959.

Below: Sex comes to the skies: Texas-based Braniff led the transformation of flight attendant imagery in the "swinging" 1960s. *Source*: *Dallas Times Herald Magazine*, 1965.

Above: School card and heart-shaped personality card game pieces from *What Shall I Be? The Exciting Game of Career Girls*, a 1966 board game for young girls where the object is to be the first player to become a career girl. Possible careers include ballet dancer, nurse, model, teacher, actress, and air hostess (when in fact at the time airline regulations made a "career" virtually impossible). Copyright Selchow and Righter Company, 1966.

Right: Despite the apparent attempt to present the "reality" of a flight attendant's life, United's main message is belied by the speech bubble emanating from the airplane cabin: "She's going to make someone a great wife." *Source*: *Look*, 1966.

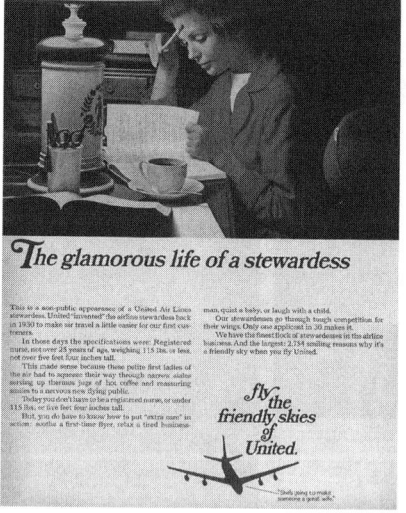

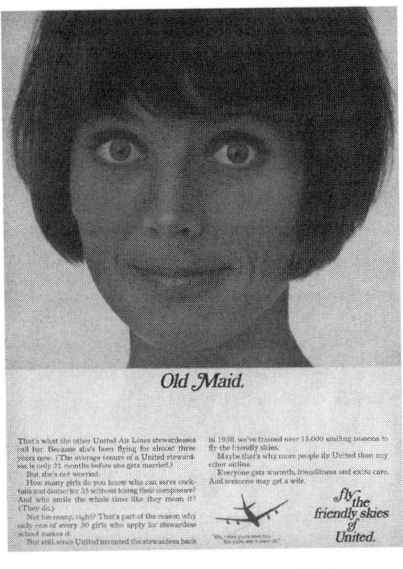

Above: Airlines encouraged rapid labor turnover. As this United advertisement suggests, women who remained unmarried after three years on the job were highly unusual. *Source*: *Look*, 1966.

Right: Airlines liked to present themselves as finishing schools, where young women could learn how to be perfect housewives. *Source*: *Time*, 1967.

Left: As the 1960s progressed, airlines became increasingly innovative in their marketing of flight attendants' sexuality, as this TWA campaign suggests. *Source*: *Time*, 1968.

Below: Emotional labor in action: flight attendants were expected to make high-paying businessmen feel special through individual attention, as the text to this American advertisement implies. *Source*: *Time*, 1969.

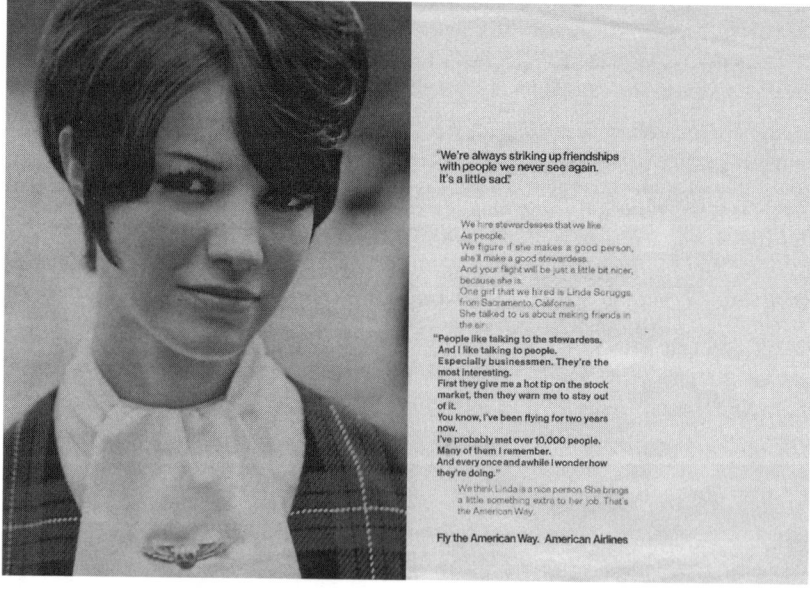

Above: The civil rights movement led to an increasing number of African American flight attendants at airlines such as Delta. *Source*: *Ebony*, 1971.

Right: By the early 1970s, the women's movement targeted sexist airline imagery, as this demonstration against National's "Fly Me" campaign suggests. *Source*: *Life*, 1971.

Left: National stuck to its "Fly Me" campaign through the mid-1970s, though in watered-down form. *Source*: *Southern Living*, 1975.

Above: As late as 1976, exclusively international Pan Am continued to place its flight attendants at center stage. *Source*: *Punch*, 1976.

Top: By the mid-1970s, Singapore International Airlines' "Singapore Girl" had become one of the most famous advertising icons in the world. 'Natural Asian charm' became a staple of marketing for airlines such as Singapore. *Source*: *Punch*, 1976.

Bottom: By 1984, Pan Am had relegated its flight attendants to the background, highlighting cabin amenities. *Source*: *Punch*, 1984.

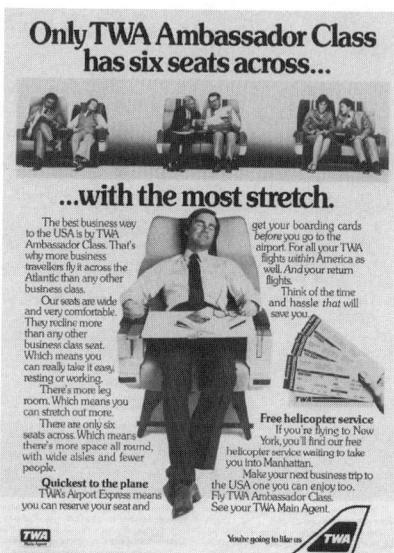

Left: TWA removed its flight attendants in this 1984 advertisement to focus exclusively on seat comforts. *Source*: *Punch*, 1984.

Below: With U.S. airlines reshaping their brand image in the 1980s, Asian airlines continued to market the attractiveness of their flight attendants, as this Cathay Pacific (Hong Kong) advertisement demonstrates. *Source*: *Punch*, 1984.

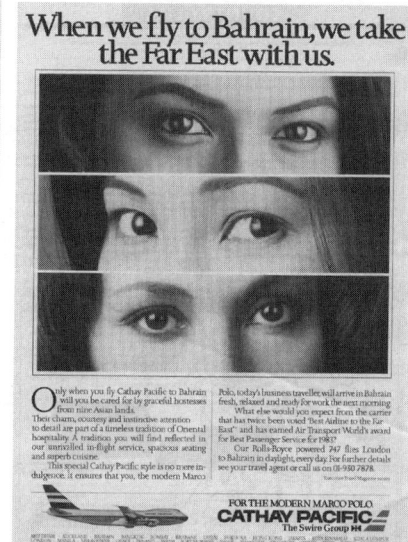

A textbook evacuation: 273 passengers and 22 crew escape a burning L1011 in less than two minutes. TWA Flight 843, July 30, 1992, JFK Airport. *Source*: Newsday Photo/Stan Honda.

American flight attendants strike in the run-up to Thanksgiving, 1993. Having been attacked by management during the 1980s, workers chose their moment—and their message—with devastating effect. *Source*: *Time*, 1993.

Left: With sexist advertising still prevalent, especially in Asia, flight attendant unions in the late 1990s sought to change public perception with an antisexism campaign. *Source*: International Transport Workers Federation, 1997.

Below: Flight attendant unions stress that safety is the number one reason their members are on board. *Source*: International Transport Workers Federation, 2000.

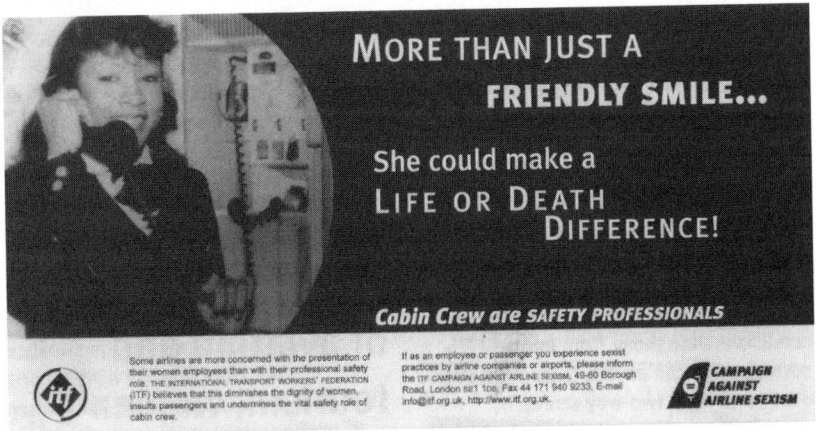

Left: The "nostalgic flight attendant": in the post-9/11 climate, popular culture resurrected the escapist 1960s "Barbie Doll" image, embodied by Gwyneth Paltrow in *View from the Top*. Miramax, 2003.

Below: Catherine Zeta-Jones falls over in *The Terminal*, another movie resurrecting sixties-style flight attendant imagery. Dreamworks SKG, 2004.

In real life, the 1960s made a comeback with Hooters Air. The woman depicted is not a flight attendant but a "Hooters Girl," there to entertain passengers. However, her presence on the safety card could confuse passengers. *Source*: Hooters Air, 2004.

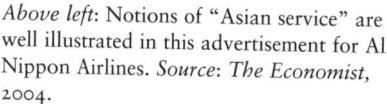

Above left: Notions of "Asian service" are well illustrated in this advertisement for All Nippon Airlines. *Source*: *The Economist*, 2004.

Above right: Asian airlines continue to flirt with sexual innuendo, as this Malaysian Airlines Systems advertisement suggests. *Source*: *Business Week*, 2006.

Right: U.S. and European international carriers focus less on service and more on sleep, demonstrated by One World member Iberia. *Source*: *The Economist*, 2006.

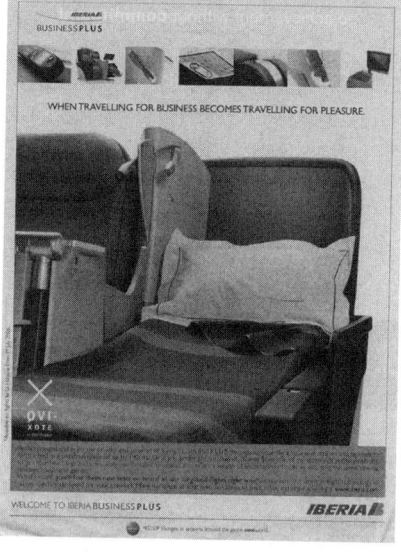

5

Cruising Altitude

Suddenly because you've got on that uniform, it's kind of like being in the army, where you would protect whoever was wearing
the same uniform you are. It's really us against the world.
—Carole, Delta flight attendant

On my way to Boston from Atlanta in June 2003, I found
myself mesmerized by the three Delta flight attendants working the Boeing 767's middle galley. Opening drawers, stocking carts, filling cups,
passing service items to each other, crouching down, squeezing past;
they worked like a slick basketball trio, each knowing instinctively
where the others were, and each with a keen sense of personal space
that ensured no collisions. For the ergonomically minded, this was po-
etry in motion.

Having completed the beverage service, the three women—who
ranged in age from midtwenties to about fifty—began conversing at
length about their lives, job concerns, and future plans. Anyone could
see there was a strong affinity between them, yet I suspected that they
had never met before the flight that morning. On my way back from the
bathroom, I asked them if this was so. "Yes," they laughed in surprise.
"How did you know?"

I "knew" because flight attendants—especially at larger carriers—
have told me that it is common for them to work with complete
strangers. "We've never met before," one Delta flier announced, pointing at her colleague in the back of another 767, this time going to
Madrid. "That's the nice thing about this job." "Yeah, it is," her colleague echoed.

The Occupational Community

Though potential strangers, workers very rapidly fall into a set of tried and tested practices enabling them to get along with the kind of synchronicity I witnessed ninety minutes out from Boston. Operating protocols prescribe some routines: standardized procedure is a basic safety tenet in any industry, and all air crew perform tasks in strict order to make sure nothing is left out. But other routines are rooted in emotional bonding that lies at the heart of what sociologists have called "occupational community," where workers identify strongly with both their profession and their colleagues to the extent that they believe, as many flight attendants have also told me, that no one else understands them.

According to Massachusetts Institute of Technology management theorists John Van Maanen and Stephen Barley, an occupational community consists of four elements, all of which apply to flight attendants: "a group of people who consider themselves to be engaged in the same sort of work; who identify (more or less positively) with their work; who share a set of values, norms and perspectives that apply to, but extend beyond, work related matters; and whose social relationships meld the realms of work and leisure."[1] Occupational communities have often been associated with high-pressure emergency work, such as police and nursing, or with male-dominated heavy industries, such as mining, fishing, and steel (an easily recognized occupational community can be found in Michael Cimino's film *The Deer Hunter,* among the steelworkers of a small Pennsylvania town).

But flight attendants' occupational community is slightly different and is in some ways more cohesive than those of other occupations. Whereas other communities are often fixed in a particular place, be it Worcester, Massachusetts, in the case of fishing, or the local hospital, in the case of nurses, flight attendants' community is a far more mobile entity. In a sense, it exists in space rather than place, and as a result has no fixed abode. At the same time, flight attendants have to work harder to maintain it because they continually confront stereotypes that undermine it.

It is also a community of strangers, very different from, say, the staff room at a local high school where people interact on a familiar, daily basis. Flight attendants' occupational community is not the product of an accident of geography. Unlike miners, they do not all live in the same town. Their occupational community is an active part of the postdestination phase of the "space-out," evolving from the greater job identification evident from the 1970s and cemented in the reconstruction of the career as full-time safety professional as opposed to short-term flying waitress.

What is important here, though, is to grasp the job's centrality in all of this. Occupational community emerged from flight attendants' collective onboard experiences and everyday practices in the air. Consciousness of their often peculiar identity—misunderstood by outsiders and misrepresented by the industry—developed on the job, in the airplane cabin, and in the rituals and routines that they constructed as part of their work lives.

This shared identity emerges in several forms, all of which embed occupational community. One is jump seat therapy, where workers exchange intimate details and problems with each other during downtime on a flight. The uniform provides a second form of identification, on the one hand part of an obsessive discipline program devised by management, but on the other a source of real pride and confidence on the part of workers. Emotional labor, where workers' emotions become part of the job, also cements identity, often in paradoxical ways. Finally, industrial action for flight attendants is often an expression of shared identity and is based on occupational community, which explains how flight attendants, in spite of gender stereotypes painting women workers as passive, can sometimes be as militant as other communities such as miners. When members of an occupational community go on strike, it is not just their jobs that are on the line but their lifestyles.

This last point is important. Though occupational communities can sometimes be useful to management, in the self-supervision and enforcement of dress codes, for example, they can also represent a threat when workplace and union issues crop up. It is no accident that one of the main casualties of the industry "squeeze-in" is the flight attendant occupational community itself.

Building Community: A More Varied Workforce, Safety, and Bigger Planes

Many workers find compensation in their jobs beyond wages, such as fulfillment, pride, satisfaction, or emotional support, and they correspondingly build networks of fellow workers with shared identities, be it around the water cooler or in the bar on Friday evenings. This sense of fraternity is hardly new: in the nineteenth century, for instance, Marx viewed it as the basis for the development of class consciousness among the factory proletariat. Nowadays, as writers like Robert Putnam point out, management harnesses the idea that the workplace, not the community outside, is the site of people's most meaningful relationships, portraying the firm as a "family" that is often more supportive and less stressful than real families at home.[2]

Though airlines have nurtured these propositions—especially family—the flight attendant community operates on a different scale: members identify with each other not necessarily as friends or colleagues they see every day but as fellow flight attendants they may only actually meet once in their lives. The uniform denotes a person as someone who will implicitly understand anything a coworker may ask of them, and from the moment they board the airplane, these workers—even if complete strangers—begin constructing identifying bonds. In fact, this identity runs so deep it unites *ex*–flight attendants, even from different airlines, as I have seen with my own eyes during focus groups with such workers.

However, I want to convey the extent to which flight attendants *built* an occupational community as part of the postdestination phase of the "space-out" from the 1970s onward. The impact of civil rights meant that flight attendants were no longer "all-American" girls from small midwestern towns, as United liked to pretend. Up to the early 1970s airlines recruited women of similar age, background, and, significantly, race, which tended to create a sorority feel among workers.[3] For one stewardess in the 1940s, for instance, "it really made a nice group of girls . . . we talked the same language."[4] But changing recruitment patterns and a more heterogeneous workforce, with more "older" women staying on the job, meant that flight attendant bonding now centered less upon class, race, and status than upon shared experience of the job itself. To put this another way, up to the 1970s most flight attendants already had much in common before starting work: "graduating" in "classes" with peers of similar ages, many flight attendants worked their eighteen-month stints together and left together. As women made the job a full-time career, though, a far wider age range developed on board so that increasingly the only thing that these workers had in common was the actual job. The longer tenure served by workers made them reflect more upon the job itself. Even if they claimed to be staying only a short amount of time, as many did, they found themselves developing greater levels of attachment to the job and to their colleagues.

Safety, and the conversion of the job into one of safety professional, also enhanced flight attendants' sense of community. Workers have a shared knowledge of flight's potential dangers, but they also know that in an emergency they have to rely without hesitation on colleagues they have only just met (possibly minutes previously, if during takeoff). In evacuations, these workers "jam," as was the case with TWA Flight 843, in which flight attendants (some of them off duty) completely evacuated a burning L1011 in less than two minutes. As in the military, wearing the uniform means that you are expected to perform your duties professionally if called to do so, and everyone else in uniform knows this. "In an emergency situation," says Eileen, at Delta, "you've got to know that Eileen Johnson is someone in the next cabin that you can rely on. And when you develop that kind of kinship, you bond for life." Flight attendants bond not necessarily around the sense of common danger, in other words, but around the unspoken fact that the colleague you just met—someone you may never meet again—may just save your life, and vice versa.

Another factor in building community was the airplane itself, which with the introduction of new wide-body models in the late 1960s significantly increased the number of flight attendants on board. As historian Frieda Rozen points out, this helped alleviate the hitherto disparate geographic nature of flight attendant work, sometimes assembling more than ten workers on the airplane together, which in turn deepened the sense of a group ethos increasingly collectivized around shared norms, issues, and solutions.[5] One major bonding ritual, jump seat therapy, was born out of this experience.

Job identification and occupational community were therefore increasingly constructed on the airplane itself. Flight attendants' first bond of loyalty became to one another. When "no one else understands," flight attendants carve out their own spaces and surround themselves with those people who emphatically *do* understand, namely, their coworkers. As former Delta flight attendant Alexandra Murphy observes in her doctoral thesis, the galley, in particular, takes on the role of "home base" in a game of tag: "Flight attendants feel safe there to say anything they want."[6] In the galley and on the jump seat, flight attendants open up to each other, cementing their identity in the process.

Jump Seat Therapy

Flight attendants from all types of airlines talk of the bonding between attendants. Kelly, a former Delta flier, takes a sip of coffee and says, "The camaraderie among flight attendants is excellent. The network of friends is really great. Flight attendants become each other's family." "I've made the most wonderful friends. It's like a sorority," echoes one Northwest worker I spoke to on my way to Detroit. "I love it, we all get on really well," says another on Hooters Air. Even outside the United States, this camaraderie is evident. Cecile, who flew for Air France, explains: "I still have friends since forty years. . . . I'm still friends with them. And that dates from 1960. Forty-four years." Mandy, who flies for a UK charter company, talks of how retired workers often express themselves: "People when they've left, if you go back to those people and say do you miss it? They say they don't miss the job but they miss the people. And working through the nights. But they miss the team and the people. They do have a laugh." The clearest demonstration of this bonding is jump seat therapy. When talking to Eileen, a Delta flier, I ask if she had taken part in this ritual, and she responds:

> I think almost all flight attendants have. We've all gone through some ups and downs in our lives and divorces and children misbehaving and all that sort of thing. You do find you can have a willing ear, I think, from most flight attendants. You sort of pick and choose. I wouldn't discuss my private life with everybody I fly with. I've probably heard more than I want to know from some people. Some people who have no compulsion [*sic*] at all about telling you the most intimate details of their life. Their latest sexual experience or those kinds of things, and your ears are going like this [wiggling them]. *Who* are you and *why* are you telling me this?

Clare, at Continental laughs as she comments: "The things you hear. I could write a book. The things you hear at 30,000 feet. People have a tendency to tell you their deepest, darkest secrets. Things you would never hear on the ground." Jump seat therapy combines two familiar human situations. The first is work as respite, in which colleagues provide emotional support outside their family or domestic relationships. As Derek, a Delta flier since the 1970s, puts it. "I want to tell them 'Dump the guy' or, you know, 'Shut up! And suck it up and just take it!'

You know? But then I've seen abuse. Abuse where you know they were beat up by their boyfriends and all that kind of stuff. You see everything. And it's just anything you can say or do would be, 'OK'"

The second familiar situation is the anonymity of strangers. Many of us have occasionally found ourselves telling people we hardly know or only just met surprisingly intimate things, comfortable in the knowledge we will likely never meet again. As Mary Ann says:

> There are always people that don't want to divulge as much about themselves, and then there are people like me that talk too much and then look back later and say, aw, I wish I hadn't said all that. There were times that you realized I shouldn't have said anything. But you know what, then it would all roll away because you'd say, ah, I won't even see them again for ten years. We won't fly again for ten years.

However, jump seat therapy is unusual in that it *combines* these situations, whereby regular office gossip, politics, and emotional support fuse with the comfort of anonymity to form a ritual that is repeated over and over again. This makes it unique, and it is worth unpacking just why it is so prevalent.

The Need to Belong, the Need to Be Different

Flight attendants inhabit a bizarre, jumbled temporal and spatial world, in which life on the ground seems remote. As Clare, from Continental, observes, "You're in a tube in the sky and you're just like in the twilight zone, and they have a way of letting it all out. It's pretty interesting." When people are spatially disoriented and fatigued, they can say things they would never say in "real world." As Eileen puts it: "You are sort of in this isolated world away from reality. You are in the metal thing that is up above the earth, and maybe it's sort of an unreal atmosphere and you just, you feel like you are sort of in this together."

Disorientation draws flight attendants together. It is unsurprising that parents, especially, will bond over tales of their respective children (many nonparents pointedly bond over their cats). Yet jump seat therapy also belies the intrinsic loneliness many flight attendants feel. As Jean, from Delta, suggests: "It could be a very lonely life, even though you're around people all the time, especially if you lived alone. You could sort of tell the flight attendants who lived alone because they were sometimes the ones that would open up the most when you are shoulder to shoulder on a jump seat." Her colleague Donna agrees: "It is lonely, solitary. You get to know the most personal things on the jump seat. It's very anonymous, and you won't see people again you confide in." Carolyn, also at Delta, explains: "Jump seat therapy gets very personal for strangers, but you are stuck in this environment. It is an extremely lonely job, and one is scheduled so much more nowadays and you may have no family life. You have your cats. The older ones put pictures of cats up in the galley, and the younger ones talk about how they don't want to end up like that." Yet jump seat therapy's most intriguing aspects involve identity, simultaneously allowing a worker to confirm her membership of the profession and occupational community and yet to differentiate herself within that profession. By engaging in jump seat therapy, workers construct a shared identity. "With your colleagues you're a different person," says Mandy, a UK flier.

To echo Carole, it's "us against the world." Jump seat therapy becomes part of a bonding ritual in which sharing information demonstrates trust and confidence in the ability of one's colleagues to cope in a crisis. "Us against the world" underpins flight attendant identity and is a declaration of commitment to each other first and foremost, above the passengers, above the pilots, and certainly above their respective airlines.

But while jump seat therapy provides a bonding experience that fuses the workers into a homogeneous mass, at the same time it allows for individuation. Having put on the uniform and become part of the gang, flight attendants then want to demonstrate that they are, after all, individuals. This sometimes emerges in competition for the wackiest stories but also lies in the fact that—as strangers—most flight attendants have no clue about coworkers' lives outside the job (i.e., the thing that makes them different). Even among flight attendant "friends," few visit each other's home. Carole explains: "A lot of us never knew last names, but we knew first names. We were very intimate, yet we were very detached all at the same time. I never talked to any of those people on my off days. I never went to their houses. It was never even suggested, not by any of us." This may be an extreme characterization, and on several occasions I have actually been in a flight attendant's house when a coworker has arrived. But flight attendants do need to individuate. The "brag book," in which they keep pictures of loved ones (including the cats), is a clear example. Kelly explains, pretending to flip open a small photo album: "This is me. This is who I am. Otherwise we're all the same people in the same uniform with the same hair and the same shoes and things like that. The only thing that's different is what we are showing you of that other life, and that's in these pictures."

Giselle, at American, explains:

> When you start a conversation with a flight attendant and you know you're going to fly with her for maybe a three- or four-day trip, you get to know each other, and she starts saying, "Oh, I miss my little baby, I have a four-month-old at home," and then you'll say, "Oh, do you have a picture of your baby?" So then she shows you her husband and her family, and she says, "Do you have any pictures with you?" So you pull out your pictures. It's always that way on that jump seat.

So jump seat therapy, where the brag book tends to be pulled out, enables flight attendants to identify with the profession and yet individuate themselves within that profession.

The Support Network

The jump seat model is a tremendously important part of occupational community. The clearest example of this can be found in the role of Employee Assistance Programs run by trade unions and airlines (though many workers avoid airline EAP programs for fear of lack of confidentiality). For the AFA's EAP, shared identity runs deep and is constructed around the kind of counseling evident in jump seat therapy. According to Heather Healy, AFA's EAP director, the program "is a natural extension of the peer support system that [flight attendants] as a culture have already developed. We are leveraging off that cultural dynamic."[7]

AFA's EAP is a network of volunteers who provide peer support at any time of the day for flight attendants. EAP acts as conflict resolution mediator between peers. When one flight attendant has had enough of another flight attendant, the EAP can often step in to try to smooth things over. It also acts as an assessment referral and a support for family or work-related problems. Last—though certainly not least—EAP provides a critical response network, with a far wider interpretation than the NTSB of what counts as a traumatic incident. According to

Healy, 60 percent of EAP's responses are not even recognized as a traumatic incident. Being robbed on a layover would qualify under the EAP. Under the NTSB, it clearly would not. "No one in the industry will respond to this as there is no bending of metal and you're not a passenger," says Healy.[8]

The importance of the occupational community's peer support network, extended through the EAPs, can be seen most dramatically in its response to 9/11. Two United airliners were lost that day, along with twelve flight attendants. Susan, a United flight attendant, takes up the story, which, despite its length, is worth hearing in full:

> I was an EAP representative for the union after September 11, and I spent many, many evenings at the airport right after that, and it was really fascinating to watch because initially the company didn't provide any assistance to the employees, the union did. It was shocking what happened in Los Angeles. There was no calling people, there was no checking on people, there was just nothing done for anybody. And there was a very heavy hand that was used to threaten flight attendants to go back to work. And then we were there, the EAP representatives were there, and we were dealing with the flight attendants, kind of on an ad hoc basis, not part of the company, and it became obvious after the first week that the company [realized] this wasn't just going to go away. The company was kind of thinking this isn't a major event. I swear I think that all of the executives just pulled the wool over their eyes and stuck their head in the sand like ostriches like this isn't a big deal. It will go away, we'll get the aircraft back in the air. And it wasn't that. It wasn't that for the country, the national psyche, for the world psyche, it was a huge event in world history, and they miscalculated it.
>
> So then they started to backpedal and say, well, maybe we should let these people who are their peers do some work. And then they said, we'll pay for you to drop your trip. This was after a week when the AFA had trip dropped us to be taking care of people. And it was very stressful and very frustrating to watch the nonsupport from your own company. I have supervisors coming to me in the evening, these are people I've known for many years, saying that they wanted to quit their jobs because of what the upper management was asking them to do. So please don't think that supervisors don't get affected and upset by what they're being asked to do. It does affect them.
>
> It was an interesting experience because then the company brought

in all these mental health professionals, psychologists and L.A. County Health Department and clinical psychologists and Red Cross psychologists and social workers, and they had a table in the front lobby area with all these individuals sitting there, and then across from them was our EAP table and our little funky sign that I did. . . . Except for that everybody that walked in the door knows me or knew that I was a flight attendant and the other flight attendants sitting there who were on the committee, and they gravitated to us, and they would not go across and talk to those people at the other table. That's when I really realized we're like police and firemen a lot. I'm married to a police officer, so I'm aware of this kind of insular brotherhood or sisterhood, if you will, where we don't trust people on the outside very much. We really don't because they don't understand us.

Though not talking about 9/11, Wendy, an EAP representative for low-cost carrier Air Tran, paints a similar picture of peer support:

It's like a family. It really is. . . . I mean, if anybody has a death, if anybody has a problem, if anybody has a need? I've had flight attendants come to me before I was in Employee Assistance, and I also have another group that I work with that helps out with flight attendants who have problems and monetary needs. And, I mean, I've had flight attendants who couldn't pay their house note because they were hospitalized or whatever. And you know you just have to get the word out. And it's, like, "Yeah, we'll help. We'll help." I mean, it's like people really do care, even though there are times, and I'm not saying there are a lot of times, that crew members can't get along, but it's going to happen occasionally. But for all practical purposes, I mean, it is just like one big family. I mean, everybody cares what happens to you if you've got a bad situation or whatever. And it's like everybody being in this very same situation being a flight crew you can really relate to what you're going through. And I think that's where the compassion comes in. They know where you've been. They feel your pain. And you know there is a lot of difference between going to work from 9:00 to 5:00 at an office job and being a flight crew. You are just thrown with each other, so you've got to build something there. When you spend four days with somebody, you eat meals with them or you are on the airplane with them all day. I mean you know you've got a pretty good feel for what's going on in their personal life after four days.

Jump seat therapy is therefore the tip of the iceberg of a far wider support network typical of an occupational community. Mining towns nearly always rally around families that have lost people in a pit disaster. But like a real iceberg, most of the body matter of support remains below the surface, invisible to the public.

When I was sitting in Mary Ann's house in a northern suburb of Atlanta, she pulled out her retirement photo album. One picture showed her with four other smiling Delta women. She pointed to one of them and explained:

> That's someone I met that day. I never flew with her but one time. This was down in Costa Rica. As I got closer to retirement, I decided to try and go to as many cities that I hadn't been to. I don't recall her name at all, but you know what, again, this is that camaraderie that I was speaking of. Never flown with these other three women, they knew I was getting close to retirement, and they were just very willing, yes, let's go out and pose for some pictures for your retirement album. To me, again as I said earlier, that's the amazing thing about flight attendants. Flight attendants are really supportive of each other. They really are.

So Mary Ann's favorite retirement picture is with a group of fellow flight attendants she does not know. But in such a strong occupational community, it did not matter one iota to her. All that matters is that they wear the uniform.

Jump seat therapy provides a good example of flight attendant bonding that underlay the development of occupational community. But what flight attendants said to one another on the jump seat was something over which airlines really had no control. Paradoxically, however, when airlines did try to exert control over how flight attendants looked and acted on board, the sense of bonding and shared identification actually deepened.

The Uniform

Most flight attendants regard their uniforms with ambivalence; workers cannot remove it quickly enough when they get home after a flight. Some uniforms—especially in the 1960s—were plain degrading, and older workers nowadays complain about new attempts to "sex up" modern uniforms, in which they feel uncomfortable. Yet as historian Dorothy Sue Cobble writes, "Flight attendants [have] historically . . . taken pride in their appearance and in the company's celebration of their beauty."[9] Undoubtedly, glamour attracted a number of women to the profession. Aimée Bratt, for instance, recalls the circumstances of her Pan Am interview in the 1960s: "There was a 'real stewardess' in there in an immaculate blue uniform, who gave me a cool glance. She looked like she belonged in places like these; the Grand Hotel was indeed a very elegant old hotel. I was very envious."

But the uniform means a good deal more to flight attendants than wearing the company brand. Putting it on and taking it off again normally marks their transition point in and out of flight attendant mode, when they switch characters from home to work. Moreover, flight attendants derive a sense of power from wearing the uniform that extends beyond just being a high-profile company representative. This is partly because it confers upon them access rights to the flight attendant community, and partly because it denotes a sense of professionalism and authority that affects workers at the individual and psychological level. As one worker claimed: "People in uniform do something for people. You look at the firemen, the policemen, the pilots. We all, just as youngsters, thought that was really cool. There is something about that. There's a real power thing with that I think."[10]

Flight attendants in uniform can move around an airplane at will, save for the cockpit. This mobility in itself is empowering, allowing flight attendants to observe passengers without their knowing, to tell them when to sit down and stand up, and to tell them when they can or cannot use the bathroom.[11] This sense of authority is something that flight attendants are loath to lose. In their minds, a proper uniform is part of being a safety professional, and when fighting against sexist imagery, flight attendants take care not to throw the baby out with the bathwater and to lose the power that even "glamorous" uniforms provide. As Karen, who works for Delta, explains, "I don't think they were ever fighting against looking attractive. I mean, they do want to look attractive; you want to feel attractive when you get dressed to go out."

As is the case with weight controls, discussed in the previous chapter, talking about flight attendant uniforms inevitably broaches the subject of surveillance and self-surveillance. Airlines enforce appearance codes partly through spot checks at airports and occasionally "ghost riders" —supervisors posing as passengers—on flights. They also attempt to do so by inculcating workers with the company ethos, so that workers discipline themselves through self-monitoring. Up in the air, despite the presence of ghost riders, airlines know that flight attendants are basically out of reach of company regulations, one of the reasons these workers like doing the job in the first place. The attitude flight attendants have toward their uniforms is not straightforward.

The Uniform as Confidence Provider

For one thing, the uniform confers confidence. I was surprised to find during interviews with flight attendants that about a quarter of them characterized themselves as lacking in confidence before joining the profession. Wearing a flight attendant uniform helps redress this. Mandy, who works for a UK charter carrier, tells me: "Maybe my husband wouldn't actually recognize me when I'm at work. When I'm at work, I'm a different person. I put my uniform on and I change. There is a definite change. It's as soon as I put my uniform on. I have more self-esteem . . . my self esteem definitely comes out when I'm in my work." We were sitting at her dining room table in St. Albans, a desirable, middle-class town near London, and I asked her if this had always been the case. She replied:

> No. I've built up a lot more confidence since I've done this. I think it's only been in the last few years I've actually really believed what I'm doing because I suppose the first five, six years I used to think, am I really doing this? This is just so unlike me. I think as a child I was always sort of teased for being nonathletic, quite chubby. I was a tomboy. And I think people think doing this job and wearing makeup and doing your hair nice, initially just wasn't me at all. I did have to pinch myself a few times. As I've gotten more adult and mature, yes, this is me and I think I do a good job.

Back in Atlanta, Amy, who flew for Delta, says:

> I was the shyest kid in the world. . . . I would just go in the corner and just stay there. Painfully shy. Just after I got out of high school, I just thought, this isn't working. I needed that avenue of safety for what I

wanted to do. Back then in the sixties, I think the airlines were safe, of course. Very upscale and upbeat. And very high end. More glamorous, of course. And I felt comfortable in that scenario. I felt very valued that I fit. I liked that. I liked wearing the gloves to work and the stockings and all that stuff. I like getting dressed up. I like the high end of life. But it was conservative enough that I felt comfortable in that and secure.

One of flight attendants' biggest gripes is not against the wearing of uniforms but against the wearing of *bad* uniforms. Things like fabric and ill-fitting garments are important, when you are spending up to sixteen hours in a piece of clothing.[12] They do not feel comfortable and, moreover, they do not convey a professional image. Especially in an age when flight attendants increasingly worry about enforcing safety procedures on a disinterested public, they feel a badly designed uniform sends the wrong message.

So, flight attendants do not necessarily object to being forced to wear a uniform. What they dislike is being told what uniform to wear when there has been no consultation with management.[13] A classic example is Delta's gray unisex uniform introduced just before 9/11. As Pauline argues: "Management wanted it. All the flight attendants that worked on the uniforms said this is not what we want. We tried to tell [management], and they wouldn't listen. So now they're going to change it again because they had so many gripes about it. It was not a uniform that shows what our true colors are." "Our" true colors could be Delta's, but in this instance I got the feeling Pauline felt that it was her profession that was being undermined. "People are depressed about the new uniform," says Carolyn. "I am embarrassed about it. You look and feel horrible." And here is Deborah, also at Delta:

It's poorly made, very poorly made, and it's just ugly. There is nothing attractive about it. In fact, passengers when we first got it would say we looked like prison guards. Nobody would tell us who signed off on that uniform. No one would take ownership of it. My granddaughter said to me, "Nanny Deborah, do you have to wear that ugly dress?" I mean, flight attendants' children are telling them, "Don't go anyplace in that dress where my friends will see you." That is how badly it is perceived. I mean, it was more than the color. Everybody's buttons popped off. You had to actually pin your dress together in the front in order to keep the snaps in place. People wore pendants so they wouldn't open up wide. You couldn't sew buttons on, because no matter how much you sewed them on, they still popped off.

Delta has recently appeared to take these complaints into consideration. In 2005, CEO Gerald Grinstein acknowledged, "The uniform they are now wearing, they uniformly don't like." The airline linked poor employee morale to the issue and took to overhauling the gray unisex uniforms, even though they had been in use for only four years.[14]

The final point about uniform and appearance in general is that flight attendants often resist strict company monitoring and in the process deepen their sense of commitment to the profession and their fellow workers. When Carolyn talks about "us against them," "them" is not just the public but management of the airline. As Murphy argues, there are a whole host of "hidden transcripts"—scraps of information passed between flight attendants—that solidify both this sense of hostility to management and, at the same time, comradeship with fellow workers. Shoe policies are a good example. Female flight attendants must have two pairs of shoes, one for the concourse and one for on board. While in the air women can wear flat shoes, but airlines insist they wear heels at all other times when in uniform, even if they are not being paid. A flight attendant can be excused from wearing heels only by getting a doctor's note. Murphy reports one worker's strategy for overcoming this regulation: "I never wear my heels when I'm not going through a base city, or especially Dallas or Atlanta. It is such a stupid policy and they bother my feet. And I'm not going to pay $50 for an office visit every 6 months to have some damn doctor write me a note."[15]

As Murphy explains: "Many flight attendants comply with these regulations in public. . . . However, they have figured out where the high risk areas are for getting caught breaking organizational rules. They then pass this information on to the other flight attendants through their hidden transcripts, limiting the power of the panoptic gaze."[16] The "panoptic gaze" refers to Foucault's writings on Jeremy Bentham's all-seeing prison, discussed in the previous chapter. Surveillance here actually increases a flight attendant's self-identity, in the process deepening a sense of belonging to an occupational community. A similar process can be found when addressing how flight attendants act as well as how they look.

I Second That Emotion: Flight Attendants as Emotional Laborers

In airline folklore, on buying an airline ticket, passengers are not just buying transportation from A to B; they are also buying the right to be smiled at and deferred to by a flight attendant. In her book on emotional labor, *The Managed Heart*, Arlie Hochschild talks of how these workers "induce or suppress feeling in order to sustain an outward countenance that produces the proper state of mind in others—in this case, the sense of being cared for in a convivial and safe place."[17]

Flight attendants mirror other workers, such as telemarketers, bill collectors, and even teachers trained to respond emotionally to interactions in certain ways and, crucially, to produce certain effects in the receiver of the exchange. Waitstaff make diners feel welcome and laugh at their jokes, ensuring a return visit and a good tip; bill collectors provoke fear and guilt in late payers, ensuring the company gets its money.

Manipulation is the name of the game. Flight attendants manipulate their own feelings in order to manipulate the customer. One of Roberta Lessor's interviewees illustrates this nicely: "The biggest thing an airline stewardess learns is manipulating people. I'm in charge and I'm the one who's running the show, and I'll always be a step ahead of you. It's my moment of victory or power. . . . It's not only learning what to say but how to say it. As long as I convey that I care, I can tell them what I want them to do."[18] In fact, manipulation starts upon deciding to become a flight attendant, with any number of advice books telling candidates how to look and behave in interviews. Here are one "mock" question and "model" answer:

Q: Tell me a time when you handled a customer complaint effectively.
A: As a flight attendant you will be placating passengers every day. It is important that you relate to your recruiter that you know that a customer complaint must be handled with professionalism, effectively and *to the satisfaction of the customer*. (italics added)[19]

Even if a customer's complaint is unjustified or delivered in a rude manner (as many are), flight attendants must keep a lid on how they really feel and substitute how they have been trained to feel.

If selected, flight attendants then face manipulation during training, with their characters molded to fit company requirements. Elizabeth Rich described her training in her book on the profession in the early 1970s: "For five weeks I was going to have to keep my mind in a straitjacket and my emotions completely repressed."[20] Things have not really changed since then. Airlines bombard new recruits with "emotion management" skills, an obvious example being how to deal with angry or obnoxious passengers. Carriers believe the best way to deal with "irates"—as such customers are called—is empathy. Hochschild quotes one instructor: "I pretend something traumatic has happened in their lives. Once I had an irate that was complaining about me, cursing at me, threatening to get my name and report me to the company. I later found out his son had just died. Now when I meet an irate I think of that man."[21] Airlines advise flight attendants to conceptualize such passengers as children and to "kill them with kindness." In other words, flight attendants must, at all times, suppress the natural urge to snap back at obnoxious passengers. Though the increase in air rage has qualified this approach, many flight attendants still feel that their company worries more about the ramifications of offending a passenger than the consequences of a passenger offending *them*. This philosophy extends beyond the United States, as an Italian flight attendant illustrates: "When dealing with irate or offensive passengers, you can't show anger because the customers are always right since they pay. Therefore it is better to avoid confrontation. . . . If someone puts their hand on your bottom, you should say 'Excuse me sir, but my bottom accidentally fell into your hand.'"[22]

Another example of emotion management is an airline's exhortation to its flight attendants to view the company as a "family" and the airplane as "home." Of course southern-based Delta—with its roots in the region's long-standing association with hospitality—particularly lends itself to this kind of construction.[23] Hochschild, who observed Delta training in the early 1980s, tells of one pilot's advice to new recruits. He said to them: "Now, girls, I want to tell you something else. . . . I want you to think of the cabin as the living room in your very own home. At home, wouldn't you go out of your way to make friends feel at ease and have a good time? Well, it's the same thing in the L1011."[24] The metaphor becomes so ingrained in workers that some end up parroting the company line without even realizing it; numerous Delta flight attendants talked to me of the "family" and "home" comparisons. As Hochschild concludes, "The analogy between home and cabin also joins the worker to her company; just as she naturally protects members of her own family, she will naturally defend the company. . . . The company brilliantly extends and uses its workers' basic human empathy."[25]

Flight Attendant Acting

But there is also good deal of acting going on here. Ellen, a Delta flier from the 1970s, laughs when she tells me, "On more than one occasion, I thought of the job as a flight attendant as acting. You were playing a role on the airplane." For Hochschild, acting frames emotional labor's central dilemma, the point at which one cannot tell where the act stops and the "real" person begins. Workers inhabit a world that is half Orwellian and half Ayn Rand, their feelings and emotions reduced to objects of commercial exchange.[26] The net result is that workers lose sight of their authentic feelings: as Holden Caulfield in *The Catcher in the Rye* suspects, the world is ultimately full of phonies.

Yet flight attendants I spoke to seemed well aware of what their company was up to, including attempts to manipulate them. Indeed, by implication, a person who is aware of being manipulated is not really being manipulated. One KLM flight attendant argues: "Of course I am manipulated. That would be a problem if I would not know it."[27] Delta workers, meanwhile, seem only too cognizant of the passive-aggressive techniques with which their company used the "family" motif, even if they appeared to go along with it. "Guilt was a big motivator for all of us," says Carole, for instance. "Our company was a big guilt-ridden cesspool. [We were] nonunion. It was the only way to motivate us. Just like organized religion." Maya, who joined Delta when her airline, Western, was bought in the mid-1980s, observes:

> I mean, for me I think when you say act, I mean, I'll smile because that's what I'm paid to do and they want to see a pleasant face. But I'm pretty much me on the airplane, and I think that's why I enjoy it because I have a good time with passengers and I get along with other flight attendants. So some flight attendants you know don't want to be there, and you can tell they're acting.

Cynicism has grown with time and changing onboard conditions. As Mary Ann says, regarding the "home" metaphor, "In later years, we all began to say we wouldn't let most of these people in our home, much less on our property. But we weren't taught that." After deregulation in 1978, flight attendants began to talk of the "Greyhound summer," when cheap fares enticed people who used to travel by bus into the air. As Lisa says: "The Greyhound bus people can't come in my home. And that's what we would see. Like when I was flying and men wore hats and women wore gloves, and then we got into tank tops during the hippie time. I don't want him in my home. I don't want him in my neighborhood."

Also, industry mergers could create havoc with an airline's emotion management. As Roseanne says:

> When I started flying, with Delta, the Delta Family I think was probably in place and it probably did work to a certain extent, but we were very small then. But then when we merged with Western, and you got this whole different, I mean a totally different group of people, because we were southerners. . . . You brought in these folks from L.A., and they were totally different than us. It was hilarious. And they thought the Delta Family was a crock of shit. They did, they did. And it was like they never bought into it, ever.

The Western merger in the mid-1980s undermined Delta's family rhetoric as an emotional management tool. In such cases, flight attendants may still use emotional labor, however, but often they do so more for their own ends than for those of the airline. They increasingly view it in the same instrumental terms that they regarded the uniform: the crucial factor is control and autonomy. As Lisa suggests, "Girls would want to do nice service. Because it reflected on them. They weren't thinking 'Oh, I hope these people like Delta Air Lines.'"

Emotional Labor Builds Solidarity

On the one hand, emotion work was exploitative, but on the other, flight attendants derived a sense of power from it that cemented their identification with the profession. As the industry has become more cutthroat, with flight attendants feeling more vulnerable to economic downturns, such identification has deepened. As Roseanne explains, "That loyalty is to each other, not so much to the corporate offices."

A recent study of UK cabin crew brings home this point. Sociologists Sharon Bolton and Carol Boyd note how flight attendants' main reason for not calling in sick, even if they are ill, is because they do not want one of their colleagues on standby to be burdened with the trip. "It is notable here how it is a sense of commitment to colleagues that is the motivational force behind this generous gesture," they write, "not successful normative control regimes implemented by the organization."[28] That is some dedication to the flight attendant community, suggesting that attempts to control appearance and emotion can actually backfire. This is a group of workers with a strong sense of identification who feel a collective injustice when an individual worker is wronged. With that kind of solidarity, it is no accident that flight attendants' occupational community can become a source of industrial militancy, and bonding rituals can make the leap to direct challenges to management. We have already seen how flight attendant unions took on carriers over sexist advertising in the 1970s. For another example, let us jump forward to 1993, when American Airlines flight attendants decided to make getting home for Thanksgiving slightly more difficult than normal.

"American's Lying, We're Not Flying!" *Flight Attendants on Strike*

American in the 1980s under CEO Bob Crandall had pioneered B-scale salaries, at which new hires were taken on at significantly less pay than that for established flight attendants. Yet still American was a relatively high-cost airline, and in 1993, as carriers struggled with the fallout from the first Gulf War, Crandall decided to tackle labor costs. The most logical target in such situations is the perceived weakest group at the airline; thus Crandall, according to Thomas Petzinger's *Hard Landing*, resolved to "make an example of the flight attendants."[29]

Crandall wanted to impose closer control over scheduling, for flight attendants to start paying toward their own health costs, to prevent the erosion of B-scale provisions in the contract, and to maintain uniform weight standards. After two years of negotiations with the Association of Professional Flight Attendants, Crandall broke off talks, imposed the contract unilaterally, and refused to go to arbitration. Though APFA talked of strike action, American's management research team thought flight attendants would buckle at the last minute.[30] In fact, 94 percent of APFA members voted in favor of strike action, targeted for the run-up to Thanksgiving, 1993. Starting on November 18, about 20,000 flight attendants walked out, crippling American's network. On the fifth day of the strike President Bill Clinton intervened, at the behest of APFA, ensuring the dispute went to binding arbitration.

In industrial relations, strikes do not appear out of nowhere, and a close reading of the dispute shows how many features of the postdestination phase of the "space-out" played a part in both its escalation and its execution. Though pay was important, a catalyst for the dispute's intensification was management pressure on flight attendants' "spatial remuneration." In one instance a very senior worker had been placed on reserve, threatening the whole seniority system that underpins flight attendants' sense of control. More directly, American canceled flight attendant vacation time for November and December, an extraordinary policy that most adversely affected senior workers, who had the seniority to be able to command time off during that period, and whose support of industrial action in the past is best described as lukewarm. American also wanted to reduce the number of flight attendants on its Boeing 727s from four to three.[31]

A second important feature was that flight attendants' emphasis on being safety professionals had never been so pertinent. From the outset, they announced that they would strike only for eleven days because this would be an insufficient time period for management to train replacements. FAA regulations prohibit passenger flights with no flight attendants, but because American had to maintain its highly complex operations schedule, it had to continue to fly empty planes around the country at tremendous expense. Flight attendants told sympathetic pilots the best way they could show solidarity was, paradoxically, to keep flying, rather than refuse to cross picket lines, because this would hit American the hardest.

Flight attendants worked very hard on getting the message right. Training a core of fifty workers to handle media relations, APFA continually outsmarted management in its attempts to get its story into the media. Sympathetic accounts appeared in magazines such as *Time* and *Newsweek*. "Have you run across anyone who wasn't rooting for the flight attendants?" the latter asked. "Such nice, cheery rebels."[32]

But the message APFA sent was one that both defied and subverted the normal image perpetrated by airlines. One press release stated:

We lift, push, pull, bend, and stoop in confined work areas. We are re-quired to work 14 hours on domestic flights, more on foreign trips. We are subject to constant changes in cabin temperature and humidity, vi-bration, turbulence and time-zone changes that disrupt our work-sleep patterns. . . . And we pay for it all with back problems, foot, knee, and leg aches, eye, ear, nose, and throat maladies, headaches, high rates of colds and infections, hearing problems, skin irritations, menstrual and reproductive problems, varicose veins, fatigue and depression.[33]

The strike gave flight attendants an opportunity to raise issues that would normally never have concerned the public. But they also used gender as a weapon, here referring to menstrual and reproductive prob-lems, and also, in one of the strike's key moments, likening American's behavior to that of an abusive husband.[34] American's response verged on the offensive, claiming the airline was a victim of a "very angry group of people," prone to activism because of "the gay and lesbian component."[35] Such rhetoric backfired on management in the same way it did during an equally bitter dispute at TWA in 1986, when boss Carl Icahn suggested that the majority-female flight attendant workforce were second incomers, not breadwinners.[36]

"Chalk up the biggest labor victory in years to flight attendants!" *USA Today* declared after the dispute went to arbitration, a move that American had flat-out refused before the strike.[37] But its significance only makes sense when viewed as a battle not just about a job but an entire lifestyle. As one organizer put it:

These people struck out of years of anger, years of being ignored, years of being disrespected. The airline never dreamed these people had the courage they proved to have, or the solidarity. The whole flight atten-dant solidarity that's come about in the last couple of years has come about as more and more flight attendants have become mature adults with children and families. When they say "enough is enough," they are looking in the eyes of their children, who rely on them for food and ed-ucation and for hope. This goes way beyond self-interest.[38]

In other words, the strike was the logical outcome of pushing an occu-pational community, with its high levels of job identification, forged through on-the-job bonding experiences, too far.

Up in the skies, flight attendants therefore build solidarity that expresses itself both on the jump seat and on the picket line. Both are expressions of a deeply felt occupational community. But what happens when flight attendants come down again and embark on a layover in a foreign city, for instance? As the next chapter shows, the "space-out" is a major factor there, too.

6

The Layover

I remember thinking when I first flew international, I'd say to other flight attendants [who'd stay in their room], "Don't fly international if you're not going to get out and enjoy the city. What in the world are you doing this for? What are you all thinking?" And then I realized this is my time, and I don't have to answer to anybody. . . . Some days I just need to have that down time. I need to have the time to be able to do whatever reading, writing, stuff I just would like to do. And at home I don't ever feel comfortable. I always feel like there's something else I need to be doing. Always something else. So my down time is treasured time on those layovers.

—Kirsty, Delta flight attendant

About an hour from London by train, the south coast English resort town of Brighton has long been a major destination for American tourists. Its pavilion, a monument to the lavish decadence of the Prince Regent, the son of George III, and its famed antique shops and pier offer glimpses of the quaintness Americans associate with the United Kingdom but sometimes have trouble locating. Brighton's seedy underbelly—historically, the city was to London what Atlantic City was to New York—perhaps adds to the appeal, immortalized in Graham Greene's *Brighton Rock,* the movie *Mona Lisa,* and tales of holiday battles between teenage Mods and Rockers in the 1960s.

Delta flight attendants hold Brighton dear to their hearts. During much of the eighties and nineties, workers from the Atlanta airline laid over in the city following their overnight flight to London Gatwick, the city's second-largest airport after Heathrow. In several interviews with Delta women, I swapped names of favorite city haunts that I knew from my time growing up near London. Having decided to quit flying after twenty-five years, Sandra viewed the city in symbolic terms. "I had an epiphany on my first flight back after my husband's serious surgery," she tells me. "Then on the day I retired, the Brighton pier collapsed into the sea. I took that as a sign I'd made the right decision."[1]

The layover is one of the job's greatest perks, yet also the site of the greatest contradiction between popular imagery and reality surrounding the profession. The dominant myth, propagated by fictional works such as *Coffee, Tea or Me?* and advertising campaigns like National's "Fly Me," frames the layover as a fusion of exotic, glamorous destinations and an opportunity for easy, no-strings-attached sex. This is a myth that has been hard to dispel, and even the contemporary independent movie *The Aviary,* written by a United flight attendant, exaggerates the layover's reputation as a site for random sexual encounters. Summer Posey, the main character and a United flight attendant, falls into bed with the first man she meets at her crash pad and seems to spend half her time looking for men while away from home.

No doubt affairs do happen (they do in any job), and a few women admitted to me to being "wild" in the early seventies. Equally, airlines lured many flight attendants to the job with promises of exotic travel. But the layover's importance these days has little to do with the capacity for the odd fling in a foreign capital—if it ever did. In fact, in many ways, the layover is central to the contemporary "space-out." As I explained earlier, when bidding according to seniority, flight attendants do not necessarily plump for cities they like (though, as in Brighton's case, this helps) but to maximize their autonomy. A long-distance trip means fewer overall flights per month, and therefore more time and space to do their own things.[2] At the same time, flight attendants view the layover as a spatial haven, and they try to maximize their time and space in which they do not have to worry about domestic responsibilities. Flying to Rome is better than going to Raleigh, North Carolina, not because it is the capital of Italy but because it gives flight attendants almost a day to themselves. Moreover, for some workers, it does not matter where they go because they often stay in their rooms for most of the time. Such flight attendants are known in the industry as slam clickers —slam the door, lock it behind you, and don't appear until it is time to go back to the airport. The layover also provides flight attendants with space to pursue different careers (I have come across antique collecting and tax advising, among others). Whatever the motivation, flight attendants cherish their layovers—indeed they *are* one of the job's perks that keeps them coming back for more.

Women and Mobility

The layover also has a deeper—dare I say philosophical—meaning for flight attendants. As Roberta Lessor found, in her study of flight attendants in the early 1980s, "There appears to be a quality or essence to the geographically vast work environment that contributes to changing consciousness."[3] Put bluntly, the layover provides women with the chance to "space-out," not just in terms of having a break from the family but in terms of having the freedom to—at the most extreme level—reinvent themselves. For many, this freedom is addictive.

In the process, women implicitly turn existing gender patterns on their head. As the geographer Linda McDowell observes, "Travel, even the idea of travelling, challenges the spatial association between home and women that has been so important in structuring the social construction of femininity in the 'West.'"[4] Certainly, travel for flight attendants conforms to this kind of challenge: there is no other female-dominated profession in which women spend so much time away from home as part and parcel of their working lives. Flight attendants have an engagement with space that is quite different from that of their contemporaries back on the ground.

As numerous feminist geographers have argued, space—as a human construct rather than an abstract concept—is loaded with gendered inequalities.[5] There is perhaps no more apt phrase for the built environment around us than "man-made": from the layout of suburban homes to the architecture of downtown business districts, the historically gendered assumption that some spaces are reserved for men and others for women is writ large across the landscape.[6] Women often curtail their movement in public spaces, especially in cities—choosing when and where they go jogging is a good example—through fear of attack (despite the far greater chance of their being attacked by their own male partner at home). Those attempting to reject such restrictions do so in explicitly geographic terms: not for nothing is the U.S. women's antiviolence movement mantra "Take Back the Night," arguing that women should be able to move around at will, without fear.[7]

It is not just fear that circumscribes women's mobility. At the practical level, in one-vehicle families, men have historically been the ones to take the car. In most major cities you can witness the early-morning pilgrimage of transit-dependent women (often of color) struggling to work as janitors or supermarket cashiers on slow and inefficient public buses. Even among middle-class double-income couples, women typically work closer to home than men and have greater responsibility for domestic chores.[8]

Logistical barriers are framed by cultural ones, often enshrined in language and myth. Society has long poured scorn upon women who are "fast" or who "get around." The tale of Little Red Riding Hood warns young girls against the dangers of straying too far from the path laid out for them (as does, in an oblique way, the socially conservative *Wizard of Oz*). Even amid such radicals as the Beat generation, male writers such as Jack Kerouac were always "on the road" between static girlfriends (and aunts) stuck at home. Freedom and mobility, in this sense, were male preserves, which was one of the reasons the movie *Thelma and Louise* was so radical.

Flight Attendant Mobility as Subversion

My point is that flight attendant mobility—all those evenings away from home in distant cities—is by definition subversive. In flight attendant families, it is typically the woman who works farther from home and who moves around. Mary Ann, who flew for Delta, tells me, "Women, particularly, find themselves restricted most of their lives, one way or the other. You're always restricted." We were sitting in her front room looking at old photos, and she continues:

> As you were ripping through my retirement album, I was noticing one of the pictures, and I remembered the feeling that I would often get in another city. You could become anybody you wanted to be, particularly international. Because you were in a different culture, there were different expectations of the kind of person you were. It was almost as if you could remake yourself.

For women, moving around or going to new places, and taking on new identities other than those prescribed to them back home, can disrupt social norms.[9] This was especially true for young women coming of age in the South after World War II and was something they were well aware of. Growing up in Fort Worth, Texas, Hazel joined Delta in the early 1950s. "I'm sure we were talked about and thought badly of," she chuckles in reference to herself and her colleagues. Escaping the traditional fabric of small-town life was one of the job's attractions. Molly, who joined United as late as 1975, tells me, "I'm from South Carolina and I thought, 'I've got to get out of here.'" Ironically, airlines such as Delta hastened the disruption of tradition, hiring flight attendants as embodiments of "southern hospitality" yet at the same time turning them into modern paid workers—with their own wants and aspirations —who were the very antithesis of the "southern lady."[10]

In becoming highly mobile flight attendants, therefore, many women entered a world of modernity, confronting themselves and their surroundings in ways hitherto unnecessary in traditional societies.[11] One Pan Am flier suggests: "It just opened my eyes. . . . I lived such a sheltered life that flying just kind of opened a whole new world to me. And, you know, just flying to different countries and meeting different people, seeing how they lived, even the food they ate was different. It was an eye opener."[12] "Many feminists," geographers Susan Hanson and Geraldine Pratt concur, "have narrated a process of uncovering multiple layers of social identity by departing from their home base."[13] On layovers, flight attendants often feel free to step out to become whoever they want to be, reinforced by the confidence the job has instilled in them. Or, instead, they do not go out at all, choosing to be a different person, not a wife or mother, for instance, within the confines of the hotel room. Parents, especially those with young children, relish the chance to get away from daily domestic chores, pamper themselves for a night, get some quiet time, and catch up on sleep. Time spent in the space of the hotel room, one woman told me, is your time: "On your layover, it's yours. It's yours. Whereas the other times are not. They are not yours at all." Flight attendant moms, in particular, count themselves lucky: "What mom wouldn't honestly want a night off from the kids?" one asks me.

But the layover is never completely insulated from the world of home, especially with the widespread introduction of mobile telephones. Layers of complexity emerge around the fact that having escaped for the night, many flight attendants subsequently experience guilt and worry about their family in their absence. These feelings are often expressed in angst over whether or not to keep in touch with home—"Should I call or shouldn't I?" Mothers simultaneously relish their personal freedom and feel guilty at having left their children. They are thankful for the free time but then may feel unneeded. They worry about missing out on crucial family moments and their child's development, and that the family is actually coping fine without them. More than one woman told me of feeling out of the picture when away from home.

In addition, although freedom can be liberating, it can also be disconcerting. Given the opportunity to be alone for a while, flight attendants can often end up just feeling lonely. A relatively common analogy I heard was that of a traveling salesman, caught in an endless pattern of monotonous journeys and hotel rooms, compounded by feelings of disorientation and jet lag. "There's an emptiness. It's a very lonely job," one flight attendant concluded.

So "being oneself" needs to be tempered with guilt, feelings of being unneeded, loneliness, and disorientation. In this context, flight attendants, having escaped their real homes and families—go about constructing alternate ones. They do this through a combination of rituals and routines. They adorn their hotel rooms with accoutrements from home; they eat meals in the same restaurants at the same time of day and with the same people (their fellow workers and vicarious family). In short, having slipped out of the bonds of domesticity, flight attendants often go about replicating them—intentionally and unintentionally—on their layover. Given the temporal and spatial chaos often surrounding their real homes, flight attendants often create a more stable alternative when away. It is in this jumbled sense of permanently coming and going, of shifting identities, that the layover represents a spatial haven in a storm.

The World at Their Feet

Though it is a cliché, the idea that glamorous travel lured flight attendants to the profession has more than a ring of truth to it. When destination was all-important to them, flight attendants consumed new locations avidly. Senior flight attendants, for instance, often wax lyrical about the places they have been in their careers. Giselle flew for Pan Am before going, in turn, to Eastern and then American. Sitting in her suburban Atlanta kitchen with another American flier, she had this to say:

> When I flew for Pan Am, you didn't fly in the United States. You took off and you went around the world. So I'd go on a ten-day trip around the world. Sometimes three-day trips, five-day trips, five-day layovers in

Buenos Aires. My favorite was a ten-day trip, you left San Juan, [Puerto Rico] and you went to Portugal and laid over in a little village called Cascais, Portugal, right on the ocean; two days there and then two days in either Barcelona or Madrid, and then two days in Rome, Italy, and an African shuttle and back again to San Juan.

When I ask Angela why she joined Delta in 1969, she replies:

Growing up as a child, I'd always been interested in seeing the world, and world history was one of my favorite subjects when I was in high school, and it was just very interesting to me to see what the other part of the world was like and people and their culture. . . . So I decided to get a job with the airlines where I'd have the flexibility of traveling more than a vacation once a year. . . . I could afford to travel and go to the exotic places that I've always wanted to travel to, and be introduced to a different culture and different people. So I've always loved working with people. I know this is like quote-unquote one of the things people always say that they enjoy, but I do.

Airlines usually offer free travel for their workers and their relatives, and flight attendants could therefore explore the world both during time off and as part of their job. Moreover, flight attendants could usually get reduced fares on other airlines, thereby expanding their orbit. Numerous Delta retirees told me about trips abroad that they had taken after leaving the airline.

Sex does appear to have been a part of the job's attraction for some flight attendants at the time. As Aimée Bratt recalls, in her memoirs of Pan Am: "We had, as I have said, very long layovers in seductive places like Tahiti and Samoa, where the so-called 'crew parties' flourished, and drinking and dancing and romancing and sex were all part of it. And it was great."[14] For flight attendant Elizabeth Rich, such themes dominated "the prevailing image of the airline stewardess and probably accounted for a majority of the fantasies which motivated thousands of young women to apply for this job each year."[15]

Airline marketing and popular culture in the late 1960s and 1970s both unquestionably overstated the profession's hedonistic image. But considering an era of changing social mores and a profession whose itinerant nature inevitably generates transient relationships among young adult workers, it would be surprising if the "party" image of flight attendants were not partly true. As one woman says:

> You know in the seventies, dating was, when you look back on it, it was just gross. Dating was as casual as talking to someone on the phone. You stayed drunk. Everybody drank. Everybody had sex. I can't say I wasn't part of it. Layovers. Drunk from the time you landed. Some of us were even drunk in the air. It wasn't a secret. Yet it was not condoned. It was kind of like the old boys' network where you know they're all doing whatever they're doing and if it's not going to hurt you, what the hell. And that's the way it was because it was so new, so exciting.

As discussed earlier, flight attendants did not resent having sex: what they resented was the fact that airlines marketed their sexuality, which is something different. But by the 1980s things had changed, for reasons that were part cultural, part economic, and part demographic. Culturally, the social backlash against the previous decades' excesses—coupled with the rise of AIDS—rendered sleeping around less acceptable (and less safe). Economically, the industry's deregulation in 1978 made airlines much more competitive, and thus stricter. Flight attendants, by their own admission, could no longer "get away" with things that they had done previously. Personnel departments got much tougher on alcohol use and eventually resorted to random testing. Additionally, layovers that once lasted perhaps two or three days became shorter. As one woman puts it, "Promiscuity would be more common, but no one has the time anymore."

The Changing Importance of the Layover

Most important, however, the demographic composition of the flight attendant group had changed. By the early 1970s, civil rights legislation outlawing company bans on marriage, children, and working beyond the age of thirty had begun to take effect. The net result was that a collection of young, single, and adventurous twentysomethings, by the 1980s, increasingly became a group of thirtysomethings, often in stable relationships, often with children, and, most salient, often with a completely different set of priorities.

As a result, the layover's significance changed, as flight attendants "spaced-out" in a different way: when the job was a short-term career, destination was everything; when it became a full-term profession, the destination became increasingly irrelevant. This point is well illustrated through looking at shifting perceptions of Hawaii. A domestic port of call, yet undoubtedly one of Aimée Bratt's "seductive destinations," Hawaii in the 1960s was one of the plum routes. In interviews several flight attendants tell me about the past attraction of cocktails, sunsets, and beaches. Pauline, who began flying for Delta in the late 1960s, claims: "We would go to Waikiki and rent a car to go around to the other side of the island. And you think, 'Oh, my God,' if you land in Honolulu, and I'm getting paid to do this? Sit on Waikiki Beach and watch the hula dancers. Getting paid to do this?" Hawaii is still one of the most sought-after trips and is accordingly often staffed by senior crew. But their reasons for choosing it nowadays have little to do with the destination itself and more to do with the number of paid hours the trip commands. Flying to Hawaii and back from Atlanta once a week means cabin crew have to do little else; thus, it is a way of maximizing time and space away from the job.

Claudette thinks of almost nothing but rest on her layover in Hawaii, especially on arrival. "It's 11:00 at night. It's muumuu time. It got to where I didn't even want to be in my own skin," she says. Though some flight attendants still talk of enjoying a cocktail in Hawaii, the route is now popular not for the exotic charms of Honolulu but because it is the highest-paying domestic trip in Delta's system.

Priorities have changed. Rest, relaxation, and renewal have become the layover's most important attraction, as opposed to all-night partying. Layovers increasingly represent spatial havens in which flight attendants explore not just the world around them but also their own identities.

The Confidence to Be

In the previous chapter I examined how the job's specific onboard requirements helped instill some flight attendants with confidence. This confidence is useful on layovers, when flight attendants display the wherewithal to negotiate potentially strange cities, often alone, in ways that challenge gendered expectations about public space, where freedom to "roam without fear" has been most associated with masculinity.[16] As the political philosopher Iris Marion Young notes, women have generally lacked confidence in their ability to *do* things. "We have more of a tendency than men to greatly underestimate our bodily capacity," she says. "We decide beforehand—usually mistakenly—that the task is beyond us, and thus give it less than our full effort." [17]

But for flight attendants, a key factor in the layover is its "boundedness." [18] It is bounded temporally and spatially, in the sense that workers know that its duration is limited, and also that if they do "roam without fear" they cannot really go *that far* in such a short space of time. This in itself is reassuring, as Ellen explains. "I think of the term 'structured deviance,'" she says, and then continues:

> You could go off and, like, be wild, but you *always* had this thing to come back to. You had your hotel room. I mean you could test the waters, I guess, you know? And to me that was the greatest thing. Things that I never would have done, ever, I felt comfortable about doing because I was with a group of people. For instance, going out with other flight attendants on a New York layover, "Oh, let's go to this disco," for example, I never would have done that on my own.

Mary Ann, another recent Delta retiree, hands me another cup of coffee, sits back down on her sofa, and recalls:

> I remember one Sunday afternoon in Paris, and I flew Paris a lot, it's my favorite city. I was sitting out in the Tuileries gardens with my feet propped up on a chair. All those chairs there that everyone sits around the little fountain and pond and the kids push the little toy boats on a Sunday afternoon. I had been sitting there under one of the chestnut trees reading for about an hour or so, and I looked up and I hadn't spoken with anybody all day except maybe at breakfast. It hit me all of a sudden that I felt very much at home there. I felt very comfortable, like I belonged. It was almost that the person I was here, in Atlanta, was not the person I was there.
>
> Somehow along the way you get the courage to try things, because there aren't people there that know you [and] that have expectations of how you will behave. And I don't mean getting into trouble morally or anything. It's just people don't know you, so it's sort of like you have a chance to start life anew. It was like that going to different cities. It was like starting life all over again. You didn't have any baggage.

It is clear here how some flight attendants come to cherish the spatial freedom available on layovers. Being a member of the flight attendant family boosts confidence, but so, to repeat, does the job itself. One particular area this relates to is technology, which, though normally a male preserve, holds little fear for task-oriented flight attendants. Several interviewees told me stories of specific technological achievements, such as hiring a car and driving it on the "wrong" side of the road (in Ireland, for instance), or other "little increments," as one put it, that combined to nurture greater self-confidence. The fact that there is no one else around to rely on (tacitly, this often means a husband) leaves flight attendants in the position of having to deal with situations for themselves. Though this very attribute is a requirement of the job, it is also extremely empowering.

One may need to qualify this, especially in a world of heightened terrorism fears. Confidence, especially in public space, has to be matched with caution, and flight attendants express anger at what they considered particularly stupid acts by their peers while abroad. One, for instance, told me with incredulity how, after the invasion of Iraq had begun, one worker had put a sign on a bar door in a European capital instructing her airline colleagues to "meet here" for drinks. Roaming without fear is a different thing in Bogotá, for instance, than it is in Paris. Flight attendants—especially those who cannot speak Spanish—seldom leave the hotel when laying over in the Colombian capital, not because they are slam clicking but for security reasons.

At the same time, it would be naive to think that race does not influence mobility, and the overwhelming majority of women I spoke to were white. In foreign cities, especially in Europe, white flight attendants may overcome gendered obstacles but never have to deal with racial ones. That said, the handful of nonwhite women I interviewed were equally enthusiastic about the layover's spatial haven as their white counterparts.[19]

The Great Escape: Getting Away from the Family

Up until the passage of civil rights legislation in the 1960s, it was widely assumed that being a flight attendant was unsuitable for a mother. Indeed, former flier Georgia Nielsen, in her work on the founding of the Association of Flight Attendants, observes that some workers themselves believed this.[20] As early as 1970, however, Elizabeth Rich noted how a "stewardess, after all, has much more time to spend with her child than the mother who works at a nine-to-five job."[21]

Flight attendant parents often regard their jobs as beneficial to their children's upbringing. They are able to devote more time to school activities than the average parent; they also see their children as independent and well balanced, though a large grain of salt may be required to swallow some of these claims. Guilt is never far from the surface.

By contrast, flight attendants often view the layover as specifically beneficial for themselves. Kelly, for instance, flew with Delta for eight years, beginning in the late 1980s, while she had young children at home. She still stays in touch with many of her ex-colleagues. "I have friends who will never quit," she tells me. "Because it's their saving grace, a lot of flight attendants say they go to work to rest. Being away from home is their time alone. For parents, there is no rest at home. But flight attendants have hours alone in a hotel room. They can lock the hotel door. There are no little creatures bothering them." When I ask her to expand upon this in a subsequent conversation, she explains:

> When I was [flying] back in Atlanta, we had great layovers, and you would have, you know, at least one out of the two nights, you would have an eighteen- or nineteen-hour layover. So you could go back in your room if you didn't want to go out to dinner. [You could be a] slam clicker, and sometimes you would just go in your room, lock it shut, and sometimes you wouldn't see anyone until pickup the next day, and you would order room service, paint your toenails, give yourself a facial, you know. When you're away from home, you don't have laundry, you don't have to clean the house, you don't have to worry about that stuff, you don't have cooking, you're not going shopping, you're not doing bills, so for eighteen hours, you have . . . basically, free time.

Not many mothers of small children get eighteen hours of free time every week. But the notion of free time and space crops up frequently in discussions with parents at all airlines and of all ages. Suzie, in her thirties, for instance, with a five-year-old son, works for Atlantic Southeast Airlines (ASA), which does not have long-distance flights to other continents and has much shorter layovers in domestic destinations. Yet still she finds the layover a spatial haven, as she explains:

We are a service-industry people. We wait on people hand and foot. You go home to mom, what does she do? Waits on people hand and foot. I lost my identity for about four years. You know, granted, I'm no spring chicken, but I like my bubble bath. I like to be able to paint my toenails. I'm a girly-girl. I like time to myself. Well, any mother that has a three- or four- or two-year-old is not going to have that. You have no privacy. I mean, the bathroom is open territory, you know. And it was really starting to bother me, and I just felt like I lost my identity. . . . If at all possible I like to pick the destinations for overnight stays, because that's my free time. That's mine, where I can be me. As a person, not a mommy, not a wife, not a flight attendant. I can have a drink. I can go shopping. I can sleep in in the morning and watch a movie on TV. That's my time, and I need that.

But senior fliers also talk about the desire to get away from domestic responsibilities. Kathleen, a United flier since the early 1970s, puts it like this:

It got to the point when I liked time for myself. I like people. I would get away, and it was an opportunity to not only be a housewife and mom. I liked having a time when I didn't feel like a wife and mom. I had short layovers, to get the minimum time. I was never twenty-four hours in a city. I didn't fly international as I still wanted to see [the kids] every day. But the hotel time alone was great.

In a similar vein, Janice flew with Delta between 1968 and 2001. She recalls:

It was very good for me, and for many years I didn't realize it. But when you are a full-time mother of four you're very busy. Especially when you are very much involved in their lives. And I have many other interests. I'm very fond of my church, so I stay busy all the time. And I didn't realize for quite a while, that that break where I would be on a layover and I couldn't do anything about getting the house clean or taking care of one of the kid's activities or baking what I had to bake, or running around doing errands, that was very good for me. That was kind of a sanity break, and I came home very refreshed after those.

The sanity break can be as much from household chores as it is from children's demands. Donna, a junior flier at Delta, married but with no children, suggests: "I enjoy being in the room by myself. I rarely go out on my layovers unless there's really something nice I want to see. It's my therapy. That's what I always tell my dad: it's my therapy. I hide in the room and I read and I sleep and you don't have to wash clothes or clean the house." Flight attendants are not always fleeing only household drudgery. Several talk about how the layover provides respite from difficult domestic partnerships. "When you're in an unhappy relationship, yeah, you can't wait to get to the airport," comments one. Returning home, recalls another, "I would never know if my husband would be there and I would have a knot in my stomach. It was good to go in those days, to get away from all this. Sometimes driving home I would just think, 'Oh God.'"

Seen in this light, the layover appears benign, something useful, an ideal coping mechanism. Indeed, it becomes an essential part of the job in which flight attendants reap the reward of the free time and free space it provides. Amid the current economic turmoil in the industry, flight attendants tell me that they would continue to fly because of the layover's therapeutic value, the chance to escape, the opportunity to have their own space and time. Yet, paradoxically, having embraced the freedom on offer, many flight attendants are simultaneously wracked with guilt and concern about what is going on at home in their absence.

To Call or Not to Call

In interviews, flight attendants repeatedly express opposing views regarding contact with home while they are away. Over the last few years, with the advent of cell phones, calling home has obviously become much easier. Some flight attendants, though not many, also use e-mail. Both strategies—calling or not calling—can be seen as manifestations of feelings of guilt and feelings that they are not actually needed. Patricia, a retired United flier, is an extreme example of a flight attendant who likes to keep in touch. Above all, she missed the everyday things while away:

> I think just the sense of having daily rituals, getting up at the same time. Doing just the mundane things that you do during the day. Get the kids'

teeth brushed. You've got to get them dressed. Get everyone breakfast and off to school. Be there when they get home. You know, just like that? Just the biggest sacrifice, of course, I did miss first words and first steps. I did, yeah, and that's tough.

Phoning home during the layover, she says, was one of the only ways to communicate with her husband, since time at home with two children was so frantic. As she describes it,

> Our communication was really by telephone when I was on my layover. When I was at home there wasn't time. [My husband] was running back off to the office or whatever had to be done. So, that's really when we talked was by phone on my layover. It cost a fortune. Because I would call home three of four times a day. I was very homesick. A lot of flight attendants, most all flight attendants—I am very unusual that way—won't call at all. They just wait until they get home, and some will call maybe once a day. This was before all these, you know, great calling rates. Yeah, now it's easier or you have your computer. But we didn't have that option. So, yeah, my phone bills were huge.

When I ask her why she felt the urge to call so much, she responds:

> Just to find out that, you know, what everybody was doing. What was going on? Is everybody OK? You know, I just felt really out of it. I was an absentee mother, and I'm very much a homebody. I'm very, you know, family is important to me, and I just wanted to keep tabs and [make sure] everything was OK at home. So I would always leave a long list of instructions on, you know, what to feed this person and what to do for that person and who has to be here on time, you know? [Laughs] I would have these lengthy lists of things for [my husband] to do. I don't know whether he did any of them or not, but it made me feel better just to think that I had some grasp on the things that were going on.

By keeping in touch, flight attendants like Patricia attempt to manage from afar, a frequent pattern among interviewees. But there is something else at work here. By calling, flight attendants reinsert themselves into the family from which they are physically separated, at the most humdrum and everyday level. They want to know "what's going on," no matter how mundane. Esther, who has flown for Delta for twenty-seven years, calls about her son regularly. She elaborates: "When he was young, I even just wanted to know what his bodily functions were doing that day. 'Cause I'm not there to do it. What have you had for dinner and so on." For all the talk of enjoying being disconnected from the domestic routines, flight attendants often feel the urge to be reconnected. "The cell phone is our best friend because we usually call home every night," explains Paula, from ASA: "And it's not really to check in, it's just, OK, there's that familiar voice that I know or to say good night to their children. We are not there with them, but we can talk with them over the phone."

Yet contact with home can resurrect feelings of guilt at not being there. Kathleen, another United flier, for instance, talks of how needy her daughter was and that she "felt denied that Mom wasn't always there." Her solution was to make sure that she was the one who initiated contact: "I usually called home at night, so she didn't have the option of calling. When she did call, it made me feel worse. There were so many guilt factors at work here. Often I'd just think to myself, 'What am I *doing?*'"

If one strategy is to keep in touch, the alternative is almost to pretend that the family no longer exists. Some flight attendants go into a cocoonlike existence. Rather than call once a trip, they do not call at all and forbid spouses and children from calling them. Andrea, a Delta flier with two teenage sons, tells her husband:

> "Don't call me unless they're bleeding." But I also say, "If someone dies, don't tell me. I can't do anything about it." It's better to let me fly home and then get in, sit down with a glass of wine, and then tell me. It has happened to some flight attendants. Someone has died, and they are overwrought. And they can't get home any quicker. Let them come home, then tell them.

Margaret, also with Delta and with two teenage children tells me:

> I don't keep in touch. When I first started flying international, I would call home. And then, it is just too expensive. So, I just don't call, because there is nothing I can do. The fastest way I'm going to get back is the trip I work. A friend of mine's husband died when she was in Eng-

land on a trip when her father called. Of course, there was nothing she could do till she got home. And they didn't want her to work the flight back, they wanted her to sit, [but] she can't sit so she worked. Just to keep her mind off [it], you know. But I mean she said, "I don't know why they called me because there is nothing I can do. I couldn't get back any sooner than what I was doing." You know. So I know that was really hard for her. Trying to get back. So I don't call.

Denise, who recently retired from Delta after thirty-four years, argues:

My theory was, and I hope you don't think this sounds too apathetic, but my theory was that once I got on the airplane, I was there to do a job, and once that door closed, there wasn't anything I could do about anything on the ground with my family. And don't be calling me on my layovers, because I can't get to you. Especially over in Europe, I thought that was very insensitive of families that would call and the husband would be saying, "Well, so and so has fallen and he's got stitches." There's not anything you can do about it.

Both of these strategies are ultimately devised to shield the flight attendant. Either she or he is sheltered from bad news, or she or he is prevented from feeling left out and possibly unneeded in the family matrix. Whatever the option, it is clear that for all the talk of free time on layovers, flight attendants exhibit a strong undercurrent of concern. This ambivalence is exacerbated by feelings of disorientation and loneliness.

The Bathroom Light and Disorientation

One major problem for flight attendants is that they inhabit a world in which airplanes, airports, and their surroundings all look pretty much alike. Hotel rooms and the hotels themselves are all fairly similar, leading to the kind of disorientating experience identified by Daniel Boorstin back in the 1960s and Fredric Jameson, in his famous elucidation of postmodernism, twenty years later.[22]

Most of us have had the feeling of waking up and not knowing where we are. Flight attendants on layovers, however, do this on a regular basis. The combination of jet lag and monotonous hotel rooms can be highly disorientating. Paula, for instance, an ASA worker, observes:

> I have to leave the light on in the bathroom wherever I go because I always get turned around. I'm never in the same place, you know, two nights in a row. You know, if it's the same hotel every week, then I get used to it. But I have to have a light on because I forget where I'm at. I have waked up many times, and people do this all the time. The alarm clock goes off and I go, "Where am I?" Because we are just somewhere different every three hours, it seems. But, I mean, after seven years, I still do that.

Ellen, who flew for Delta from 1973 to 2001, also left the bathroom light on. She explains:

> That was probably the hardest thing, especially when we were doing domestic a lot. Because they were short layovers. I mean, you had like four legs, you spent the night, three more legs, spent the night, and you just had no idea, you just kind of followed the pattern, followed the plan and just followed the leader. Captain will just take you. Many times you would wake up and have no clue where you were. No clue.

To help orient themselves, flight attendants often go through the same routines on waking. Shelly provides a good example of this:

> When you wake up, right away you go through all those things. Where am I? OK, there's the bed, I'm in a hotel. I'm in California. My sign-in is, you always keep your clock by the bed and always have a pen and always a piece of paper on the bedside table because if the crew desk calls you in the middle of the night to say the trip you thought you were going on is canceled or is rescheduled, it's the middle of the night and you have to write this down, otherwise you think maybe it's a dream.

Being regularly disoriented is bound to have psychological effects, especially if one is physically cut off from loved ones. One result can be loneliness. Clare, who flies for Continental, compares the sensation to the movie *Lost in Translation,* in which Bill Murray plays an insomniac actor "stuck" in a Tokyo hotel. Murray's plight (and that of costar

Scarlett Johansson) is analogous to that of many flight attendants, she suggests:

> Though it wasn't the best movie in the world, I think the way that they would stare out of the hotel rooms sometimes and his phone calls back to his wife when she's talking about something that is more focused on the kids and this guy, all he wants is somebody to talk to. He's un-plugged. He's lost. And this is meaningless, what she's saying to him. And you can get some of that sometimes. Those psychological and emotional feelings. Definitely. You're up in the middle of the night some-times, your sleep patterns are interrupted, and it definitely has a toll on you, emotionally, psychologically. You feel like you are, where are you? Your first thought in the morning is, where are you?

Loneliness

Several factors may compound this loneliness. International fliers may not be able to speak the local language and may not be "adopted" by those workers who can (and who often have their own networks of friends abroad). Regional fliers may work alone and literally have no one else to talk to, save for the pilots. Though flight attendants tend to open up to each other more readily than most workers, the transient na-ture of many of their relationships leaves them feeling that they have no real companions. More than one person indicates that, paradoxically—given the image—airlines are a very difficult place to make friends.

For some, especially those who live alone, the work trip may be the only social outing of the week, which can inevitably lead to disappoint-ment. "They're lonely," Claudette suggests of many of her fellow work-ers. "They think in their mind 'I have this glamorous job, I'm an attrac-tive person, and I should just have men falling at my feet.'" Staring at the walls of the hotel room, wondering where you are, wondering what your loved ones are up to—this is not a permanent condition for all flight attendants; but nearly all have found themselves in it at some point.

But flight attendants find and actively create anchors of stability within this world of apparent anomie. Disconnected from the routines and rituals of their real homes, they set about re-creating them when away. They begin with the hotel room.

Rituals and Routines: Getting Reconnected

Flight attendants have a tendency to domesticate the space around them in the hotel. Having showered—nearly every worker talks of "washing the plane off"—they often adorn the room. This both creates and re-creates an alternative home-space. Among the items flight attendants bring from home to put or use in their room are favorite pillows or blankets; pictures of family and/or pets (in albums and frames); favorite pajamas, robes and nightgowns; toys and stuffed animals; candles and incense; favorite wine glasses; hot water bottles; relaxing music, tapes, or CDs; favorite shampoos, soaps, washcloths, and other toiletries (even though toiletries are supplied by the hotel). Paula, a regional flight attendant at ASA, described this activity:

> I like to make a little bit of, you know, this is my home away from home, is what it is. I have an alarm clock, and it has a picture of my husband and me in it. It sits by my bed when I go on my trips. People carry pictures of their children, or their families on their IDs. They have a pouch, and they carry it with them there so it's closer to their heart. They're either pictures, or we can have one pin that has nothing to do with the airline industry or anything on our uniforms. You know, they'll have a picture of their child there. Some people do take the candles to the hotels. They take certain sheets or a pillow or something in their suitcases, so they can make their home away from home, because basically that is our home away from home [for] whatever how many nights of the week that we are there. A lot of people bring their own food with them. So they have the home cooking there.

United flight attendants in Narita, Japan, have the most elaborate system I heard about. One of them, Shelly, tells me:

> We go to the grocery stores there and gather up some things for our room because we always have a fridge in our room. And there's a lot of girls that bring movies. There are VCRs in the room. And then there's a big screening room. The hotel is international, and they tend to cater a little bit more to us with, like, the screening. So there are comfortable chairs and all with a big-screen TV. So there's a little clipboard at the front desk, and you can say, "OK, I brought over whatever movie," and

you sort of sign in and say, "I'll be showing it tomorrow at 4:00." At 4:00, bring your popcorn, bring your beer, whatever.

Regular fliers to Narita keep a permanent bag at the hotel in which they place items such as sneakers, bathing suits, and reading material. For Shelly, one prized possession is a wine glass, which she washes, carefully wraps, and places back in the duffle bag upon leaving. "That's a comfort of home, if you're a wine drinker," she says. Paying bills, writing letters, sorting out doctor's appointments, doing work on correspondence courses, studying for professional examinations, creating scrapbooks, and arranging photographs in albums are among the things that other flight attendants attend to in their hotel rooms.

Doing the Same Thing

Flight attendants also anchor themselves by adopting quite predictable routines, where possible. Theresa, a Delta flier since the early 1970s, observes:

> I think flight attendants nest. I think a lot of us, from my perspective, make friends with the same shop owners. They get into a routine to make it more comfortable. I did fly with people who had to go to the same exact places. First we go here and then we go here and then we have a pint at the Pump Room, and it was exasperating to me in that there are other things to do and see. However, that's where you got your comfort level. A lot of flight attendants got their comfort level, I think, on layovers by the routine. By knowing that the same things were there as last week. I mean, that's where you end your chaos and you get control again.

Ending chaos and getting control again is an idea worth repeating. For flight attendants, "chaos" consists of many things: physical and psychological displacement from home; jet lag, loneliness, unfamiliar surroundings, disorientation, stress from the flight itself, attending to passengers' whims, and trying to stay civil in the face of constant rudeness. Equally, "control" comes in numerous forms: slam clicking, taking a leisurely bath, going for a long walk. But control is at least partially dependent on familiarity and predictability, and it is in this sense that flight attendants often find themselves doing pretty much the same things, week in, week out, on layovers. Though of course some may still explore foreign cities, more appear to become immersed in the minutiae of everyday routines. Though some still rave about the exoticism of exciting destinations, most of the flight attendants I interviewed are far more likely to talk about the apparently mundane. Sarah, a Delta flier, provides a good example:

> Brighton is one of my favorite places in the whole world. I get in, I take a hot bath, usually have a beer. And I'm dead. Sleep three to four hours and make myself get up around 1:00 or 2:00 and that's the hardest part. Hitting the floor with feet that are still hurting from the night before. And just get out and go. Go get a cup of coffee up at Café Nero up on the back street and walk and sometimes exercise walking, sometimes just browse, depending on what I want to do. Meet back at the hotel with the crew, have happy hour 5:30 to 6:00, break off and go to dinner at one of the fabulous places, come back to somebody's room. Put on jammies and have some wine, talk, laugh, giggle, try to not have too much, so you don't hurt the next day and take two Bayer PMs at 10:00, and lights out.

We are sitting in a coffee bar in Buckhead, Atlanta's upscale northern suburb. As Frank Sinatra croons in the background, I ask Sarah what she does in the morning:

> I'll get up and run out the back door of the hotel, get coffee and an egg sandwich. I'll go to the sandwich shop; you've heard about the sandwich shop? These little ladies make the best chicken salad you ever put in your mouth, and they open at 7:00 because they know we come at 7:00, and we get the little paper plate, and it's wrapped in cellophane and it's these four quarters of this fattest chicken salad with avocado and bacon. And we take it with us on the plane. I do that and then we go to the airport and then we start the whole thing over again.

Deborah, who started at Northeast Airlines in 1965 and moved to Delta following the former's acquisition in 1973, also talks about familiar layover routines:

On my layover in Japan I do have a routine because I'm so tired. I have a favorite restaurant that I go to, and then I stop at Mr. Donut and have coffee, and then I go back to the hotel and go to sleep. When I was flying to Brussels—I did that for a number of years—I had, again, favorite restaurants that I went to, and you do some shopping in Grand Plaza Square. Years ago when I flew to Amsterdam, I loved the hotel and the restaurant in the hotel, so I never ever went out. I ate there all the time. With Delta flight attendants, they say it's all about food.

Janice, a Delta flier from 1968 to 2001, flew mainly to California from Atlanta. Her layovers followed a predictable pattern:

And so we used to go out walking when we would get in, change clothes, go out and go for a walk, and then have kind of a lunch or whatever and then lay down for a nap. And sleep for a while. And then everybody would get up on their own. Some would have room service, and some would meet and go down for dinner. I usually would have room service so that I could sleep as long as possible. And then get ready and go down for the trip and work coming back and get home.

Obviously, options vary according to location. Those flight attendants who travel to Rome, Barcelona, and other European cities, especially, do still tend to appreciate their surroundings. By contrast, as one ASA flier puts it, "There's not a lot to do in Dothan, Alabama. Columbus, Georgia, there's not a lot to do there." A colleague endorses this: "You can only go to Valdosta, Georgia, for thirteen hours on an overnight with so much enthusiasm for so long. [Laughs] Now we go to Gulfport."

When I ask what flight attendants do in those kinds of places, Paula says:

You stare at the walls. You find a restaurant; you go get something to eat. You know, hopefully it's nice outside and you can walk around or go by the pool. But if it's not, then you just kind of take a book. [Laughs] Or take your computer or something. But just recently we started getting the really good types of cities to actually go out and do things. And it also depends on where we stay. If we stay in a hotel that doesn't have anything around, then it's very hard to get somewhere.

Fayetteville, Arkansas, is the best example of that. The airport is twenty miles from anything. Once you get to that anything, it's nothing. There are two hotels side by side, and that's it. So, it depends on where you're at and what you've got around you. Usually we make the best of our surrounding.

Layovers and the "Space-Out"

"One needn't be a sociologist," writes Roberta Lessor, "to recognize that distance acts more rapidly than time to change one's outlook and sense of self."[23] The layover is a precious space, one that flight attendants value above most other aspects of the job. It provides a spatial haven in which flight attendants can relax and, if they so choose, explore not just an unusual city but, equally, their own characters and identities.

Layovers, essentially, represent a hybrid space. Workers inhabit what sociologist Ray Oldenburg has called a "third place" where they are obviously not at home but technically are not at work either.[24]

When flight attendants leave on the bathroom light in a hotel, it is to remind themselves when they wake up that they are not at home. And yet, in the spaces of the hotel rooms and the cities in which they wander, they go about constructing rituals and routines, adorning their surroundings with personal, sentimental effects that build an alternate home to their real ones. In their spatial havens flight attendants are perhaps *at* home, though they are not *in* their homes.

This spatial haven represents something solid in a world of paradox and contradiction. Flight attendant parents, especially, juggle the freedom and spaces of the layover with feelings of guilt and not being needed. Cravings for solitude are counterbalanced by straightforward loneliness. A job that once captured recruits because of the exotic layovers now retains them because of their stable, predictable mundanity. Time and space spent with the alternative family become more predictable and relaxing than that spent with the real one.

Of course layovers mean many different things to different people. For some, such as Wendy at Air Tran, "good layovers are what keep you coming back." By contrast, a couple of flight attendants I spoke to despise them. Carole, for instance, a Delta flier with one child, tells me:

I hated layovers. And I hated the hotel room. I began to hate room service. It's just like any kind of traveling salesman. I would have felt guilty sitting in that room. I want to be home. That's probably the control factor in my life. That's probably where I have to be in control all the time even though I think I'm not. I think I have to say I probably am because I wanted to be home. And it wasn't so much that I wanted to be where she [my daughter] was, I just wanted to be available to her in case something happened.

Like everything else in the airline industry right now, the spatial havens flight attendants created for themselves are becoming increasingly squeezed. Airlines have cut the length of time spent in hotels; flight attendants who would once get a whole day and night in a city now get only one night. There has been an increase in turnaround flights: whereas once flight attendants would be taken to a hotel, they are now often required to fly the return journey. Not least, fears of terrorism have made foreign cities less attractive. In short, the sanctuary that the layover once represented is itself eroding. Flight attendants no longer get as much quality time with their alternative family. Donna, a reserve flight attendant for Delta, sums up the growing mood among some workers: "Before, it was, 'Look! Oooh! Where am I going tonight?' This is so exciting. Now it's like, 'Where the *hell* am I going? Where am I sleeping tonight? When am I going to be home?'"

Unfortunately for the Donnas of the world, coming home, as the next chapter argues, is in itself less than straightforward.

7

The Return

The first thing you've got to do is get that uniform off your body. Don't talk to me. Don't talk to me, don't touch me. I love you. I'll talk to you in six hours.

—Taylor, Delta flight attendant

I have to say that was one thing that I really remember that got on my nerves because my poor dad would be sitting there trying to get everything nice and neat, and she would come home. Mom wouldn't have to say anything. You'd just know. She'd just start cleaning. She would start doing this and that, and it was a very clear message. It wasn't anything personal toward me, but I do remember feeling a sense of sympathy for my dad, who I knew tried so hard and it was never quite right.

—Jenny, flight attendant's adult daughter

Flight attendants often like to claim there is a neat separation between work and home. Like actresses, they tell me, once you're on, you're on; but once you're off, you're off. As Caron, at Delta, says, "There is a demarcation between work and home. . . . You don't bring the job home." But things are not actually so black and white. Though removing the uniform and getting in the shower may seem like ceremonial transition points between the two spheres, the relationship between work and home is often complex and muddled.

Balancing a career and family is never easy, but flight attendant moms are in a particularly unusual position. In most families outside the profession, mom comes home before dad; with flight attendants the reverse is usually the case.[1] More than anything, moms need space on their return, but in demanding to be alone they run the risk of hurting those closest to them, especially because they have not seen them for a few days. Being away so much can also lead flight attendant moms to overcompensate by what I call "conspicuous mothering." In contrast to the vicarious mothering that goes on in preparation for being away, conspicuous mothering involves overcommitment in volunteering for things like the PTA, as though flight attendants have to demonstrate to the community at large—and, I suspect, themselves—that they are not bad mothers after all. Conspicuous mothering can also take place in the home, when the flight attendant mom ostentatiously embarks upon all the chores that dad had or had not done in her absence, which can lead to resentment by those left behind when she is at work.

Flight attendants therefore have to work hard at keeping their families going, often using rituals and routines—mealtimes being a common one—similar to the ones other families adopt. Yet it is not easy. As Terri Ballard, an occupational health expert who has conducted research among Italian flight attendants, reports, "Many talked about the stress of always having to adapt to home life after returning from a long tour of duty, or of feeling 'cut in half' between the public self and the private self, in particular when they had children."[2] "It really is like two separate lives," says Ellen, from Delta. But these two lives impinge on each other: just as many flight attendant moms on layovers worry about their families, when at home they find the job's peculiar characteristics—the disorientation, perpetual cycle of arrival and departure, and, after 9/11, safety concerns—more constricting than they might like to admit.

Getting through the Front Door

"Dating the Flight Attendant" is a short piece that has been making the rounds on flight attendant message boards over the past few years.[3] Purportedly written by a man, Chad Childers, and with such an unpromising title, at first it may appear to be a predictable guide to picking up "stewardesses." In fact it is a decidedly poignant piece expressing despair at the difficulty of maintaining a relationship with someone for whom he clearly cared deeply. "Is it worth it?" he asks eventually. "No. Not if you love her, because it hurts you to see someone you love getting ripped apart inside. It's a bad situation, and although it gets better with seniority, a relationship with a flight attendant doesn't come anywhere near having enough benefits to outweigh the tribulations." Childers focuses particularly on what he terms "post-flight syndrome." This has "a lot to do with exhaustion and just wanting to be alone, tired of playing the part, serving people and catering to others' needs and wants." A bad case "can get your head bitten off," and turning up at the airport with flowers to meet your loved one is not recommended.

Of course, many do cope where Childers could not, and perhaps he should have taken advice from other flight attendants. Not one of my interviewees, for instance, mentioned being met at the airport by their partners, an idea I am sure they would consider absurd. Partners, though, are often on their mind on arrival back from a trip: at Atlanta's Hartsfield-Jackson Airport, you will see many a homeward-bound Delta or Air Tran flight attendant marching through the terminal wedded to her mobile phone, warning of imminent home arrival. "On return I call," says Andrea, a Delta flier: "I'm on my way. Mommy's coming, pick up!"

When they finally get through the front door, flight attendants go through a readjustment process. "I call it decompressing," says Taylor. First, almost universally, they change out of the uniform and take a shower. "I demand a shower," says Sarah, at Delta. "[I say to my husband,] tell me everything but come to the bathroom with me. I will peel off everything, and you just talk all you want, but I've got to get out of that uniform." Suzie, an ASA flier, tells a similar story:

> The uniform wear is off and I'm in the shower. I worked fast food when I was growing up, and I have never felt as nasty as I do when I get off of a plane. I feel nasty because it's the same air that we are circulating, and they never change or clean the seats. People are in and out like cattle. They are herded in and out, and some people are just nasty. There is no other word for it. I mean, the first thing that I do, before I even let my child touch me, I'm in the shower.

As with other jobs that require uniforms, especially those requiring emotional labor, changing out of "work attire" often coincides with a change of character. As anthropologist Joan Volpe observes, for flight attendants, removing the uniform and showering constitutes a "purification" ceremony that marks the transition out of flight attendant mode and back to the "real world."[4] This is as true for male flight attendants as for females. For Ben, a United worker, removing the uniform is symbolically important, as if he were shedding the job's actual skin: "Actually, physiologically, something will happen to you when you do that. I find myself coming home being very tired because I've been in this uniform for so long and I feel like I have to get it off me. And as I remove it from me, my energy comes back and I feel great." However, having removed the uniform, flight attendants also seek psychological and physical spaces. According to Linda, at American: "Sometimes I come home, and without ever doing anything I'll just go to the refrigerator, sit down and have a beer, and just go, 'Aaaaah.' And just sit there for a minute." Mary Ann, at Delta, says, "I would head straight to the bath, draw myself a nice bath and usually a glass of wine and I'd sit." Most flight attendants, even if they have come back from Europe (and thus been up for some twenty hours), cannot switch off immediately and go straight to bed.

"Leave Me Alone!"

Needing space can cause problems. Those half frazzled by their jobs may insist on their partners leaving them in peace for a while. "Sometimes when I come home I tell my husband that I don't want to talk to anyone," says Roseanne. "You know, just leave me alone." Mary Ann echoes this: "I felt that when I got home, it needed to be my time. I didn't want to share it with other people right then. I think being on all the time in that job, when you do get home, you've got to turn off. That lasted all the way up until retirement. My husband and son knew that when I came in from a trip, don't bother me. Do not talk to me for a while."

"There's a period I call coming down, where you switch gears, switch lives," says Lisa, a United flier, at one focus group held in Atlanta. "I feel like every time I come home from a trip, I need a little bit of space and I do need to get the uniform off, get the suitcase put away, and just kind of relax for a minute before I go right into my mom mode."

"Because on board you've got 400 chirping mouths who need you," adds Dave, at Northwest, immediately. "Where's the 'me' time? Where's the time for me?" "It used to be that the minute I walked in, I would get bombarded with questions," says Margaret, from Delta. "[My kids] knew when to push the button, and so I would say, 'You have to give me an hour!' Then I can get on with things." "Oh, I was very resentful at times," comments Denise, also at Delta, who then continues:

> My sister-in-law came and lived with us for a year, and as soon as I walked in off of a trip she was, you know, talking to me, yak, yak, and

one time I snapped at her and I said, "Please stop right now and just let me get this uniform off." Usually you smelled of smoke when everybody was smoking. And my son said to his aunt, "See, I told you not to talk to her when she first comes in." She got the picture. I was not always in a great mood when I first came in. I just needed to be away from people.

The image here is one of workers so agitated by the demands of the job that they cannot switch off: not exactly the hallmark of a group not taking work home with them. Moreover, their need for psychological and physical space is often manifested in a temporary anxiety about being touched. At one focus group in Los Angeles, one flight attendant demonstrates this by leaning over and squeezing a colleague's arm. "Don't be doing this," she says, mimicking instructions she gives to her partner. "I find that," her friend echoes. "For the first thirty minutes. Just let me unwind." Taylor, from Delta, takes up this theme at a focus group in Atlanta:

> Don't touch me. . . . You have had a thousand people grabbing at you. You're hit. You come home with bruises. And your husband or boyfriend is like, "How did you get bruised?" and you're like, "I don't know. By Mr. 3C with his elbows." But people have been grabbing at you, Miss! Waitress! Stewardess! Whatever! And your husband or your boyfriend don't understand that. You've been gone for three days, [and they say,] "I miss you." And I've missed you too, honey, but please just give me like an hour to get the uniform off. Let me take a shower and say hello to the cats. [They] don't talk back and don't ask anything of me. And just have dinner ready.

In these scenarios, it is not hard to see how feelings can be hurt. Flight attendants have been away from their nearest and dearest for three days. Their loved ones are happy when they return and want to display physical affection and to fill them in on what has been going on in their absence. And the flight attendants are too exhausted, or too wound up, to respond. Most do not even want to be touched by their significant other. They have used up all their emotion on the airplane and, like other emotional laborers, tapped out.[5] One flight attendant's daughter sums up how she used to feel when her mother returned: "Hi! We're not passengers. We're your family now! You need to step out of your job and stop. You know, it was like she had to smile for so long and be nice and so accommodating to all these people for so long that she didn't want to do that when she got home." Coming home can be a difficult experience, and maintaining relationships can be stressful. For all their claims not to bring the job home, flight attendants do little else, and this can easily be a source of rancor.

Being Apart

In her research, Terri Ballard found older women flight attendants more concerned than younger workers about their marriages and the difficulty of maintaining relationships.[6] From my interviews, I found a similar pattern. For instance, Kelly, in her thirties (though no longer flying), says, "It's a break, it keeps the marriage freshened. The break helped."

However, spouses of flight attendants seem to conform to the "intermittent husband syndrome" identified in families of offshore oil workers, among others, where husbands are away from home regularly, and partners and children have to deal with a steady procession of partings and reunions.[7] Indeed, in situations where male pilots are away and their female partners are left at home, research suggests that families suffer from more stress-related illness and marital difficulties than those where husbands do not travel. Family routines become disrupted, with negative effects on wives and children.[8]

Both partners of flight attendants and flight attendants themselves worry about being apart. One Australian study in the early 1990s found "reunion distress" a major problem for workers who left partners behind at home. Flight attendants "reported anticipation of a warm reunion with their partners, but found them 'indifferent' or 'too busy' getting on with their lives to be 'bothered overmuch.' "[9] Australian flight attendants tend to fly much longer trips than their American counterparts, and their feelings of anticlimax may not be fully replicated in the United States, where the reverse scenario seems to operate and partners are most aggrieved. Either way, reunion can be a source of tension more than joy.

Getting the "right" partners seems imperative if flight attendants are to avoid many of these relationship strains. Ballard claims younger workers have been more adept at this, being fully aware of the job's pitfalls, and thus they "specifically chose the right type of partners to avoid the type of problems their older colleagues experienced."[10] It is also the case that young women today have different expectations—even if they are not always met—regarding their partners' role in relationships. Among my interviewees, older workers tended to express more dissatisfaction that younger ones with their partners' commitment to child care, suggesting, if anything, that younger workers had found more amenable spouses. In terms of partner selection, a number of interviewees were married to pilots, other flight attendants, or industry workers, who tended to be more understanding of their work schedules and demanding routines.

Those with partners outside the industry often struggle with images circulated by such titles as *Coffee, Tea or Me?* Jealousy is not uncommon. One of Maya's boyfriends was "insecure" and "had a big problem with her flying." Another long-term boyfriend "didn't understand when [she] came home from work and didn't want to be bothered for the first few days." "Trust breaks up a lot of relationships," says Donna, at Delta. "Men can't handle their wives being gone. They call all the time on layovers even when they say not to." Clare, at Continental, elaborates: "The guys are jealous back home because the girls are leaving and possibly meeting other people and seeing other situations without them and they're insecure. . . . I know of guys that have called girls constantly, that if they're not in their room they're like, WHERE ARE YOU? And it drives people mad."

If not worried about infidelity, partners can sometimes be envious of flight attendants' ability to get away. Marion, who started flying for Song in her late forties, talks of how she would be given trips when on reserve: "My husband would get kind of mad because I would say, 'Oh, good! I got a three-day trip!' You know, and he would of course like it when I would get those one-day trips where you just go to the airport and you do your thing and you come back. So he is a big baby about me being gone."

Meanwhile, some partners seem to think flight attendants do not actually do any work and that the job involves hanging out in a series of exotic locations while the partners are stuck at home with a list of chores. They have little sympathy for how tiring the job is. As Rebecca, at United, notes:

> My husband even said at one point he was jealous because being in D.C. we do a lot of international flights to London and Paris and Milan

and Germany, all those kind of places, and it was the very thing. He thought, oh, me going to London, how glamorous is that, and you can go do all these things and go sightseeing and all this, why are you always complaining that you're tired and this and that and I don't get to go? And it was just like, you don't understand.

As a consequence, to make things work in a relationship, flight attendants, according to Dave, at Northwest, "need a person that's very secure, because you're gone a lot, and a person that doesn't mind being home on their own." Yet, despite popular misconceptions I have heard repeated by flight attendants themselves, divorce in the profession is relatively low. In the early 1970s, it was one in forty-seven, as opposed to the national average of one in four, though this was undoubtedly skewed by the fact that marriage for flight attendants had only recently been allowed.[11] Even though at one in five it is nowadays closer to the national average, it is still, according to Heather Healy at the AFA, significantly below that average. "Flight attendants have long partner histories," she says. "It fits their lifestyle of transience here and there. I'm going to make every month my choice of where I go. And I'm going to make this month my choice of whether I stay in this relationship. And this spills into relationships. A control and flexibility issue."

Healy's analysis hints at an intriguing dynamic. Just as some flight attendants often stay in the job through a series of short-term decisions, building an incremental career, some stay in relationships for similar reasons. When they consume time in "chunks," and where bidding requires every minute of the next month to be accounted for, the "future" —be it a career or a marriage—is never anything other than a short-term thing. This may be an extreme proposition, and I am not suggesting that flight attendants do not make plans. But they do so in the knowledge that, because of their job—whether they are stuck in a foreign land or reassigned to a base on the other side of the country— everything can unravel alarmingly quickly.

The Challenges of Being a Flight Attendant Mom

At both philosophical and highly practical levels, flight attendants' incremental approach to their jobs and relationships runs in opposition to their status as mothers. Philosophically, few mothers would claim parenthood is a short-term thing; practically, the rites of passage of their children, marked by ritual and ceremony, illuminate the fact that time is, indeed, moving on.

In a recent questionnaire administered to Italian women flight attendants, more than 75 percent of the 1,955 respondents felt that flight attendant mothers "had more difficulty being good mothers compared to working women with other occupations."[12] Moreover, "tension with the partner over child care" contributed to distress. In a separate U.S. study (with 73 participants), 29 percent reported "imbalance between their job demands and obligations outside of work (including family)." The imbalance was greater for flight attendants who had preschool children.[13]

Some flight attendant moms welcome the greater participation from their partners. "Every man with a child should marry a flight attendant," quips Kelly. "My husband had to assume so many parental roles. Very few husbands play the role of sole provider for three or four days." "My husband did things then that he wouldn't do when I was home," says Kirsty.

> So he played the father role more strongly because when I was there it was OK for me to do all that. When he was there it was like he had to. He took the role of what he needed to do, and it was good. A good thing for him. To see him in that respect. I feel like that was another opportunity that maybe if I had been a stay-at-home or nine-to-five mom or something it would have looked differently in our family.

Fathers whose wives are flight attendants by necessity become more hands-on in the raising of children, a pattern that resembles that in families outside the industry in which mothers work nonstandard hours.[14] However, it is often a temporary role, not a reflection of a deep-seated shift in their partner's thinking, as Kirsty indicates in her earlier comments. Dad substitutes for mom when she is away; when she is back, she becomes the chief caregiver again.

Despite an apparent gender reversal, flight attendant mothers often still find themselves doing the household chores when they are at home. In a study conducted in the 1980s, two-thirds of flight attendants claimed to have done all or most of the housework, and only 27 percent claimed that the housework was shared equally with their partners.[15]

In this, families with flight attendant mothers do not really differ from other dual-earner couples, where wives not only do more housework than their husbands but also do more low-schedule-control tasks (i.e., those that have to be done at a particular time).[16]

Not Trusting Dad

Flight attendants often worry that even when their partners are left in charge of the chores and the child care, they will not actually do them properly. According to Stacey, who flies with Delta and who has an infant son: "I remember when he was first a baby and I left, it was really hard because I just didn't know how my husband was going to be able to handle it, me being gone overnight and by himself, and it used to just tear me up." Suzie, at ASA, echoes Stacey's concerns: "It was hard with Damon when he was a baby. Because men and babies, I'm not saying they are not capable, but my husband would be like, 'He's driving me crazy!' Well, he's just a baby!"

Flight attendant moms seem convinced that their partners have special difficulty in dressing their kids properly. "It was funny," says Sandra, at Delta. "One time a trip was canceled, and I came home to see my daughter getting off the school bus dressed up in the most outrageous clothes. My husband didn't really exert control there." Maggie, with four children, seemed to regard her husband as virtually incapable:

> Here's a man who couldn't make a decision, so I had to tell him what to do. He could make a decision, but it was not a good one. She wants to wear a swimsuit, let her wear a swimsuit. I mean, the interviews I would go to for parent-teacher [night]. "Oh, we all love to take Julia to the bathroom because we never know what she's going to be wearing under that coat" [her teacher would say]. What I lived through because I didn't put out something for her to wear. Anything she wanted to wear would do.

Of course, many moms would fret about the appearance of their children if they look slovenly; given social conventions, unkempt children would be a walking advertisement to the neighborhood of bad parenting, a subject that flight attendants already worry about. But perhaps subconsciously, flight attendant moms worry about what, exactly, their role is in the domestic setup, when they are gone so much. As psychologist Francine Deutsch argues, even in families where mother and father share parenting duties because of alternating shift-work patterns, mothers still think of themselves as the number one parent: "Dads may take over many of the functions that mothers have traditionally performed," she writes. "They may feed their children, give them baths, read them bedtime stories, kiss their boo-boos, but the mother is still 'the mother.'"[17]

Overcompensation

Anthropologist John Gillis has talked about the difference between families people live "by" (the mythical and societal construct of the "proper" family) and those they live "with" (the time-pressed, contradictory mess that exists in reality).[18] In many ways, flight attendant moms, in particular, struggle against the logistical odds to maintain their presence as "mothers." They try to conform to a socialized notion of what a "good" mother is and worry not only that they are coming up short but also that "substitute" dad is, too. Patricia, from United, for instance, always left a long list of instructions for her husband. When I ask her whether she then checked off the list on her return, she replies:

> Oh, I did. I tried to. I tried to, and that was a source of friction too. If this hadn't been done and that hadn't been done or the kitchen was a wreck and Jenny [her daughter] didn't have her medicine or whatever. I would get really upset or really mad, you know. And then Doug [her husband] in turn said, "Well, you're not here and I can't keep everything in." I'd try and monitor myself and, you know, just ignore what wasn't done. But it was very hard and it's very hard to hide something like that especially, you know, a really messy kitchen when you come home.

But later I was lucky enough to interview Patricia's daughter, Jenny, who paints a slightly different picture: "My mother, as much as she tries to be level-headed a lot of times raising us when she was younger, there was a lot of neuroticism there, and I think that really played in when my dad would take care of us, for sure. And I think a lot of their arguments were about that. It's maybe a sense of guilt from my mother."

The adult daughter of another flight attendant tells a similar tale of mom coming home and being dissatisfied with dad's parenting:

> You know, there was some kind of line that had been drawn that she couldn't cross over about knowing things or disciplining because she wasn't there. I think for all three of us, me and my dad and my sister, there was some kind of resentment of, well, you know, you weren't here. So, you know for my dad, my dad being like, "I've done this with the girls. Well, this is the deal that I made with the girls, or this is how we've done it." And she would come in and try to take back over, and I think that caused my dad to feel a lot of resentment. It was like she would go away and then she would be here, then she would go away and then she would be here. And on the times that she was here, she would try to make up for those times that she wasn't here and try to be a mom five days a week when she's only here three, and I think that all of it was very difficult.

So the scenario is as follows: Mom flight attendant goes off to work, leaving dad to look after things. Dad looks after things. Mom comes home again convinced that dad hasn't quite coped and then tries to find the evidence to support her suspicions. Dad gets mad.

Flight attendant moms feel especially out of the loop in terms of what is going on within the family in their absence. This is one of the reasons they call home when away, even if it is just to say good night. One way for them to assert their motherhood is to become stronger disciplinarians than their partners. The dynamic here often revolves around "fun daddy," who takes over, with laxer rules, when mommy leaves. Kathleen and her daughter, Alice, had the following exchange while I was sitting in their kitchen in suburban Washington, D.C.:

> *Alice*: You were different parents. Dad was more lenient and fun.
> *Kathleen*: They used to dance, and Dad would sing "Party, Party" on the driveway when I left. I was resentful, as I was the bad guy who had to do all the work.
> *Alice*: When you came home everything was done.
> *Kathleen*: But it wasn't done. Dad had the opportunity to watch TV and go out for pizza. I resented that.

I ask Maggie who she thought her children would tell me they got along with better, and she answers:

> Absolutely their dad. Because he provides. The reality is, I accept it. I know they would do that because he's the one with the deep pockets and he's the one who's been here. He's their playmate, he's their buddy. No, I had things to do. I had to take care of things before I left the house, so that dad could be the playmate. It made me resentful. Extremely resentful. Well, now we've established a pattern that dad's the good guy and mom's the bad guy. And so, it just became more and more divisive, since I was gone.

The potentially problematic pairing of "fun daddy" and "discipline mommy" can be found in many American families. But the emotional exhaustion of the job makes it particularly hard for flight attendants. As Clare says:

> A lot of women will come home, and their house is in a shambles. They've left it perfect, they've set this house just how they wanted it as if they were never coming back. And the house could go on display. They come back, it's all destroyed. They've been working hard, and you lose that mask once you walk out of the airport again. You lose the flight attendant mask. And you become who you were when you left again. You become either the wife or the mother. And what's bad is, we have a face that we could sit there with the meanest person in the world and smile and say, "How can I help you?" and not lose it. But you have a tendency because you've built all this up for nine to ten hours, you get home, and the first person you unleash on is the one you love the most. And I guess it's just because you let that guard down. And it just all comes out. Everything that you've bundled up and buckled up.

Some flight attendants, when seeing the mess that confronts them at home, want to turn around and go back to their occupational community. Though female flight attendants reverse gendered expectations by being the ones who go away, leaving domestic responsibilities to their partners, they often return home and consider that those responsibilities have not been satisfactorily carried out. Perhaps, subconsciously, these women do not *want* their husbands to have done the chores properly because this would exclude them from a family from which they already feel distant. Flight attendant moms, in particular, struggle to find a role in the family, even as they "space-out" in the job specifically with the purpose of giving them more family time.

Family Rituals: The Importance of Mealtimes

In trying to reconcile the family they live "by" and the family they live "with"—the ideal versus the real—flight attendants set aside special times in which the family "acts" like a family. Moms, especially, throw themselves into school and volunteer activities that demonstrate to everyone else, and perhaps themselves, that they are good parents.

When I ask flight attendants about the kinds of routines and rituals they have for maintaining a family unit, mealtimes and food figure highly in their responses. Eating as a family unit is especially important. "We would have dinner together," says Deidre: "The three of us. In fact, my husband took over the cooking. He was a wonderful cook, anyway. And I don't think he ever liked my cooking to begin with, even when I wasn't working. And his mother was a good cook, and he learned from his mother, and he just took over all the cooking."

Sofia's husband spends much of his time studying law in Florida. During his brief weekend sojourns back in Atlanta, "We'll have our dinner together," she says. "I'll make something or he will have something ready or we'll get take out. And then Sunday we'll have a relaxing morning and we'll have our breakfast together."

Mealtimes are one of the most important times for family continuity, when family members actively construct stories that bond them to each other.[19] It is not just the eating that flight attendants view as essential. It is also important that their families are sitting together around the table, not off elsewhere doing their own thing. Derek, who is married to a fellow flight attendant, has one son, Calvin. Sitting at his dining room table one weekday morning, he points out who sits where:

> Oh yeah, mealtime, that's Calvin's, that's where I sit, and that's where mom sits. But we always have it. Dinner is always not sitting in front of the television set. No. That's a no-no. The television might be on in that room over there, but we're not sitting there watching television while we're eating. We cook stuff pretty much from scratch. You know, even when either one of us is gone it is still, "Sit down here to have dinner."

Even when flight attendants realize that eating together around the table is increasingly difficult, in purely logistical terms, they insist on at least one special meal a week. Kirsty, for instance, still flying at Delta, had two children; for her, meal times were treasured moments:

> We used to do things so we could eat meals together. I start setting the table. We're just not going to do anything else but eat at the table. I think it's real important. And as the kids got busier and all, it was harder to find those moments to sit down at a table and eat. Even if it's once or twice a week, you're going to sit down together and have a meal together without the television being on. So that's special.

Maggie, also at Delta, tells a similar tale:

> Family time, we have one night a week we must eat together, one night a week. So, we do have a ritual, one night it's mandatory. We don't care if it's the same night every week, but if we haven't had dinner together as a family by Thursday night, it's mandatory. So, that's it, once a week, we say you must eat together as a family. Now, we may get two nights, which is wonderful, but one is mandatory. If we haven't accomplished it by Wednesday, then everybody knows no matter what your plans are for Thursday, you have to break them, because Thursday night we must have dinner together. That's the extent of our together time. With four kids, I think it's a lofty ambition to think you're going to get more than that.

Flight attendants are probably no different here from many American families, settling on "one special meal" a week as a practical solution to a logistical problem.[20] Yet moms still appear to need to prove their maternal competence in other directions.

Conspicuous Mothering

Despite their hectic schedules, many flight attendant moms throw themselves headfirst into things like school and other volunteer activities. Amy, at Delta, says this: "I was on the PTA. I was at all the board meetings, and I was in the classroom doing the things. I would just schedule to be there. And it was tough. You had a lot of juggling. But the freedom of this job means if I can't work on Monday, I can [get someone] to swap with me for Friday. And it worked out great. But some things we missed." Sarah, also at Delta, was president of her PTA for two years. When I ask her whether she had already got enough on her plate without the PTA she says this:

> I don't know why I did it. Both of my girls were still in elementary school, third and fifth grade, and I did it, and I did it one more year, and then it just killed me. It was a killer, but this is my last year at the elementary school. I'm like the adviser, so we have different programs coming up, and I go and help the new officers, saying what we've done before and kind of guide them.

Shelly, at United, claims, "Some people don't even think that we really work. I know a lot of people at my son's school, and they don't think I work because I'm there so much." But Shelly, like Amy and Sarah, takes part in what I call "conspicuous mothering," volunteering as much as possible to demonstrate they are good mothers despite the scheduling difficulties. As Francine Deutsch argues, being around to pick up kids from school, or being there when they come home, is an important display of mothering for women in "split-shift" families. As she says, such times are not called "mothers' hours" for nothing.[21]

Conspicuous mothering helps flight attendants rationalize that their jobs help family ties because they can be around for their kids more, and for longer stretches of time, than workers on conventional schedules. Yet they also claim that time away from home is good for their kids because it makes them more independent. "I had the best kids," says Sandra, from Delta. "They were self-sufficient and quite independent. If I think about it, it's almost as if the kids raised themselves." "I think it probably made my children more independent," says Patricia.

When I ask adult daughters of flight attendants about the balance between their moms going away and being home, I get mixed responses. Jenny, in her early twenties, for instance, says:

> It's all I've ever known, and so it was so normal to me, but in comparison to some of my other friends and watching their mothers and fathers who had nine-to-five jobs and would come home and go to work every day, I actually felt privileged because while my mother was away for two or three days at a time, then she would come home, and I would

have this big block of time when I could really hang out with her and get some quality time. I knew she would be there after school. And be there in the mornings. So for me, it was a fair trade-off. I really enjoyed having her gone and then back for a couple of days too.

Josie, also in her early twenties is less sanguine:

> I was real attached to my mom when I was younger. So when she left it was really difficult for me. Yeah, probably every time I would be upset or I would call home from school not wanting her to leave. Because I knew that when I got home in the afternoon from school that I would be with a babysitter. Or I would have to wait till my dad got home before I was with a parent. Until I got older.

When I flippantly asked a thirteen-year-old boy, Francis, what it was like having a mother as a flight attendant, he looked at me and said one word: "Confusing."

It is difficult to extrapolate from a few conversations with children how much they have been affected by having a flight attendant parent. Jenny could be happy for a number of reasons, Josie may have been unhappy for a host of others, and Francis could be, simply, at a confusing age, period. Moreover, I am not a psychologist, and I am not constructing a causative model proving a direct relationship between flight attendant parents and child well-being. Yet many flight attendants *do* claim the job helps their kids, though in ambiguous and often contradictory ways. Here is Shelly, for example, talking about her son, Travis:

> He always wants to know who's picking him up from the school. He just wants to know that because our life is chaotic. It's sort of organized chaos. It's kind of, like, OK, we've got a lot going on, but who's on first and who's on second. And I think Travis maybe is more of a scheduling hound than other kids his age. Because he says, "Who's going to pick me up? Daddy or you?" And "Who's taking me to practice tonight, and now wait a minute. When do you go to work again?" So our kids always want to know "When's your next vacation or when are you off?" "How long are you off for?" Well, for six days. "All right, let's see. So that means that you go to work next Tuesday?" And so they know that you are theirs until next Tuesday. And so I don't know maybe they are even more appreciative of you. It's not so dependable that you are going

to be there. It's not so ho-hum that you are going to be there, but it's more exciting maybe for them?

As her question at the end of this passage suggests, Shelly's perspective on how her job affects her son is rooted in speculation and, by default, rationalization. It is as though she is trying to justify the job by persuading herself that her child actually enjoys the arrangement, when in fact she is less sure. Maybe he does, maybe he does not, but Shelly is not going to allow feelings of guilt to prevent her from continuing to be a flight attendant.

Most moms are busy people, and flight attendants are no exception. But most moms are not feeling the effects of jet lag and worrying about leaving the country every week. For all their talk of free time, flight attendants seem to overcompensate, partly out of guilt at being away and also—maybe this is the same thing—out of concern that they may appear to be bad mothers. Their role models are often their own mothers, summoned from a mythical past in which families were "stable"—a family to live "by" as opposed to "with." Carole, who flew day trips for Delta from Atlanta (known as Early Bird flights), provides a good example here:

> All the Early Bird turn ladies all had a system. The husband went along with it. We were all married for a long time. For some reason the Early Bird turn people ended up in a little group, and we all shared the same horrible, horrible, almost impossible schedule. Up at 4:00 in the morning, out the door to the airport, fly up to Washington, fly back, home, home by 2:00 or 3:00, car pool, get home. And for some reason, I don't know why we tried to do what our mothers did and still bring home a paycheck. My husband used to say, "You don't have to." Yes, I do. It's just a matter of how. It was sick. I didn't have to, no. [When the school asked for volunteers,] I could have said, "Are you kidding, lady? I work. 'Bye." Oh, no, I'll bring the crepe paper. I'll do the cupcakes. And we all did it. We were all raised by mothers who stayed home. Those who had nurturing mothers wanted to repeat that cycle, but we didn't know how to do it and work. Why I never said I'm quitting, I don't know.

The question of why she never quit is a good one and is best addressed through a further consideration of safety.

Staying on the Job

A good way of appreciating attendants' attachment to their jobs is to consider how they deal with family members' concerns for their safety. Flight attendants inhabit a strong safety culture and are very sensitive to anything that compromises security. Though they are aware that things can go horribly wrong occasionally, they also know that statistically the most dangerous part of their jobs is driving to and from work.

Flight attendants with young children sometimes say that their perspective on safety changes with childbirth. "I was never afraid to fly until I first had a baby," says Kelly. "On my first flight back, my baby was sick and I was flying to Frankfurt and I was thinking 'What am I doing?'" "Before I had my son," says Suzie, "I only had myself to think about. I mean, if I want to go up on a dangerous airplane and get killed, that's my own business, but you know I've got someone that I'm responsible for that needs me." Suzie was talking in the aftermath of an ASA crash, when numerous flight attendants worried about the safety of one particular propeller airplane at the airline:[22]

> There is no one that can replace your mother. I very seriously considered another job. I did go into the General Office shortly after that and took a break. I mean, I'm not saying that the jets are perfectly safe, nothing man-made is, but I feel safer on those. Now when that first crash happens, and it will, I don't know how I'll feel. But I'm just the type of person that I believe that everyone has a time, and when it's my time to go, then it's my time to go.

Suzie was not complaining about airline safety in general, just one airplane type. Though Kelly eventually quit her job, safety was not a factor in her decision. She could no longer juggle the job with two young children.

Flight attendants' families, though, can perceive the job as unsafe. Lisa, who flies for Delta, says:

> My son wanted me to quit when Delta had the crash in Dallas in 1985. He became very afraid of flying. He wanted me to quit. He was four years old. He really was terrified, and it was a very difficult thing. And I tried, I said, I know you're nervous, I'm nervous too. But I also know

our pilots are highly trained and I feel very safe and I wouldn't dare do anything to take your mommy from you. I would have to say, that really bothered me.

Unsurprisingly, after 9/11, families expressed particular concern. Heather Healy of the AFA explains:

> In immediate response to 9/11 we had flight attendants having a normal trauma response, and that included flight attendants being concerned about getting on a plane, and pressure added to it was their family members being concerned. Many of them have called in and said, "I'm OK to fly, but my children are crying as I walk out the door." Or, "My children have hidden my uniform." Or, "My children saw the airplane crash into the towers, they saw the United emblem and my daughter now says, 'No. Don't go.'"

There is no doubt that flight attendants were traumatized after 9/11. As Taylor says, echoing comments I heard many times in interviews, "Somebody asked me one time what was the bravest thing I've ever done. And it is getting on that airplane for the first time after 9/11. That's the most scared I've ever been."

But 9/11 was exceptional, and flight attendants across the board tell me that they have actually never felt safer, though random air rage worries them. An equally representative comment comes from Andrea, a Delta flier: "After 9/11 my eleven-year-old son wanted me to stop flying, but why would I want to quit?" She enjoyed the job far too much to entertain the thought. Though both Lisa and Suzie knew their children wanted them to stop flying, and even considered quitting, ultimately they stayed on the job.

When I began research for this book, 9/11 was not yet a year old, and it loomed over the industry like a horrible cloud that showed no signs of lifting. I spoke to a good number of flight attendants who had recently retired, but not one listed safety concerns after 9/11 as a primary reason for doing so. I am not suggesting that no flight attendants quit from fear—anecdotally, I heard stories suggesting this was the case. I just did not meet any. And the profession remains massively oversubscribed in terms of new applicants and recruits, which suggests that it cannot be seen as unreasonably dangerous.

Reasons for Staying

Why do flight attendants stay on the job? And what would make them leave? They stay because the longer they do so, the greater the seniority. The greater the seniority, the more they are able to "space-out," exerting control over their movements and being rewarded with "spatial remuneration." However, the job itself creates a lifestyle for which flight attendants constantly need to compensate. Be it PTA meetings, special meals together, or double-checking lists of their partners' chores, when they have time off, flight attendants fill that time up to the brim. They can become exhausted. Donna claims, of her three days off, only one is truly hers: "On day one I sleep; day two is my fun day, and then on day three, I do all the chores in preparation for leaving again." For Carolyn, "The notion that flight attendants have stayed in the profession because of time off is a fallacy. If you work three days on and three days off, you are working ten hours a day, thirty-two hours a week. You have the appearance of time off, but flight attendants don't really realize that they have hard schedules."

Far from being clearly demarcated, as many flight attendants like to claim, work and home are actually inseparable. Herein lies the paradox. Flight attendants gain control over their home life through doing a job that places extreme strain upon that life, so much so that the only release from it, ironically, is the job itself. So flight attendants are caught in an endless cycle, whereby their occupational community and alternative homes created at work become an escape from the pressures of home that are often created by the very job they do. In overcompensating for their absences, moms, in particular, end up putting so much pressure on themselves to live up to the family they live "by," rather than settle for the one they live "with," that the only break they get is the job that produces so much pressure in the first place. And so they do not quit because they need the job, more than anything else, for themselves.

So what does make them quit? A lack of spatial remuneration. Following 9/11, "spacing-out" started becoming increasingly difficult, and the flight attendant profile began more and more to represent "spacing-out" in the destination phase. Airlines had finally figured it out. To get rid of expensive, long-serving, high-seniority workers, they had to literally squeeze them out of the industry.

8 | Debriefing

I've been very sad for the last two years about United. Very sad. Sometimes I just spontaneously cry. I just feel bad about everything that's happening to my flying partners, to myself, to families. It's just devastating and it's sad.

—Susan, United flight attendant

At other airlines, you have these "flight attendants for life" who just sit around and bitch. It's not a fun job to have for twenty years.

—Ann Rhoades, head of human resources, JetBlue Airlines[1]

At 9:47 A.M. on December 14, 2005, Alain Gaspard, a flight attendant supervisor based at Chicago O'Hare Airport, sent a congratulatory e-mail. It read:

Folks,

This morning, we issued the 400th LOC & yet, we have two more weeks before the year is over. In 2004, we only reached 251 and this latest "milestone" truly reflects everyone's focus and hard work.

Just wanted to let you know!

Sheelah and Alain[2]

"LOC" stands for "letters of charge," which are notices issued to workers for perceived misdemeanors and which can lead to disciplinary hearings and, ultimately, termination. Unfortunately for Gaspard, he inadvertently sent the e-mail not just to his own staff but to United's flight attendants as well, confirming suspicions they had had for a while that regulations were getting tighter at the airline's main hub. A trend in stricter management suddenly looked like a deliberate policy, something United vehemently denied but which was hardly assuaged by Gaspard's attempt to recall the e-mail at 12:50 P.M. that same day. Greg Davidowitch, leader of United's AFA section, declared: "We have confirmation after years of denial by management that United Airlines measures the performance of flight attendant supervisors by the number of disciplinary letters of charge they issue. . . . The image of managers and supervisors 'high-fiving' each other over every new letter of charge is despicable."[3] United, at the time, was in Chapter 11 bankruptcy, having faced the biggest squeeze between costs and revenue among the leading U.S. carriers in the post-9/11 industry fallout.[4] For a couple of years at least, the future of what was once the world's largest carrier was in doubt.

As is often the case when cutbacks are required, flight attendants found themselves in management's line of fire, as the company tried desperately to reduce costs. About 2,500 senior fliers—including Patricia and Kathleen—were enticed into leaving, with guarantees that benefits and pensions would be protected. Those promises turned out to be hot air when United filed for Chapter 11 protection in late 2002. Other workers left or were furloughed and chose not to return when recalled. In total, the number of flight attendants at the airline fell from 25,000 to 17,000.[5]

It was particularly poignant to see flight attendants so unhappy and desperate at the airline where Ellen Church launched the profession back in 1930. "I take great pride in what I do in my job," says Suzanne, a United flier, "and it bothers me that that's not recognized at all in the company." Many flight attendants felt that the airline just wanted to get rid of them, period, and would find ways to do so if necessary. But then in late 2005, in a new twist, United, having persuaded 2,500 senior flight attendants to leave, promptly began advertising for 2,000 new ones. In just three days, the airline received more than 16,000 online applications, enough to force it to suspend its recruitment drive almost as soon as it had started.[6]

According to the airline, new hires could expect to start at about $23,000 a year. This figure was based on flying eighty-five hours per month, which is considered full-time, yet new hires' pay was guaranteed for only seventy-five hours per month. The figure also included per diem payments, which not all flight attendants receive. The AFA suggested a more likely starting salary for new hires would be $16,000 per year, down from $19,500 before bankruptcy.[7]

While airline and union argued over figures, they both seemed to leave the most important statistic out of the equation: the annual salary of those senior flight attendants who retired after 9/11. Patricia, for instance, was earning about $40,000 a year. As a rough estimate, if 2,000 senior fliers had not left, it would have cost the airline an annual sum of $80 million in salaries. In contrast, 2,000 new hires would now cost United only $48 million—at its own estimates—or, at the union's projected figure, $32 million. That is an annual saving of between $32 and $48 million a year, on salaries alone, with even greater savings coming from reduced benefits and pension plans. This could help offset the estimated $300 million legal costs United incurred as part of its Chapter 11 filing.[8]

Reducing Costs by Squeezing-In

Flight attendants may think about space, but their employers never stop thinking about money. Since deregulation in 1978, airlines have attempted to reduce their cost base, with differing pay scales introduced for flight attendants in the 1980s, and new "lean and mean" management in the 1990s.[9] All carriers have been obsessed with cost reduction. By 2001, however, 44 percent of all airline revenues were still swallowed up by labor costs, and an increasingly dominant view in the industry was that the business model supporting this wage structure had become unsustainable.[10] Major carriers faced the highest costs: American's cost per available seat-mile before 9/11 stood at 11.7 cents; in contrast, JetBlue's was 6.4 cents.[11]

The major carriers felt they had to reduce their cost base, and the post-9/11 economic crisis gave them their chance. Though the media widely presented the terrorist attacks as a financial calamity for the industry, for some airlines it was simultaneously an opportunity to change radically their existing business model and to drive through the kind of restructuring that management had been itching to implement for at least a decade. That they had been prevented from doing so was in no small measure due to the strength of flight attendant unions, which, as in the case of the APFA strike in 1993, had shown themselves ready to fight if necessary.

Strikes are costly exercises, doing great damage to a company's reputation. Though management has not been averse to provoking them in the past, in the post-9/11 context more subtle measures were at hand. Rather than trying to demolish a wall with a sledgehammer—very messy and requiring a lot of effort—why not methodically chip away at the cement holding it together? For flight attendants, that cement consisted of the occupational community they had formed on the job. More than anything, management had to reinvent the job as a short-term rather than long-term prospect. And though they hit flight attendants in the pocket—through pay and benefit cuts—airlines found that the most effective policies in undermining a group of workers for whom "spatial remuneration" was one of the job's most important features was to squeeze those very spaces they enjoyed so much. Thus began the industry "squeeze-in."

Undermining Seniority

In the last chapter, I argued that many flight attendants enjoyed the sense of control that the job gave them, so much so that it overrode feelings of guilt about regularly leaving their families, even when those families were concerned about their safety. The foundation for this feeling of control was the increasing significance of seniority from the 1970s onward, a significance that went hand in hand with flight attendants emphasizing their safety professional status. Seniority brought control incrementally and was the main reason flight attendants who had "only joined for a year or two," as most senior fliers I spoke to told me, ultimately stayed on the job for more than thirty years. Consistently, inexorably moving up the rungs of the seniority ladder provided a continuous sense of progress and a perpetual incentive to stay.

After 9/11, airlines had a window of opportunity to come up with disincentives to staying on the job. They found ways to persuade expensive senior fliers to leave and then, thinking of the long term, ways to prevent junior, less-expensive workers from staying around long enough to become senior, expensive workers. The starting point for effecting this transition was to change the bidding system.

Preferential Bidding

In the middle of 2003, Delta introduced a scheme of "preferential bidding." Under the old system, flight attendants bid for "lines" of trips, say Atlanta–New York–Los Angeles–Atlanta over Monday, Tuesday, and Wednesday. With preferential bidding, using a fully computerized system, flight attendants give their choices a weighting, which they can change each month according to their priorities. As Sofia, at Delta, explains:

> It's more personalized. Where before they would give us a schedule and this is the way it is and it's going to be every Wednesday you fly to Madrid. It was every set day of the month. But if I happened to have a doctor's appointment on Friday of the third week that I'm flying Wednesday, Thursday, Friday, I'm going to have to do something with that trip. So what we used to do is try to find somebody we could change with. Now, if I know this ahead of time, I would bid a different trip. So, for the week of the doctor's appointment, I want to fly Monday, Tuesday, Wednesday or Saturday, Sunday, Monday and have that Friday off.

Rather than select from the airline's itineraries, flight attendants under preferential bidding construct their own. Trips are allocated according to a mixture of seniority and the weighting a flight attendant places on a particular trip.

On the surface, and indeed in its actual name, preferential bidding seems like a form of increased worker control, with flight attendants able to exercise more choice over their schedule. But the people it benefits the most are workers lower down the seniority ladder. For one thing, older fliers are less computer literate than younger ones, and several I spoke to clearly had even more difficulty understanding how the computer-generated system worked than they did the old seniority system. Under preferential bidding it is easier for junior workers to secure good trips. Taylor, for instance, one spring day in 2006, sitting at a bagel shop on the west side of Atlanta, tells me:

> Seniority in the past determined your pay, your flying, your reserve. Things are so different now. Even me, being only ten years seniority or only thirty-one years old or however you want to look at it, things have changed so much so fast; we're still in that old mind-set of seniority is the only thing that matters. If you don't have it, you have nothing. But things have changed so much. I mean, I got to fly Paris.

Preferential bidding rewards junior fliers far sooner than used to be the case. Paris, Mary Ann's favorite layover, is a senior trip that, under the old system, Taylor could never have commanded on a regular basis.

It may be, as Delta told its flight attendants, that the system "gives you more scheduling flexibility."[12] But the point is that under the old system, flexibility operated within the developmental structure of the profession as a long-term career. Preferential bidding flattens the pyramid, making better trips more easily accessible at a far earlier stage in that career and thus, by default, reducing the effect of the seniority "carrot." New flight attendants can secure high-time trips now, not in fifteen years' time.

Alongside preferential bidding Delta also made three other important changes. First, it abolished the old system of reserve. Second, it removed maximum flight hours, so that instead of a limit of ninety, flight attendants could fly as much as they liked. Third, it introduced "blended pay," a complex formula that mixed base pay and flight pay.

The reserve program was replaced by "access days," which gave Delta flight attendants "greater control over [their] schedule," the airline claimed.[13] But this greater control applied only to those who were already on reserve, who, rather than being summoned to the airport at any time, could specify in advance what days they would be on standby. Delta applied the system to 70 percent of its flight attendants, which meant that workers with more than twenty years' seniority suddenly found themselves working on a reserve basis for three days a month all over again.

Delta sweetened the pill by saying that flight attendants could "swap" their access days, which reserves could not do under the old system. But, because of the abolition of the maximum-time restrictions, flight attendants are finding that they have nothing to swap. This is because under "blended pay" flight attendants are realizing that they have to fly up to twenty hours a month more to make the same amount of money as under the previous system. There are fewer flights around, as Delta cut back or farmed out domestic services to its subsidiary carriers such as ASA or Comair. And so, as Roseanne puts it, when schedules are published it is "something of a feeding frenzy," with flight attendants who were once constrained by maximum limits trying to grab as many trips as they possibly can. Some are flying 150 hours a month.

Using warm terminology involving "preference" and "access"—Delta actually calls its system "customized bidding"—the system sounds like a good thing for the workers involved. But, as the linguistic anthropologist George Lakoff has argued, such language also falls under the rubric of "framing," the construction of a concept around a word or metaphor whose good-natured fuzziness makes it difficult to oppose.[14]

Moreover, if we look at where preferential bidding has been introduced, or unions have agreed to its introduction, and also where it has not, a revealing picture emerges. Alongside Delta, the three main airlines to change their bidding systems since 9/11 are United, US Air, and Northwest. Unions at the first two agreed to change to preferential bidding, whereas Northwest, which already used the system, changed the way it was implemented. All four have spent a good deal of the period since 9/11 in Chapter 11 bankruptcy, where agreements with workers can be nullified and where unions such as AFA have been forced to accept such changes or, allegedly, see their members' jobs go to the wall. Under Railway Labor Act regulations, unions negotiate with individual companies, not across the industry, and are always vulnerable to carrier threats of liquidation, which would take away not only their members' jobs but also their treasured seniority because this would not be transferable to a new airline.

Two noteworthy carriers have had nothing to do with preferential bidding: American and Continental. American's flight attendants' union has "no interest in preferential bidding" and recently ratified a new contract at the airline that contained no mention of it.[15] Continental's flight attendants also agreed to a new contract in early 2006 in which preferential bidding played no part, with most workers indicating an "overwhelming desire" against it.[16] Neither American nor Continental entered bankruptcy after 9/11. Entering Chapter 11 was therefore a useful tool to ram through new workplace procedures, under threat of liquidation, though in the case of Delta their nonunion flight attendants never had a contract in the first place.

Though seniority still retains an important place within a preferential bidding system, it is no longer the system's be-all and end-all. There is no longer a built-in incentive for workers to construct long careers in the industry, even when those careers develop more by increment than by design. When you are able to fly as many hours as you like, why not, for example, just do that for a few years, get the travel bug out of your system, and move on to something else?

Pensions

Of course, seniority was not just important for bidding. It was also important for company pension schemes, and these became a second target for airlines. Like thousands of other companies in the United States, carriers found themselves saddled with increasingly expensive commitments to older workers. A pension scheme provides an incentive for workers to stay in a job. Greater longevity means a greater number of contributions, while many premiums are determined by an employee's final salary on retirement, which tends to increase with time served. All these conditions existed at U.S. airlines before 9/11. But with carriers claiming they faced an economic apocalypse, pensions became a convenient and relatively easy target, and reducing or eradicating them became a good way of convincing workers that hanging around in the job might not be in their best interests.

Initially, some carriers used pensions and benefit changes to persuade older workers to leave. Under the Pension Plus program, Delta, for instance, added five years to either age or seniority, and threw in continued free travel and benefits for retirees. In spring 2003, United increased the age limit for early retirement from fifty to fifty-five and then told those affected that if they left by the end of June, their benefits would be protected. The irony of the short notice was not lost on Kathleen, when I spoke to her two weeks before the deadline:

> I always envied the older gals when I was young and I was thinking that, wow, look at that, they can fly whenever they want. They can go where they want. Isn't that neat? And actually I bid for next month, I bid a line and I got my first choice. The perfect line, the perfect trip, exactly what I'd want to be doing. And it's like, finally I've gotten to this, and now it's being taken away.

Sitting on the lawn adjoining a swimming pool in Chevy Chase, Maryland, on a glorious June day, Kathleen told me she had to think long and hard about what to do with her future. Ultimately she quit the airline.

But having got a large number of senior fliers off the payroll, these carriers then got even tougher. Despite assurances to the contrary, United slashed benefits under bankruptcy court; Delta's retirees, who have no contract, live in perpetual fear of having their pensions and benefits abrogated.[17] For airlines, such action was both a material and a symbolic masterstroke. They saved millions from former flight attendants, and they sent a clear message to those still in employment: look how you will be treated if you hang around in the job too long. Think you have a pension waiting at the end of all that jet lag? Think again.

In case those flight attendants who were still around could not read the messages being sent, airlines changed their pension schemes too. Delta switched from a straight defined benefit plan to a cash-balance program, applying it to all new employees except unionized pilots.[18] The latter penalizes senior fliers because it removes the number of years of service from the multiplier used to calculate pension premiums. Cash-balance pensions accumulate more quickly than under the former scheme and are also portable. In short, there is no longer a financial incentive to stay on the job, and you can take your pension with you when you go.[19]

By changing the bidding system and pension plan, airlines sent the message that the flight attendant's career was really not long-term. But well-established carriers have long cultural histories that take time to change. The brand-new carriers did not need to even *pretend* that the career was long-term.

The Nonpermanent Workforce at JetBlue

JetBlue, the New York–based low-cost carrier, began operations in February 2001 and has been one of the few success stories of the post-9/11 environment.[20] JetBlue's founder, David Neeleman, has presided carefully over the construction of a strong corporate brand, hoping to reach the point where, like Google, the Internet search engine, "JetBlue becomes a verb."[21] JetBlue nurtures a cohesive corporate culture in which all employees are "crew members" and are showered with stock options.

When it comes to hiring flight attendants, however, JetBlue has made it abundantly clear that it does not want any of them to stay at the airline very long. As Barbara Peterson, a biographer of the airline, says, "Neeleman had imagined that he'd draw his flight attendants from the ranks of recent college graduates, who might see it as a way to live in New York City for a few years before moving on to more serious pursuits."[22] What could be more serious than rescuing someone in a crash or keeping a passenger from breaking his neck during turbulence is unclear. In any event, the airline's recruitment advertisements drew a far more diverse cross section of applicants than graduating seniors with a touch of wanderlust. But JetBlue was not going to give up its dream of a nonpermanent workforce, and thus set up three different flight attendant groupings: regular full-time, job-share, and one-year contracts, the latter specifically aimed at college students wanting to take a year off. JetBlue's "full-time" workers sign five-year contracts, in which the airline promises not to lay them off. JetBlue does not offer a traditional pension scheme, and its workers pay a large part of any health care costs.[23]

The JetBlue model of fixed contracts is not new. It is common at charter carriers in Europe, where workers have to leave after a certain period of time. It is also, as I have discussed previously, a feature of some of the world's most prestigious airlines, such as Singapore International and Emirates Air. Song, Delta's low-cost spin-off, flirted with the idea and then abandoned it. But with JetBlue, the subject of budding business school entrepreneurs and currently one of the industry's most profitable operators, its model points the way to the profession's future. As one worker put it on a flight attendant message board: "Contract work is fine for some, but I want a career! It seems like many of the airlines are looking for ways to make that less and less of a possibility for their front-line employees."[24] In removing incentives to stay long-term, airlines also strike at the heart of union power among flight attendants. The rise of strong flight attendant unions went hand in hand with the growing sense of occupational community that was the product of the job becoming permanent. As any labor expert knows, an impermanent workforce is very hard to organize. JetBlue, vehemently opposed to unions, specifically designed its three-part flight attendant workforce as a way of "[making] it far more difficult to unify these workers into a single force."[25]

For JetBlue, and for other airlines, though, it was not so much the presence of older workers as long-serving workers that was seen as a problem. In fact, both JetBlue and Song hired quite a few flight attendants in their fifties. These attendants will never climb very high up the seniority ladder, and they also conform to a growing trend of people wanting to "see the world" before settling down to retirement rather than, as was the case in the 1960s, before settling down to marriage.

In all these developments—different bidding systems, changes to pensions and benefits, fixed contracts—the net result is a reconfiguration of the flight attendant profession back into a short-term career. The spaces that seniority opened up have been squeezed as airlines have pulled the rug from under senior workers' feet. Airlines have apparently learned that attacking wages is not enough to get rid of expensive workers. What is needed is structural change within the industry that removes the incentives for those workers to stay.

Worn-Out Workers

One of the ways flight attendants "spaced-out" in the postdestination phase was to commute. With good seniority, flight attendants could live in one city and be based thousands of miles away, as was the case with United workers I spoke to living in Atlanta but based in Chicago. Commuters are quite often senior fliers, normally because they are away from their base cities for family reasons, often because their partner has a more lucrative job in another city.

It is an arduous lifestyle. Let us take the case of Shelly, for instance, who joined United in 1977, living in Atlanta with her partner and teenage son. Before the "squeeze-in," Shelly flew to Narita, Japan. "I'd fly up on Monday morning from Atlanta, getting in to Chicago about 7:30 and then check in at 10:30. We'd take off at noon." Shelly would then have a twelve-hour flight and land in Japan at 4:00 P.M. Tuesday, local time. She would then fly back on Thursday arriving back in Chicago at a time earlier than when she took off from Japan, to catch an afternoon flight back to Atlanta, to get back home about 7:00 in the evening.

Such a routine is disorienting and, with what amounts to a forty-hour day on the return journey, exhausting. But "spacing-out" was worth it. The Asian flights were high time, Shelly learned to speak Japanese in her hotel room, and still felt able to be a good mom while helping out at her child's school. But then came the "squeeze-in," and Shelly's world contracted. As part of the cutbacks, United removed the early morning flight from Atlanta, which meant to fly the Narita route Shelly had to leave not on Monday but on Sunday evening, possibly Sunday afternoon to make sure she could get on the flight to Chicago. On her return she also might not be able to get on an afternoon flight and could end up walking in the door in Atlanta at 11:00 P.M., instead of to a nice meal cooked by her partner at 7:00. That's pushing a fifty-hour day. For

Shelly the remunerative spaces of the trip no longer existed. When I spoke to her in the summer of 2003, she had taken a leave of absence. "Things are kind of unraveling," she told me. She never returned to the industry.

The "squeeze-in" affects flight attendants in numerous ways. In the year after 9/11, the AFA surveyed its members to ascertain levels of traumatic disorder and how airline restructuring had impacted on flight attendants' lives. More than half of respondents claimed that changes at work were having a negative effect on their quality of life, and 40 percent claimed that they could no longer hold the same lines as they could before 9/11. Roughly 80 percent had experienced some kind of upheaval, such as base closure, involuntary furlough, or being forced to change their commute.[26]

Many flight attendants were affected by the industry fallout after 9/11. Granted, the airline industry has always been unpredictable, with ebbs and flows in the business cycle, but the scale of change and the intensity with which airlines have pushed for major restructuring—such as changes to the bidding system—make this current period exceptional. Flight attendants have to fly more hours to make the same amount of pay. More sophisticated crew scheduling systems mean workers are often utilized up to their maximum legal hours on a regular basis. They make more trips per day, with more taking off and landing, which in itself is draining on the body. Add boarding and deplaning multiple sets of passengers, extra rounds of nodding and smiling and greeting and saying good-bye, and it is easy to see how this group of workers is becoming increasingly stressed.[27]

Before 9/11, fatigue was a problem.[28] After 9/11, with the "squeeze-in," it has gotten worse. In 2005, Congress expressed concern that FAA minimum crew rest regulations might not be sufficient for flight attendants charged with new security responsibilities. Congress also noted that "reduced rest" flexibility—the rule by which airlines could ask flight attendants to work fifteen instead of fourteen hours in an emergency—was now becoming "common practice" at some carriers. "It is likely that many flight attendants are performing their duties with no more than 4 to 6 hours of sleep," Congress concluded.

Flight attendants are therefore worn out, with greater workloads when on board. In October 2005, for instance, Delta reduced the number of flight attendants on board its overseas flights, creating more work for the others. But, inevitably, it is senior fliers who find such an increased workload more of a strain. Jet lag, for instance, affects workers in their fifties up to three times more than those in their twenties.[29] With flight attendants having to fly more punishing schedules, they inevitably become physically exhausted. Several flight attendants in their fifties told me that they thought it was time to move on because the job was now for the "younger crowd." But if it is for the younger crowd, airlines do not want this group turning into the "older" crowd. So schedules for new hires are so heinous they almost appear designed to make a good number of them quit not long after starting. Sitting in a coffee bar in Decatur, a pleasant suburb of Atlanta, Jill from Air Tran spelled out for me how bad things were for new flight attendants:

> I train a lot of flight attendants, and I tell them when they came out of training, I say, "It's abuse. The way you're treated on reserve is abuse." . . . They'll send them out on a trip and they'll finish a trip and then they'll make them sit at the airport for the rest of the eight hours, even though they only flew two or four hours. They can't go home, they have to sit at the airport another four hours. I try to prepare them. But for the company, it's cheaper to train them than to keep them, so they just keep putting them through the mill. As far as management is concerned, they would rather just keep pushing that meal through.

According to Jill, Air Tran loses about thirty flight attendants a month, but they are continually replaced by new hires fresh from training. In 2005, Air Tran had 6,000 inquiries about its flight attendant positions, interviewed 1,200 applicants, and hired 400.[30] Flight attendants who work under this kind of system have very little spatial remuneration.

Disappearing Spaces

But what about the other spaces the job provides in the postdestination phase? What about the camaraderie and onboard community and relaxing layovers? Flight attendants still create these spaces, but they are harder to maintain. For one thing, bidding is much more competitive. Through the introduction of pay cuts the airlines have, ironically, made the job more about pay, as flight attendants sacrifice their free space to maintain their standard of living. With the removal of maximum hour limits, airlines make flight attendants more cutthroat. Carolyn, a senior

Delta flier, is drained as we share a coffee near Emory University, in Atlanta. She explains:

> The scheduling is physically taxing, and the relationships with coworkers are tricky. Commuters are virtually exhausted, and workers try to outdo each other. People get so difficult that I want to avoid them. There are increasingly difficult personalities on board. There is *no* camaraderie at all. Flight attendants used to cover up for each other, but now it has got highly competitive.

Meanwhile, layovers are being squeezed. Airlines have cut back on the quality of places flight attendants stay. While Delta pilots still stay in picturesque Brighton by the sea, the flight attendants now stay in Crawley, a commuter town with very little personality that is about fifteen miles from Gatwick Airport. Even if destination was not so important, staying in Crawley destroyed many of the old Brighton routines. The pint in the Pump Room, the antique collecting, and the little sandwich shop—through which workers gained "spatial remuneration"—are now farther away.

With more intense scheduling, the length of layovers has also been reduced, and some have been abolished altogether. For instance, most United flights from the West Coast to Hawaii are now turnarounds, with workers flying out and back on the same day. Those who do get a layover now get twelve to fourteen hours whereas they used to get twenty-seven, and if eight of those hours are spent sleeping, there is little time to do much else.

When it comes to jump seat therapy, where workers create community with their colleagues through sharing stories, pictures, and problems during down time in flights, a larger number of flight attendants are finding they do not have anyone to talk to. Passenger growth at regional airlines, such as ASA, is likely to be twice as fast as that at major carriers.[31] Not only do lone flight attendants have no one to share their world with, they also have no one to consult when things go wrong.[32]

Finally, what about the balance between work and home, which flight attendants found so appealing about the job and one of the reasons for continuing to do it? We have already seen how Shelly has fared at an older carrier, squeezed from the profession because she now lived in a world of work-home *im*balance. But at newer carriers, such as JetBlue, the only way work and home can be balanced is through job sharing, where workers would struggle to make $8,000 a year, hardly enough to raise a family, especially if based in New York. Applicants needing to work full-time are warned in advance by the airline that they may be gone from home for up to six consecutive days. There is a covert vetting procedure here that is as powerful as JetBlue's overt demand that applicants meet the "organizational fit for the JetBlue culture, that is, exhibit the JetBlue values of Safety, Caring, Integrity, Fun and Passion."[33] Covertly, JetBlue is telling potential applicants that there are no spaces outside the job.

The old spaces of the postdestination phase—camaraderie, commuting, jump seat therapy, layovers, and spaces away from the job—have all been squeezed by an industry that has de facto removed much of the spatial remuneration the job once offered. Again, the message is clear: this is not the sort of job you will want to do for a long time. But this is not the end of the "squeeze-in." At both a metaphorical and a literal level, airlines are now squeezing flight attendants into (and out of) their own uniforms.

Body Wars

Outside the United States, carriers have been coming up with novel ways of weeding out unwanted flight attendants. Dubrovnik Airways, a Croatian carrier, subjects its (mainly female) flight attendants, but not its (mainly male) pilots, to a swimming pool test, rather like that which goes on at Singapore. A special "company jury" presides over the exam, which all new recruits must take while in training.[34]

Meanwhile, Air India has contracted a new branding consultancy to help the aggressive carrier deal with equally aggressive regional rivals in the fastest-growing market in the world. As part of the revamp, flight attendants, according to the airline, had to lose weight. The carrier claimed "significant numbers" of workers between age forty and fifty-five were "overweight, obese and morbidly obese."[35]

Aer Lingus, the Irish carrier, was forced to acknowledge the existence of a company memo listing ways to make life difficult for workers. One of the suggestions in an internal document, *Business Plan—HR (Human Resources) Strategy 2004*, was to make cabin crew, including older flight attendants (at whom this was clearly aimed) wear jumpsuits rather than their normal uniforms. The overall strategy was to create "environmental push factors" that would encourage staff to voluntarily quit, incorporating such measures as changing shift patterns that would be disruptive to workers with families. The airline claimed the plan was only a discussion document.[36]

Finally, from Australia, Virgin Blue, owned by Richard Branson, asked applicants to perform a song-and-dance routine to demonstrate they had "Virgin Flair." Eight former Ansett Airlines workers took the company to court for age discrimination. The women argued the airline had not employed a single woman over thirty-five years old, and that interview panels equated the ability to have "fun" with youth—largely because the panel itself was staffed with relative youngsters. A Queensland court agreed with the workers and awarded damages against the carrier.[37]

It seems a woman's bodily appearance is once more important to the airlines, as carriers harken back to images more akin to the 1960s: young, bubbly crew out for a good time. However, let us not forget developments back in the United States. When designer Richard Tyler came up with a new uniform for Delta, he "planned it so that the flight attendants who were walking down the concourse . . . would look like a runway show."[38] But it is at Delta's low-cost spin-off, Song, where the most interesting picture emerges. As at Virgin Blue, Song's recruits had to do a song-and-dance routine or some similar theatrical performance, even though they were all current, safety-qualified Delta flight attendants. "It's a much more playful, happy airline," Song's vice president told the *Atlanta Journal-Constitution* in 2003.[39] Part of that happiness involved resurrecting the "nostalgic flight attendant" figure from the 1960s. With its flight attendants in their Kate Spade–designed uniforms, according to one commentator, "Song may be the most ambitious attempt by an airline to brand itself with fashion since the now-defunct Dallas airline, Braniff."[40]

In October 2005, Delta, in Chapter 11 bankruptcy, announced that Song would be "folded back" into its mainline operation. "We are incorporating the best of Song into the best of Delta," said CEO Gerald Grinstein.[41] The "best of Song" includes those all-singing, all-dancing "ex-Delta" flight attendants who have been put through reprogramming and are now being presented back to the old Delta workforce as the handpicked cream of the crop. The "Song Stars"—as they are known internally—are overwhelmingly junior fliers who jumped at the chance to join Song and improve their seniority in the process. Song, in its short existence, provided a new model for the Delta flight attendant, one that made more senior workers like Roseanne uncomfortable. As she explains, "It's worrisome to me because the Song Stars, they are younger, they have sexy uniforms, and the persona is like Southwest. I'm just not that kind of flight attendant, you know."

Part of the "squeeze-in," it seems, involves the airlines resurrecting a flight attendant "norm"—or, as JetBlue puts it, an "organizational fit" —that sends a strong message not only to potential customers but also to workers themselves. With their new uniform designs and emphasis on "fun" and "passion," airlines once more implicitly fall back on gendered notions of the perfect female body rooted in imagery from the 1960s but perpetuated and disseminated in most consistent form since the 1970s by Singapore Girl. Singapore Girl remains the template for airline flight attendant branding, where older women workers have no space, and where, squeezed hard enough, they will de-select themselves from being part of the industry.

"They Won't Let Me Do My Job"

In interviews with flight attendants, one of their most common complaints is that airlines are actually preventing them from doing their job properly. Flight attendants increasingly feel their notion of what the job should be about is very different from that of the airlines. Of course we have seen this before with differing conceptions of safety, where flight attendants stressed their role as safety professionals and airlines rarely mentioned it. But this disagreement extends into the service side of the job, where workers—as airlines constantly like to remind them—are ambassadors for their carriers. Time and again I hear from flight attendants that the problem with management is that it is increasingly populated by those who have never been flight attendants themselves. Here, for instance, is Susan, from United:

> United used to exclusively only hire or promote people to a supervisory position for flight attendants if they've been a flight attendant. And then somewhere along the line there was a culture change probably that came from higher up that decided they weren't going to do that. And they started hiring people from all different walks of life. People that worked at the phone company and all different types of people to

make them people managers. And that's when we saw a real significant change because it's hard to sit in an office talking to somebody about something that's happened on the aircraft . . . if they have no frame of reference really for what you're doing. And what's shocking about that also is they're able really to emotionally detach from you as a supervisor. They don't show any empathy. And it engenders a kind of an adversarial relationship with the management of your company, which ultimately doesn't do anybody any good. It just seems to be the way it is across the board in our industry. I can't speak about other industries, but in our industry it's very prevalent.

In former years, company presidents or CEOs often retained the respect of flight attendants because they had grown up in the industry and, as in the case of Eastern's Eddie Rickenbacker, been pilots themselves. In contrast to modern management, they knew what it was like up there in the clouds. Time and again I hear from flight attendants who say their airline is now run by people who "aren't airline people"—especially their own line managers. To break down this distrust, and to give management some insight into what goes on in a flight attendant's world, supervisors sometimes take trips with flight attendants, to see what things are really like at 35,000 feet. But they always fly the easy trips. As Steve, at United, describes:

My biggest thing is, I've always had this argument. The supervisors pick four trips a year . . . with forty people going to somewhere easy. I'd like to see that they be required to do a three-day trip every month. And I've had a conversation with the supervisors, and I'm an ex-policeman, and I said, when you see the sergeants and lieutenants out on the streets, yeah, they've got paperwork, they're in the offices and all that, but you know what, then they become patrolmen. They're out there patrolling, they're a supervisor out on a patrol. And then I turn around and I said a fireman, when you see guys fighting fires, a captain or battalion chief, he's sweating like a dog fighting this fire. He's a fireman. But I said, you guys aren't a flight attendant. You have no idea what I'm going through. I said, I want you to meet those passengers, I want you to work those trips, then you're going to start to see some changes.

For United flight attendants, nothing could better illustrate the gap between them and management than a town hall meeting held by Jane

Allen, senior vice president of onboard service, in Chicago in November 2004. At 12:40 P.M. she declared to the flight attendants who had gathered for the session, "Guys, I have to stop here—I've been on my feet since 9:30 this morning." According to one attendee, "It was an *unbelievable* moment." The audience collapsed in incredulous laughter as their head supervisor revealed she found it difficult to stay on her feet for longer than three hours, while telling flight attendants—some of whom had just arrived from ten-hour-plus international flights—how to do their job.[42]

Emotional Dissonance

The lack of correspondence between what flight attendants think their job is about, and what they think management think it should be about leads to what psychologists call "emotional dissonance" and, relatedly, actual embarrassment. Emotional dissonance is basically the difference between displayed and felt emotions. Smiling at irate passengers and saying, "Of, course, I totally understand," while inside wanting to yell profanities at them is a good example. We have all experienced emotional dissonance at some point, acting in a way that disguises our true feelings.

In a job where acting plays a major part, flight attendants experience emotional dissonance constantly. In an important study, two Dutch psychologists, Ellen Heuven and Arnold Bakker, suggest that emotional dissonance is not necessarily a problem—a good dose of "healthy" emotional dissonance reminds workers that they are, in fact, acting half the time. They can go to work, go home again, and get on with their lives. "If I were in flight attendant mode all the time, I'd burn out," one San Francisco–based United flier tells me, clearly aware of the acting component on the job.

But under certain conditions emotional dissonance can become a substantial problem. One distinguishing feature, according to Heuven and Bakker, between cabin crew displaying "healthy" and "unhealthy" emotional dissonance is levels of perceived control over how they expressed themselves. Those who feel they can be flexible in their dealings with passengers tend to be more relaxed on board than those who feel they have to stick to a set script, with no personal autonomy involved. As one flight attendant described it, "I had the feeling that, in the short time a passenger sees me, he needs to get a positive image of our airline, and that therefore I had to be a laughing object."[43] The Dutch authors conclude: "A structural mismatch between emotions that need to be displayed and inner feelings makes an important contribution to explaining why cabin attendants get emotionally exhausted and detach from their jobs."[44]

But increasingly, flight attendants find the source of this structural mismatch the fact that the scripts airlines ask them to present are simply preposterous. The "mismatch" between how flight attendants act and how they feel often results in plain embarrassment at no longer being able to do a proper job. As John, a United flier, says: "I don't feel burned out but just really insulted. Management takes everything away that you can use to do a good job. They take away the food, they take away the stuff that makes the presentation nice. There's not a whole lot you can do with what you have to make it really good." When I put to Taylor that it seemed she was mad at Delta for ruining the job, she agrees:

Yeah, I am. That's a good way to put it. That pretty much sums it up in a nutshell. I've got a lot of anger. I feel embarrassed when I'm at work. We don't have pillows, we don't have plastic spoons anymore. There are little things, you know, people say, can I have a pillow or can I have salt and pepper? I'm really sorry we don't have that anymore. We don't have plastic wings anymore. Kids love those wings. I'm so embarrassed to say, we don't carry pillows anymore because Delta is a cheap ass. I can't tell you how many times I get stuff out of my own personal supply to give to passengers. Embarrassed is a good word.

In March 2004, an internal memo sent by American's northeast regional managing director berated flight attendants for, among other things, telling customers they are unable to accommodate them "due to cost cutting by AA." "Exactly what should we say that would meet management's expectations?" union representatives asked in response.[45] It may be that emotional dissonance in this instance has actually disappeared altogether, but flight attendants are still left feeling guilty and placed in an awkward position.

Flight attendants therefore have one more thing to add to their list of reasons for no longer hanging around too long on the job. They have lost remunerative spaces; they have lost incentives to stay, in the form of pensions; they have seen resurgence in imagery that questions their status as safety professionals, and older workers no longer feel comfortable in the job. To top it all, they often feel that they are no longer able to do the job as they feel it should be done. Where once they were proud to don their uniforms and stride up and down the aisles of an airplane, some are now ashamed of the company they are supposed to be representing. In telling me why she had quit the job, Sandra could be writing the epitaph for a whole profession:

> When I joined Delta I had wanderlust. The job was great. . . . And then I needed the freedom of being able to go away when I could, and the flying was a break from the day-to-day. But I always liked the job itself. I liked the passengers. This changed, though, and I knew it was time to go. I started to get embarrassed in the industry, embarrassed at being the only white-haired thing on the airplane. And it is not the job it was. You were there to solve problems, and it is hard to lose this part of the job as we never had the time anymore. Now you hand passengers over to the agents, and they are twelve years old and haven't a clue what to do. We were supposed to empower ourselves according to the airline some time back. So we did, and they realized that flight attendants were doing everything to accommodate the passenger. So that didn't last long. . . . It used to be that "keep your head down" was advice for dealing with emergency situations. Now we say "keep your head down" to avoid talking to the passengers.

The Industry's Future

Making predictions about the notoriously fickle airline industry's future is perhaps not the wisest move, especially with the rising price of oil and greater focus on airplane emissions as a contributor to global warming. But in industry circles, the thinking is that there will eventually be two types of airline. Domestic travel—in the United States—will be provided more and more by low-cost carriers with few frills. Some of these may be foreign-owned, if rules that protect U.S.-based airlines are relaxed. Richard Branson's Virgin Atlantic, for instance, has long wanted to set up a low-cost model in the United States along similar lines to Australia's Virgin Blue (though hopefully without its hiring policies). The major U.S. airlines, on the other hand, will increasingly view international travel as the most profitable side of their business. Should market deregulation continue, a handful of consolidated international megacarriers loosely based around existing alliances such as One World are likely to emerge. At the very least, the merger trend in the industry will likely account for one big U.S. airline name before too long.

Flight attendants joining the industry face a very different future from their predecessors. They will face numerous disincentives to stay for thirty years (given the job's health dangers, perhaps that is no bad thing). Fixed-term contracts, lack of pensions, and a more punishing workload will almost certainly increase the attrition rate. Some may continue to "trade up" airlines, starting in the low-cost sector and then moving to bigger carriers when possible.

However, in an increasingly globalized industry, "trading up" may be less feasible than before. Some U.S. carriers seem predisposed to looking overseas for cheaper international crew. In May 2006, for instance, Delta began to employ all-Indian-based crews on its daily Chennai– New York flights, costing the airline about one-third as much as for an American-based crew.[46] Behind strife-torn Northwest lurks the suspicion that the carrier would like to get rid of all its U.S.-based international crew. Moreover, emerging megacarriers are likely to be of the ilk of Dubai-based Emirates Air, with no shortage of applicants but among whom few are likely to be college graduates from the Midwest. And those who sign on will do so for a limited period of time. In short, the low-cost sector, which is still expanding, may be the best hope for those still wanting to fly for a living. Jobs here are less well paid, are more intensive, involve a more restricted route network, and provide few of the spaces flight attendants could find at larger carriers.

The most significant change facing flight attendants is the reduction in the relative importance of seniority. In an increasingly short-term career, seniority will no longer be viewed as the Holy Grail, an incentive luring flight attendants into the future and persuading them to stay on the job. Part of the "incremental career" was that things did get better in increments; now that is less often the case, and flight attendants who perceive no improvement and, perhaps more important, no *prospect* of improvement, are unlikely to hang around in the job once they have got the travel bug out of their system. With airlines once again recruiting on the basis of the job being a great way to see the world, destination once more becomes all-important. The UK airline Monarch, for instance, tells would-be recruits: "As part of Monarch Cabin Crew . . . you may have the opportunity to visit exciting destinations that include: the Car-ribean [*sic*] USA, Africa and India. . . . Forget routine, but expect to work hard and play hard too!"[47]

New (and Old) Beginnings

In his poignant book, *All That Is Solid Melts into Air,* Marshall Berman writes of how human beings engage in a continual battle to make sense of the world around them, to put down roots, to build homes and com-munities and meaningful lives even while the forces of modernization (now read: globalization) undermine almost all that they have achieved. The greatest fictional representation of this tragedy is Willy Loman, the main character in Arthur Miller's *Death of a Salesman,* who always wants to own something completely before it goes out of date. At his funeral, his wife speaks words to Willy's grave that encapsulate the heartbreaking irony of modern life: "I made the last payment on the house today. Today, dear. And there'll be nobody home."[48]

Flight attendants, whose situation resembles that of miners, steel-workers, and those in the fishing industry, have had their occupational communities—their homes away from home—ripped up before their very eyes. Nothing is the same anymore, they tell me. Kirsty, still at Delta, smiles with resignation as she comments: "It's just a different job. It used to be considered a career. They don't really want us to consider it a career anymore. I think that's one of the biggest changes. Manage-ment probably won't admit this, but I think they want us to do it five years and go on to something else." Another Delta flier is more blunt: "It's my feeling that the powers that be and some that have just de-parted with Delta Air Lines have raped and pillaged our company."

In these final pages, however, I want to emphasize that, though the old flight attendant lifestyle may have disappeared, life itself still goes on. The "job" may be dead; but long live the job. Rather than a paean to a lost world, this book is a story of women workers carving out spaces for themselves. Though those spaces have closed, as the industry has systematically squeezed workers, I think it does flight attendants a disservice to suggest that they have become merely passive victims at the whims of global capital. Even if the job no longer offers the kind of full-time career it may once have, there is no reason that flight attendants cannot continue to shape it in the best ways they can.

Nursing Revisited: The World of Certification

The first flight attendants were nurses, and it is therefore perhaps apt to turn to nursing as a comparative profession. Nurses have much in common with flight attendants: most are women, and their jobs are overwhelmingly associated with "feminized" traits of nurture and care. Though nursing's emotional labor component is not necessarily driven by the company bottom line, the job is still draining, requiring workers to bite their lips on occasion in the interest of producing a desired state in the patient. Nurses also face irregular hours and often problematic power relations with predominantly male doctors and surgeons. As for flight attendants, since the 1980s, real wages in nursing have not kept pace.[49] At the same time, the average age of nurses has increased. Nurses also work and live amid an occupational community in which only fellow workers really understand what they do.

In the early 1970s nurses—like flight attendants—began to reshape their profession. The growth of the nurse-practitioner field, in which nurses became the first port of call in locations physicians tended not to touch, such as remote rural areas or inner cities, increased their status. At the same time, greater technical specialization within the health industry led to the beginning of a professional nursing certification movement, whereby nurses would acquire extra, recognized, and respected credentials above and beyond their basic registered nurse status. The American Nurses Credentialing Center (ANCC) now offers thirty-seven different certificate courses.[50]

The plethora of certificates available to nurses has its drawbacks, as some in the profession note, not the least being that few outsiders know what the string of letters on a nurse's name badge actually mean.[51] But, overall, certification has been a good thing. It has increased the portability of nurses' skills, where a nationally recognized certificate is seen as a mark of distinction from Hartford to Honolulu. The growth of multistate licensing, enabling a nurse to live in one state and work in another (especially important for the growth of the telehealth industry), has also given nurses more geographic flexibility.

Perhaps more important, certification seems to have helped nurses feel better about their jobs and to have improved morale. In a 2000 survey, respondents talked of how certification enabled them to "experience personal growth," "feel more satisfied as a professional nurse," "feel more competent in my skills as a professional nurse," "be seen as a credible provider," "feel more accountable as a professional nurse," and "experience more confidence in my practice."[52]

Recognition among their colleagues, or public recognition—such as an awards ceremony or announcement in newspapers—was cited as a greater reward than financial benefits. Certification gave workers "autonomy" and "allowed them to assert control over their practice." "My employer offered no rewards for my certification," commented one respondent. "But I didn't do it for them. I sought certification because it was important for me."

Autonomy, control, and nonfinancial rewards are all familiar concepts to flight attendants. In a period of rapid change, could certification give the flight attendant profession the shot in the arm it needs?

The Safety Professional (Again)

In the aftermath of 9/11, flight attendants successfully pushed for federal certification, a goal they had been hoping to achieve for some fifty years. At a time when the public was being served up a plate of images centered upon the "nostalgic flight attendant," workers themselves were still insisting they were safety professionals even if, as my experience on Independence Air illustrated in chapter 3 suggests, it is sometimes an uphill battle.

Given the structural changes in the industry, it is unlikely that asserting their safety function will be enough to cement the job as a long-term career, as it once did in the 1970s. But airlines will always need flight attendants, and even if the time frame of the job has changed, it does not mean flight attendants cannot benefit from certification and continually stressing their safety professionalism. If it increases their self-confidence and transferable skills for when they leave the profession, so much the better. In restressing the job's safety aspects, enshrined in new federal safety certification, flight attendants can continue to shape their lives as best they can. To that end, bringing the occupation under the auspices of the Occupational Safety and Health Administration remains a laudable—and achievable—goal.

Formalizing the job's safety component could help offset the decline of its old lifestyle. It could make flight attendants, like nurses, more portable. Armed with such qualifications, they could become more geographically mobile, "spacing out" in a new sense, moving from carrier to carrier to search out the best terms and conditions. In fact, airlines may find their attacks on the power of seniority coming back to haunt them. Flight attendants used to be so obsessed with seniority that it acted as a brake on those wanting to switch airlines, because they would have to restart at the bottom of the ladder. Now, in a world with no company pensions and where seniority matters less, flight attendants have less to stay for. Airlines may find themselves in the paradoxical position of facing severe recruitment problems for their new short-term jobs. The only way to retain staff may be to raise wages, thus incurring all those costs that they had tried to get rid of. Lest this proposition be deemed far-fetched, the UK low-cost carrier easyJet provides a possible pointer to a more common future pattern. Having become one of Europe's leading new airlines, in summer 2006 the company found itself having to cancel flights due to a lack of cabin crew. Twenty percent of easyJet's 2,000 cabin crew leave annually, many for more attractive jobs at British Airways or Virgin Atlantic. EasyJet was left in the surreal position of recruiting on board its aircraft, asking bemused passengers if they would be "up for the challenge" of a career at the airline.[53]

Of course being more portable may not gel with family commitments, but new contract agreements, such as that recently signed at Alaska Airlines, have more generous provisions concerning leaves of absence. Workers can take off up to three years' unpaid leave while retaining seniority—which, notwithstanding my earlier arguments, still means something—and be guaranteed a job on their return.[54]

Continually stressing safety would also directly challenge the rise of the "nostalgic flight attendant." Though airlines may like to take hiring patterns back to the sixties and resurrect titillating images to boot, there is, in fact, no going back. Anyone who has sought out an old childhood haunt or taken a trip down memory lane knows that there is a point where nostalgia comes face-to-face with harsh reality. That is why it can be so painful. Women may be forced to sell their bodies again, using sexist imagery and chic uniforms. But they are doing so under different conditions and in a world that has, thankfully, changed much from the 1960s. In a symbolic twist, not long before I finished the manuscript for this book, Hooters Air stopped flying its scheduled service, though it remains in the air as a charter operation. It was losing too much money.

Women flight attendants will continue to fight for their rights, even in difficult circumstances. There is an assumption, for instance, that globalization means a lowering of standards and that overseas crews will somehow sell the profession short. In fact, when it comes to fighting for their rights, some of the most vociferous flight attendants—as the ITF's antisexism campaign suggested—can be found among the smiling, supposedly deferential Asian workers from the Pacific Rim. Cabin crew at Hong Kong's Cathay Pacific, for instance, who admittedly have never been a group to back down in a fight, are currently battling legislation that allows airlines based in the city to retire them at forty-five, when the retirement age for workers based elsewhere is fifty-five. Possibly they may resurrect what they considered a powerful weapon in a previous dispute: for one hour on each Cathay flight, their cabin crew would simply refuse to smile at the passengers.[55]

So long as there is a body on board as a representative of an airline, that body has power. In the skies of North America, workers are still rumbling with discontent: Northwest's flight attendants look set to dump their union in a 1970s-style coup d'état, and Delta's nonunion flight attendants are organizing a Committee of the 1000, aiming at reviving the union drive scuppered by management in the immediate aftermath of 9/11. Even United's flight attendants have not quite lost their spirit, registering anger at their own union as much as at the company that destroyed their pensions. Here is Rebecca, for instance, who settled quite happily at her new base and, despite everything United has thrown at its workforce, is still intent on dancing in the sky:

> I'm real excited about coming out of bankruptcy because I'm hoping that within the next couple of years we'll be able to start up another union because nobody is happy with AFA and what they do and what they quote-unquote fight for. They fight for all the wrong crap and not the important crap. They don't fight for things they can change. They only fight for things they can't change and then turn around and say, look, we tried. Bullshit.

Rebecca does not sound like a worker at the end of her tether. In her words I hear the ghosts of the Lowell mill girls who, in Massachusetts in 1834, struck for a better world. Indeed, more than ever, Rebecca sounds to me like a flight attendant. "So anyway," she continues, "I got off on a tangent. What were we talking about?"

Notes

NOTES TO THE INTRODUCTION

1. Amy's first name was Madeline, though to her friends she was always known as Amy. Tributes to all the flight attendants killed on 9/11 can be found at the Association of Flight Attendants Web site at http://www.afanet.org/memoriam/. Information here is also taken from Gail Sheehy, "Stewardess ID'd hijackers early, transcripts show," *New York Observer,* February 16, 2004. This online current affairs journal can be found at www.observer.com.

2. Audio recording and written transcript of Betty Ong's phone call can be found at the investigative Web site "The memory hole," at http://www.the memoryhole.org/911/911-ong-tape.htm.

3. Sheehy, "Stewardesses ID'd hijackers early."

4. See BBC News report, September 21, 2001, at "The last moments of Flight 11," http://news.bbc.co.uk/2/hi/americas/1556096.stm.

5. Philip Roth, *The Plot against America* (New York: Houghton Mifflin, 2004). See also Robert Wohl, *The Spectacle of Flight: Aviation and the Western Imagination 1920–1950* (New Haven, CT: Yale University Press, 2005), and Dominick Pisano, ed., *The Airplane in American Culture* (Ann Arbor: University of Michigan Press, 2003).

6. *The New Shorter Oxford English Dictionary* (1993) gives Greek etymology for "nostalgia": *nostos* (a homecoming) and *algos* (pain). Intertwined with Homer's *Odyssey*, nostalgia, for the Greeks, represented a sometimes-fatal condition of not being able to find one's home or familiar surroundings.

7. Fred Davis, *Yearning for Yesterday: A Sociology of Nostalgia* (New York: Free Press, 1979), 13.

8. All interviewee names are pseudonyms.

9. According to the Bureau of Labor Statistics, there were 115,750 flight attendants in 2001, up from 111,170 in 1998. The most recent figure available (2002) puts the number at 104,360.

10. Bruce Handy, "Glamour with attitude," *Vanity Fair,* October 2002, 215–227. See also Sandra Thompson, "A hip-filled flight experience recalls the days of in-flight elegance," *St. Petersburg Times,* November 29, 2003. See also David Graham, "Coffee, tea or me hardly the high life," *Toronto Star,* April 5,

2003; Steve Knopper, "Flight attendants' image is up in the air," *Chicago Metromix*, April 3, 2003; and Debra Waltman "Flight attendant longs for coffee, tea or milk," *Star Tribune*, March 27, 2002.

11. The quotation is taken from Barnes and Noble bookseller's Web site at www.barnesandnoble.com. Trudi Baker and Rachel Jones, *Coffee, Tea or Me? The Uninhibited Memoirs of Two Airline Stewardesses* (New York: Bartholomew House, 1967). In fact the book was written by Donald Bain, with the publisher originally employing two ex-Eastern fliers to front it on publicity tours. My thanks to Donald Bain for this information.

12. Ernestine Bradley, *The Way Home* (New York: Random House, 2005).

13. *Plane Crazy* official Web site, at http://planecrazynymf2005.com.

14. Aimée Bratt, *Glamour and Turbulence: I Remember Pan Am 1966–91* (New York: Vantage, 1996).

15. Most of the praise for *The Aviary* came from the same IP address, and Web site moderators discussed banning what appeared to be fee-free advertising.

16. Heather Healy, director, Employee Assistance Program, Association of Flight Attendants, interview by author, Washington, D.C., January 9, 2003.

17. "Airlines hope new fashions make financial statement," *USA Today*, July 6, 2005; Scott Kirsner, "Song's startup flight plan," *Fast Company* 71 (2003): 98–104.

18. Aliya Sternstein, "Unfasten your seat belts," *Forbes*, February 17, 2003, 52.

19. Amit Roy, "Jumbo at hand, Virgin eyes bedroom in the skies," *Telegraph*, January 19, 2005.

20. "Delta orders redesign of uniforms," *USA Today*, February 4, 2004.

21. "Airlines hope new fashions make financial statement." On the origins of Singapore Girl, see Ian Batey, *Asian Branding: A Great Way to Fly* (Singapore: Prentice Hall, 2002), 115–138. On airline branding in general, see Keith Lovegrove, *Airline: Identity, Design and Culture* (London: Laurence King, 2000).

22. "Singapore Airlines: A nice girl like you," Belgian video documentary, Evangelische Omroep, 1997.

23. Breanne L. Heldman, "Flight attendants see red," *New York Daily News*, April 28, 2005.

24. For an overall perspective on flight attendant imagery, see Johanna Omelia and Michael Waldock, *Come Fly with Us! A Global History of the Airline Hostess* (Portland, OR: Collectors Press, 2003).

25. Cate Corcoran, "Runway fashion," *Slate*, September 15, 2003, http://slate.msn.com/id/2088054. On JetBlue's uniform design, also see James Wynbrandt, *Flying High* (New York: Wiley, 2004), 184.

26. Suzanne Lee Kolm, "Who says it's a man's world? Women's work and

travel in the first decade of flight," in *The Airplane in American Culture,* ed. Dominick Pisano (Ann Arbor: University of Michigan Press, 2003), 147–164.

27. Tom Wolfe, *The Right Stuff* (New York: Bantam, 1979).

28. An exception to this was Helen Richey, who worked as a copilot for Central Airlines for ten months between 1934 and 1935.

29. To my knowledge, the only woman ever to head an airline is Barbara Cassani, who was put in charge of British Airways' low cost carrier, Go. U.S. airlines, especially in the formative years, tended to be headed by male egomaniacs, such as Howard Hughes (Transcontinental and Western), Juan Trippe (Pan Am), and Eddie Rickenbacker (Eastern). Carriers enshrined masculinity through the use of company newsletters that regularly presented men in technical roles. See Albert Mills, "Cockpits, hangars, boys and galleys: Corporate masculinities and the development of British Airways," *Gender, Work and Organization* 5 (1998): 172–188.

30. Kolm, "Who says it's a man's world?" Also see Georgia Panter Nielsen, *From Sky Girl to Flight Attendant* (Ithaca, NY: ILR Press, 1982); Paula Kane, *Sex Objects in the Sky* (Chicago: Follett, 1974).

31. Susan Faludi, *Backlash* (New York: Anchor, 1992).

32. In 2002, 39.2 percent of American Airlines (the largest carrier in terms of emplanements) passengers were women. See Airline Entertainment Technology "Sky Radio" Web site at www.skyradionet.com/mediakitaa.cfm.

33. "Fly Hooters Air," online forum, *Atlanta Journal-Constitution,* February 14, 2003; and subsequent "Should women fly Hooters Air?" Woman to Woman, *Atlanta Journal Constitution,* February 28, 2003, www.ajc.com/opinion/content/opinion/woman/archives.html.

34. Loe uses the wonderful pseudonym "Bazooms" in her ethnographic account of the restaurants. See Meika Loe, "Working for men at the intersection of power, gender and sexuality," *Sociological Inquiry* 66 (1996): 409.

35. Alex Waterfield, "Hooters Air is flying high," *Columbia News Service,* November 8, 2005. See also "Fly Brand X!" *Travel Weekly,* November 3, 2003, 70.

36. Global rankings on the Internet may need to be taken with a grain of salt, but a Skytrax cabin crew survey received more than 2 million nominations for a ten-month period between 2003 and 2004. Of the top ten airline cabin crew, ranked by passengers (ninety-three different nationalities), eight were Asian, one (Qatar Airlines) was from the Middle East, and one (Air Tahiti) was from Oceania. See http://www.airlinequality.com/2004/Staff_04.htm, August, 21, 2005.

37. Though female travelers are the fastest-growing group in the Asian-Pacific region, much of this growth is in the low-cost airline sector. Singapore International Airlines still places great stock in attracting business class passengers. On the changing Asia-Pacific market, see "Asian-Pacific travel set for more

growth in 2005," press release, Abacus International Travel Agents, www.aba-cus.com.sg, June 3, 2005.

38. At American Airlines, for example, high-revenue first-class and business class passengers continue to be overwhelmingly male (75 percent). See www.sky radionet.com/mediakitaa.cfm.

39. According to historian Katie Barry, "Men comprised anywhere between five to fifteen percent of the occupation from the 1930s to the 1970s and their enduring presence both hastened and complicated flight attendant activism." Kathleen Barry, "Femininity in Flight: Flight Attendants, Glamour, and Pink-Collar Activism in the Twentieth-Century United States" (Ph.D. diss., New York University, 2002), 8. Barry also argues that women stewardesses were content to let male stewards take the lead in union matters because they felt men would hold more authority in the eyes of management. Also see Cathleen Marie Doo-ley, "Battle in the Sky: A Cultural and Legal History of Sex Discrimination in the United States Airline Industry, 1930–1980" (Ph.D. diss., University of Ari-zona, 2001), 32–33.

40. In Alexandra Murphy's ethnographic research, she recounts a male flight attendant's complaints about how "people just assume that if you are a man, and you are in this job, you must be gay." She then describes how, once the man had gone, a woman flight attendant leaned over to inform her, "The truth is, al-most all the men that fly are gay, but I didn't want to say that in front of him because I am not sure if he is or not." "She continued," writes Murphy, "in her conspiratorial manner by telling me how 'straight' men handled their initial in-teractions with the crew. 'They will immediately point out some woman with big boobs; or tell a joke about gays. Or they will talk about their girlfriends.'" Alexandra Murphy, "Managing 'Nowhere': The Changing Organizational Per-formance of Air Travel" (Ph.D. diss., University of South Florida, 1998), 104.

41. Carl Solberg, *Conquest of the Skies* (Boston: Little, Brown, 1979), 335.

42. Airlines were more surprised at the number of male applicants in the early 1970s than by their sexuality.

43. Roberta Lessor points out an interesting difference in male pilot atti-tudes toward male flight attendants in the 1940s as opposed to the early 1980s. In the earlier period, pilots would prefer meals to be prepared by male stewards because they regarded meal preparation as skilled work. With rationalization of meal preparation, modern pilots were more likely to ask for "one for the girls" to be sent up to the cockpit. Women flight attendants generally welcomed the presence of male cabin crew, even if, in interviews I conducted, they were some-times welcomed as being "one of the girls." See Roberta Lessor, "Unanticipated Longevity in Women's Work: The Career Development of Airline Flight Atten-dants" (Ph.D. diss., University of California, San Francisco, 1982), 148–157. However, gay men's "acceptance" by U.S. crew may not be replicated else-where, as homophobia seems more common among Australian workers. See

Claire Williams, "Sky service: The demands of emotional labour in the airline industry," *Gender, Work and Organization* 10 (2003): 538–541.

44. Carol Herburger Pollard, "Sky Goddesses: the Cost of an Image" (master's thesis, Sonoma State University, 1991), 149.

45. See, for instance, Marcelle D'Argy Smith, "Sex after sixty-the last taboo?" *SAGA Magazine*, August 2004.

46. "Airlines hope new fashions make financial statement."

47. Handy, "Glamour with attitude," 215.

48. David Harvey, *The Condition of Postmodernity* (Oxford: Blackwell, 1989).

49. Elizabeth Rich, *Flying High: What It's Like to Be an Airline Stewardess* (New York: Stein and Day, 1972).

50. On flight attendant activism in the 1970s, see in particular Barry, "Femininity in Flight," and Frieda Shoenberg Rozen, "Turbulence in the Air: The Autonomy Movement in the Flight Attendant Unions" (Ph.D. diss., Pennsylvania State University, 1988). Also see Dorothy Sue Cobble, " 'A spontaneous loss of enthusiasm': Workplace feminism and the transformation of women's service jobs in the 1970s," *International Labor and Working Class History* 56 (1999): 23–44.

51. Pat Friend, president, Association of Flight Attendants–Communications Workers of America, telephone interview by author, March 16, 2003.

52. This trend was in full swing before 9/11. See Paul Blyton, Miguel Martinez, John McGurk, and Peter Turnbull, *Contesting Globalization: Airline Restructuring, Labour Flexibility and Trade Union Strategies* (London: International Transport Workers Federation, 1998).

53. Harriet Bradley, *Men's Work, Women's Work* (Cambridge: Cambridge University Press, 1989).

54. Jeremy Rifkin, *Time Wars* (New York: Simon and Schuster, 1989), 1.

55. The "working families" literature is dominated by time obsession, a good example being Phyllis Moen, ed., *It's about Time* (Ithaca, NY: ILR Press, 2003). Despite a chapter on journey to work issues, the work contains not a single map, suggesting that space is completely irrelevant.

56. Barbara Ehrenreich, *Nickle and Dimed* (New York: Metropolitan Books, 2001); Michael Ende, *Momo*, trans. J. Maxwell Brownjohn (Harmondsworth, UK: Penguin Books, 1984).

57. Juliet Schor, *The Overworked American* (New York: Basic Books, 1991), 150.

58. In chapter 10, "The Working Day," perhaps the core chapter of *Capital*, space never gets a look in. "What is a working day?" asks Marx. "What is the length of time during which capital may consume the labour-power whose daily value it has paid for?" Karl Marx, *Capital*, vol. 1, trans. Ben Fowkes (Harmondsworth, UK: Penguin Books, 1976), 375.

59. As Ernst Fischer writes, "The relationship between capitalist and worker presupposes a struggle from the outset: struggle for the *rate of surplus value,* i.e. the proportion of surplus labour-time to that labour-time necessary for the maintenance of labour-power—in other words, first and foremost, the length of the working day." Ernst Fischer, *Marx in His Own Words,* trans. Anna Bostock (Harmondsworth, UK: Pelican, 1973), 104.

60. E. P. Thompson, "Time, work discipline and industrial capitalism," *Past and Present* 38 (1967): 56–97.

61. For a theoretical exposition of probably the most important argument in geography of the last thirty years, see Harvey, *The Condition of Postmodernity;* Doreen Massey, *Space, Place and Gender* (Cambridge, UK: Polity Press, 1994); Ed Soja, *Postmodern Geographies* (London: Verso, 1989); Neil Smith, *Uneven Development* (Oxford: Blackwell, 1984).

62. Henri Lefebvre, *The Production of Space,* trans. Donald Nicholson-Smith, (Oxford: Blackwell, 1991).

63. "Air travel health news," a Web site run by Diana Fairechild, http://www.flyana.com/index.html, June 14, 2005.

64. In 1977, the *Vocational Guidance Quarterly* reported: "It appears that many of the [flight attendant] respondents chose this occupation because they perceived it as a facilitator toward a new and exciting style of life, at least for a certain period of time. It must be recognized that most entered the occupation knowing it would probably be a limited-duration commitment. Consequently, it is likely that many viewed being a flight attendant as a stage in life before settling down either in a permanent work position or as a housewife." H. Lytle Givens and Albeno P. Garbin, "Social-personal characteristics and occupational choice processes of female flight attendants," *Vocational Guidance Quarterly* 26 (1977): 121.

65. See Iris Marion Young, "Throwing like a girl: A phenomenology of feminine body comportment, motility and spatiality," in *Throwing Like a Girl and Other Essays in Feminist Philosophy and Social Theory,* ed. Iris Marion Young, 141–159 (Bloomington: Indiana University Press, 1990).

66. Susan Hanson and Geraldine Pratt, *Gender, Work and Space* (New York: Routledge, 1995).

67. American effectively "freezes" flight attendants' seniority if they are out on leave, so over time Amy Sweeney would have found her bidding power effectively eroded. My thanks to "Sluggo," an American flight attendant message board contributor for help with this point.

68. On burnout, see Joan Volpe, "Study of flight attendant subculture" (unpublished report prepared for Employee Assistance Program, Association of Flight Attendants, Washington, D.C., 1984); also W. Parker Nolen, "An Exploratory Study of Stress, Depression and Burnout in Flight Attendants" M.B.A. diss., Concordia University, 1996).

69. Madeline Amy Sweeney Award for Civilian Bravery 2005 Nomination Form, http://www.mass.gov/portal/site/massgovportal/menuitem.6d3b3f7541d7 31c14db4a11030468a0c/?pageID=eopsutilities&L=1&sid=Eeops&U=sweeney_ award_form.

70. "Madeline 'Amy' Sweeney, The Final Call," paid notice in the *Boston Globe,* http://www.legacy.com/bostonglobe/Sept11.asp?Memorial=AA11&Page =TributeFullText&PageNo=4.

71. Arlie Russell Hochschild, *The Managed Heart,* 2nd ed. (Berkeley: University of California Press, 2003). The book was originally published in 1983.

72. Claire Williams, *Blue, White and Pink Collar Workers in Australia* (London: Allen and Unwin, 1988).

73. Differing airlines have differing names given to flight attendants' alumnae organizations. United Clipped Wings began in 1941, American's Kiwi Club in 1952, and Eastern's Silverliners International in 1954. Helen McLaughlin, *Footsteps in the Sky* (Denver: State of the Art Press, 1994), 312–315.

74. Lessor, "Unanticipated Longevity in Women's Work," 56.

75. Perhaps the best starting point for postmodernism is one of the original essays written on it by Frederic Jameson, "Postmodernism, or the cultural logic of late capitalism," *New Left Review* 146 (1984): 53–92.

76. Marshall Berman, *All That Is Solid Melts into Air* (New York: Verso, 1983).

77. Historically speaking, women from the 1920s onward found new communities in shop work and restaurant work. See Frances Donovan, *The Saleslady* (Chicago: University of Chicago Press, 1929); Dorothy Sue Cobble, *Dishing It Out* (Urbana: University of Illinois Press, 1991); and Susan Porter Benson, *Counter Cultures* (Urbana: University of Illinois Press, 1986).

78. Heather Healy, interview.

79. Dooley, "Battle in the Sky," 20.

80. Divorce rates in the industry run at about 20 percent. Heather Healy, interview.

81. Interviews were semistructured. Some of the focus groups were conducted in conjunction with Bobbie Sullivan, an independent research psychologist based in Hawaii, and the owner of AircrewHealth.com.

82. Interviewees fell into two groups. Between October 2002 and February 2005, I conducted single interviews with any flight attendant expressing a willingness to speak to me, irrespective of whether he or she was still working. Given the difficulty in pinning down this group of workers, I made no attempt to achieve a scientific statistical cross section of the flight attendant population. Interviewees would often be friends of friends, who would then recommend their own flight attendant colleagues. That said, I did end up interviewing a broad section of workers, ranging in age from their twenties to their seventies. I spoke mainly to women, though also to more than ten men. I spoke to married,

divorced, widowed, and single flight attendants. The majority were white, though several were black. A few were openly gay. Most interviews lasted for approximately an hour and were conducted at the attendant's home, in a café, or occasionally on the telephone.

Second, I did repeat interviews, two or three, with a handful of working flight attendants over the same period, but adding a final round of interviews in February 2006. Among this group were parents, junior fliers (whom I thought were underrepresented), and senior fliers who had seemed to me particularly perceptive in their analysis of change in the industry. In strict methodological terms, I realize this last group moved from being "subjects" to "informational experts," but this to me seemed less important than getting up-to-date information from people inside the job.

I additionally grabbed what opportunities I could to talk informally with flight attendants working on the fifty-odd flights I took since starting the project in 2002. However, I was keenly aware of intruding on flight attendants and would attempt to talk to them only if the flight was long or if it was half empty. As a man, for a start, I was wary of approaching women workers, especially if wanting to talk about balancing home, work, marriage, and children and so on. I always told them up front that I was writing a book or doing research and tried to have my business card ready.

All names have been replaced by aliases in this book. British crew came from British Airways, Britannia, Monarch, Virgin Atlantic, and easyJet (the latter two interviewed in 2000). Flight attendants in the United States had also worked at the following now-defunct carriers: PSA, Pan American, People Express, Trans World, Braniff, Western, Northeast, Republic, and Flying Tigers.

NOTES TO CHAPTER I

1. Vida Hurst, *Air Stewardess* (New York: Grosset and Dunlap, 1934). 12. I would like to acknowledge the perceptive essay by Chrissie Brodigan, a graduate student at George Mason University, that alerted me to this work. See Chrissie Brodigan, "Flying girls, super sleuths and sex goddesses: The transformation and disappearance of the airborne heroine from popular fiction," http://chnm.gmu.edu/cabinandcrew/essays/heroines/index.html.

2. Barbara Dorger, *Turbulent Skies: Run-away Thoughts from a Senior Flight Attendant* (n.p.: Xlibris, 2004), 23.

3. Bayla Singer, *Like Sex with Gods: An Unorthodox History of Flying* (College Station: Texas A&M University Press, 2003).

4. This story was reprinted in *Scientific American* 283 (2000): 12.

5. Marshall McLuhan, *Understanding Media* (London: Routledge and Kegan Paul, 1964).

6. Eileen Lebow, *Before Amelia: Women Pilots in the Early Days of Aviation* (Washington, DC: Brassey's, 2002). 162.

7. Ibid., 6.

8. Though she eschewed the term "feminist," Earhart obviously saw the world through a gendered lens. For instance, in her autobiography she placed the blame for women being held back in aviation and society at large on the education system, which "goes on dividing people according to their sex, and putting them in little feminine or masculine pigeonholes." Amelia Earhart, *The Fun of It* (Chicago: Academy Press, 1977), 143–144.

9. Margery Brown, quoted Claudia M. Oakes, *United States Women in Aviation 1930–39* (Washington, DC: Smithsonian Institution Press, 1985), 4.

10. Deborah Douglas, *American Women and Flight since 1940* (Lexington: University Press of Kentucky, 2004), 176.

11. McLaughlin, *Footsteps in the Sky,* 86

12. For a summary of various accounts of Church's approach to Stimpson, see Nielsen, *From Sky Girl to Flight Attendant,* 8–10.

13. Suzanne Lee Kolm, "Women's Labor Aloft: A Cultural History of Airline Flight Attendants in the United States, 1930–1978" (Ph.D. diss., Brown University, 1995), 64–65.

14. McLaughlin, *Footsteps in the Sky,* 14.

15. Nielsen, *From Sky Girl to Flight Attendant,* 8. In her doctoral dissertation, Katie Barry notes how historians often slighted Church's role in crafting the stewardess occupation, with one book claiming that Stimpson got "his [*sic*]" idea from a "girl friend." Barry, "Femininity in Flight," 52n35.

16. Omelia and Waldock, *Come Fly with Us!* 12.

17. Kolm disputes the argument that a timid stewardess would give male passengers heart. However, her sources for this claim come from 1937 onward, by which time initial fears about aviation had surely subsided. Kolm, "Women's Labor Aloft," 47–50.

18. Hochschild, *The Managed Heart,* 7.

19. Kolm, "Who says it's a man's world?" 149–150.

20. Women made this argument when defending apparently "unequal" treatment in labor conditions, especially when they benefited from legislation at state level. As a consequence, many working-class women opposed any move toward an equal rights amendment. See Dorothy Sue Cobble, *The Other Women's Movement* (Princeton, NJ: Princeton University Press, 2004), 60–66

21. *Safety and Accommodation in European Passenger Planes No. 3* (New York: Daniel Guggenheim Fund for the Promotion of Aeronautics, 1928).

22. Omelia and Waldock, *Come Fly with Us!* 18.

23. W. David Lewis and Wesley Phillips Newton, *Delta: The History of an Airline* (Athens: University of Georgia Press, 1979), 72.

24. Birdie Bomar and Kathryn Bankston, *Birdie* (n.p.: 1st Books, 2002), 127–157.

25. Ibid., 156.

26. McLaughlin, *Footsteps in the Sky*, 19.

27. Robert Serling, *The Only Way to Fly: The Story of Western Airlines, America's Senior Air Carrier* (Garden City, NY: Doubleday, 1976), 151.

28. Brodigan, "Flying girls, super sleuths and sex goddesses."

29. None of the Original Eight was flying by the time of introduction of the Douglas DC-3 workhorse in 1936. See Nielsen, *From Sky Girl to Flight Attendant*, 15.

30. Kolm, "Who says it's a man's world?" 150.

31. Omelia and Waldock, *Come Fly with Us!* 25.

32. B. R. Mitchell, *International Historical Statistics: The Americas, 1750–1988*, 2nd ed. (New York: Stockton, 1993), 589, 593.

33. Nielsen, *From Sky Girl to Flight Attendant*, 30.

34. Bomar and Bankston, *Birdie*, 260–261.

35. Before the war a handful of carriers experimented with "non-nurses" as stewardesses and found them to be up to the challenge of passenger service. Barry, "Femininity in Flight," 67.

36. Douglas, *American Women and Flight since 1940*, 33.

37. The RLA was part of an attempt to prevent a nationally strategic industry collapsing as the result of a strike. Harry Rissetto, "The National Mediation Board and the Railway Labor Act in the 1990s," in *Airline Labor Relations in the Global Era*, ed. Peter Capelli (Ithaca, NY: ILR Press, 1995), 116–128.

38. Nielsen, *From Sky Girl to Flight Attendant*, 22–28.

39. However, in the late 1950s Delta Air Lines lost no time in stressing the speed of its jet service in comparison to Eastern's turboprops. Lewis and Newton, *Delta*, 278.

40. Frieda Rozen, "Technological advances and increasing militance: Flight attendant unions in the jet age," in *Women, Work and Technology*, ed. Barbara Drygulski Wright (Ann Arbor: University of Michigan Press, 1987), 225.

41. Ibid., 226.

42. Omelia and Waldock, *Come Fly with Us!* 59.

43. Kolm, "Who says it's a man's world?" 158.

44. Airlines continually liked to boast about their role in preparing the future wives of America and reveled in the notion that young women joined the profession in search of a husband. In fact, right from the start, some women disputed this. In 1938, one stewardess declared in the journal *Popular Aviation*, "Just because a third of hostesses and stewardesses resign during a single year to be married does not mean that all of us sit on a perch in the sky waiting for Dan Cupid to soar by and take a pot shot at us with his 'poison' arrow." Quoted in Barry, "Femininity in Flight," 98.

45. Drew Whitelegg, "From smiles to miles: Delta Air Lines and southern hospitality," *Southern Cultures* 11 (2005): 9–29.

46. Lewis and Newton, *Delta*, 95.

47. Delta Air Lines, *Annual Report* (1956), penultimate page (no page numbers).

48. Alice Cook, "Introduction," in *From Sky Girl to Flight Attendant*, xviii.

49. Kolm, "Women's Labor Aloft," 133–148.

50. Irene Zimmerman, "Language occupations: The airline hostess," *Modern Language Journal* 34 (1950): 227.

51. Omelia and Waldock, *Come Fly with Us!* 55.

52. Nielsen, *From Sky Girl to Flight Attendant*, 94.

53. Drew Gilpin Faust, "Clutching the chains that bind: Margaret Mitchell and *Gone with the Wind*," *Southern Cultures* 5 (1999): 8.

54. My thanks to Marie Force, of Delta Air Lines Heritage Museum, for unearthing these figures.

55. Whitelegg, "From smiles to miles," 10.

56. Barry, "Femininity in Flight," 170.

57. Cobble, *The Other Women's Movement*, 76.

58. "Stewardesses map TWA jet walkout," *New York Times,* October 10, 1959.

59. In 1968, annual resignations amounted to about 30 percent of the workforce. In 1978 it amounted to about 3 percent, with average job tenure now seven years. M. Smolensky, E. Lee, D. Mott, and M. Colligan, "A health profile of American flight attendants," *Journal of Human Ergology* 11, Suppl., (1982): 104.

60. Cobble, *The Other Women's Movement*, 76.

61. Douglas, *American Women in Flight since 1940*, 159.

62. Mitchell, *International Historical Statistics*, 593.

63. John Nance, *Splash of Colors: The Self-Destruction of Braniff International* (New York: William Morrow, 1984), 32.

64. Lovegrove, *Airline*, 22.

65. Laura Jacobs, "Stewardess," *2wice*, Fall 1998, http://www.2wice.org/issues/uniform/stew.html.

66. Nance, *Splash of Colors*, 35.

67. Excerpt from Braniff International hostess recruitment brochure, http://www.braniffinternational.org/image/braniffhostessnew.htm.

68. Holiday Dmitri, "Reviving high culture," *Chicago Criterion*, May 2003.

69. Omelia and Waldock, *Come Fly with Us!* 102–103. The television advertisement can be found in "Tailspin," Enterprise Series Video, 1983.

70. Nance, *Splash of Colors*, 36.

71. Omelia and Waldock, *Come Fly with Us!* 106. The television advertisement can be found on "The Lipstick Years: Fly Me," BBC documentary, 2000.

72. "Summer stewardess uniform," *Delta Digest,* May 1969, 2.

73. Omelia and Waldock, *Come Fly with Us!* 91.

74. Kevin Freiburg and Jackie Freiburg, *Nuts: Southwest Airlines' Crazy Recipe for Business and Personal Success* (New York: Broadway, 1998).

75. Lamar Muse, *Southwest Passage: The Inside Story of Southwest Airline's Formative Years* (Austin, TX: Eakin Press, 2002), 82–83. In fact, PSA claimed the same thing.

76. Southwest's culture should *not* imply that the airline skimps on safety. It does not. Its safety record, with only one (nonfatal) crash in thirty years (a runway overshoot at Burbank), is second to none.

77. Louise Taylor, "Stewardesses, stereotypes and air rage," *Aviation Safety International* 4, no. 3 (1999): 6.

78. Ibid., 7.

79. http://planecrazynymf2005.com/.

80. Rich, *Flying High,* 25.

81. Baker and Jones, *Coffee, Tea or Me?* back cover.

82. Ibid., 133

83. Elizabeth Moles and Norman Friedman, "The airline hostess: Realities of an occupation with a popular cultural image," *Journal of Popular Culture* 7 (1973): 309.

84. Kane, *Sex Objects in the Sky,* 13.

85. National Airlines former flight attendant Web site, http://www.national sundowners.com/images/70/parting_shots_large.jpg.

86. Omelia and Waldock, *Come Fly with Us!* 82.

87. Kolm, "Women's Labor Aloft," 183–188.

88. Rozen, "Technological advances and increasing militance," 230.

89. Dooley, "Battle in the Sky," 137–145. Union activist Barbara "Dusty" Roads tells a nice story in this respect. Turning up at the local EEOC office, she and her sister flight attendants filed the first grievance. "We walked in and looked around at a sea of black faces," she says. "This woman came up to us, two blondes in stewardess uniforms, and she said 'What are you doing here?' And I said, we have a problem. She said, 'You're white, you're free and you're 21. What is it?' I said, 'Honey, sit down, I got a long story to tell you." "Interview with Barbara 'Dusty' Roads," *Peoples Century: Half the People,* http://www.pbs.org/wgbh/peoplescentury/episodes/halfthepeople/roadstranscript.html.

90. Kathleen Heenan "Fighting the 'Fly Me' airlines," *Civil Liberties Review* 150 (December 1976–January 1977): 58.

91. Cook, "Introduction," xxii.

92. Cobble, *The Other Women's Movement,* 77.

93. C. J. Blanc, R. Digo, and P. Moroni, "Psychopathology of airline stewardesses," *Aerospace Medicine* 40 (1969): 187.

94. Nielsen, *From Sky Girl to Flight Attendant,* 101.

95. Cook, "Introduction," xxi–xxii.

96. Cobble, *The Other Women's Movement,* 208.

97. Dooley, "Battle in the Sky," chap. 5.

98. Nielsen, *From Sky Girl to Flight Attendant,* 18–20.

99. Ibid., 19.

100. Lewis and Newton, *Delta,* 357.

101. Dooley, "Battle in the Sky," 223.

102. Cobble, *The Other Women's Movement,* 209.

103. In *United Airlines, Inc. v. McDonald,* 432 U.S. 385 (1977), flight attendants eventually won their eighteen-year-old lawsuit in 1986, which reinstated 475 attendants, with a further $37 million back-pay settlement for 1,725 flight attendants.

104. On the Diaz case, see Barry, "Femininity in Flight," 480–499, and Dooley, "Battle in the Sky," 178–187. Airlines unintentionally raise the stakes by falling back on the bona fide occupational qualification (BFOQ) clause to the Civil Rights Act. Essentially, the clause stated that a commercial enterprise could reserve an occupation for one gender if it could demonstrate that it was in its economic interests to do so (and that it would otherwise suffer commercially). In striking down the airlines' BFOQ defense, the appeals court effectively ruled that the profession could not be limited to women.

105. Rozen, "Technological advances and increasing militance," 230.

106. Ibid., 232.

107. Roberta Lessor, "Social movements, the occupational arena and changes in career consciousness: The case of women flight attendants," *Journal of Occupational Behavior* 5 (1984): 37–51.

108. Kolm, "Who says it's a man's world?" 155.

109. Douglas, *American Women and Flight since 1940,* 161.

110. "SCLC threatens boycott: Delta gets ultimatum," *Atlanta Constitution,* September 3, 1970.

111. Muse, *Southwest Passage,* 103.

112. See Jacqueline Agesa, "The Impact of Deregulation on Racial and Gender Employment: The Case of the Airline Industry" (Ph.D. diss., University of Wisconsin–Milwaukee, 1996).

113. Nielsen, *From Sky Girl to Flight Attendant,* chap. 5.

114. Ibid., 115.

115. Mark L. Khan, "Airlines," in *Collective Bargaining: Contemporary American Experience,* ed. Gerald Somers (Madison, WI: Industrial Relations Research Association, 1980), 325.

116. Peter Capelli and Timothy Harris, "Airline union concessions in the wake of deregulation," *Monthly Labor Review,* conference papers, June 1985, 38.

117. "Air stewardesses fight weight rule," *New York Times,* March 4, 1972.

118. AlexSandra Lett and Harold Silverman, "Coffee, tea and dignity: Knocking down employment barriers 37,000 feet up," *Perspectives: The Civil Rights Quarterly* 12 (1980): 8.

119. Dooley, "Battle in the Sky," 322–345.

120. Ibid., 233.

121. Elizabeth Bailey, David Graham, and Daniel Kaplan, *Deregulating the Airlines* (Cambridge, MA: MIT Press, 1985).

122. Thomas Petzinger, *Hard Landing* (New York: Random House, 1995).

123. Avishai Gil, "Air transport deregulation and its implications for flight attendants," *International Labour Review* 129 (1990): 323. This is not to suggest airlines have no control over oil price fluctuations. Southwest, for example, has long kept its fuel costs low through successful hedging.

124. "A candid conversation with David Garrett," *Delta Digest*, June 1983, 4.

125. Petzinger, *Hard Landing,* 147

126. Gil, "Air transport deregulation and its implications for flight attendants," 324.

127. Peter Capelli, "Competitive pressures and labor relations in the airline industry," *Industrial Relations* 24 (1985): 333.

128. Capelli and Harris, "Airline union concessions in the wake of deregulation," 38.

129. O. Robinson, "Employment policy and deregulation in European air transport," *Service Industries Journal* 14 (1994): 15.

130. International Transport Workers Federation, *The Globalisation of the Civil Aviation Industry* (Geneva: ITF, 1992), 40.

131. J. Gallacher and M. Odell, "Airline alliances: Tagging along," *Airline Business,* July 1994, 25–42.

132. Drew Whitelegg, "Delta Air Lines 1970–1995: Sowing the seeds of globalization," *Transportes, Servicios y Telecomunicaciones* 6 (2004): 98–99.

133. Doug Cameron, "People movers," *Airline Business*, March 1997, 50–51.

134. I gained this impression during interviews with Virgin Atlantic workers in the United Kingdom, as well as Delta workers in the United States.

135. International Transport Workers Federation, *The Globalisation of the Civil Aviation Industry.*

136. Yet at the same time, with globalization, flight attendants at Asian airlines have embarked on such battles. See Drew Whitelegg, "Cabin pressure: The dialectics of emotional labour in the airline industry," *Journal of Transport History* 23 (2002): 73–86; Stephen Linstead, "Averting the gaze: Gender and power on the perfumed picket line," *Gender, Work and Organization* 2 (1995): 192–206.

137. Lessor, "Social movements, the occupational arena and changes in career consciousness," 48.

1. Cobble, *The Other Women's Movement,* 72.
2. James P. Spradley and David W. McCurdy, *The Cultural Experience* (Chicago: Science Research Associates, 1972), 193.
3. Such experts are often senior flight attendants and charge between ten and twenty dollars.
4. Some also receive "base" pay, a nominal retainer, while those staying overnight receive a per diem. This latter payment can be significant because it is not taxed. According to Suzie, an ASA flier, it "adds up to be a nice chunk of change when you are gone for three and four days a week. It's what I live on. I pay my bills on my hourly rate and per diem is what I live on."
5. I came to appreciate this point when trying to set up interviews. "Call me back after bidding" was a common refrain, with numerous flight attendants suggesting they could not make any plans until they had got their bids sorted out.
6. Flight attendants from smaller carriers pepper message boards such as flightattendant.org with requests for interview tips from colleagues at larger ones. The posting "HELP! I GOT AN INTERVIEW AT AMERICAN!" by "ASA Fly-Girl" is typical. Even very senior flight attendants at ASA are restricted in their movements because of the carrier's limited network. There are no "high time" lines comparable to, say, an American Airlines return trip from Dallas to Paris.
7. Airline histories sometimes resemble complex family trees. Since 1970, for instance, Delta has merged with Northeast and Western, bought part of Pan Am, bought ASA, started Song, sold ASA, and gone bankrupt.
8. Kiki Ward, *The Essential Guide to Being a Flight Attendant* (n.p.: Kiwi Productions, 2002), 32.
9. Alyce Desrosiers and Arthur C. Emlen, "Airlines, flight attendants and dependent care" (unpublished manuscript, Portland State University, 1997), 9.
10. Out of respect for their confidence, I will not disclose any of the schemes used.
11. Jeffrey E. Hill, Alan J. Hawkins, Maria Ferris, and Michelle Weitzman, "Finding an extra day a week: The positive influence of perceived job flexibility on work and family life balance," *Family Relations* 50 (2001): 49–55.
12. Quoted in Maggie Jackson, "The ultimate guide to flexibility," *Working Mother,* September 2004, 42. During the 2004 presidential election, Bush told an Ohio crowd, "I think the government ought to allow employers to say to an employee, 'If you want some time off, and work different hours, you're allowed

to do so.'" Janet Hook and Peter Wallsten, "President pushes flextime," *Los Angeles Times*, August 6, 2004.

13. Lonnie Golden, "Flexible work schedules: What are we trading off to get them?" *Monthly Labor Review* 124, no. 3 (2001): 8.

14. Pollard, "Sky Goddesses," 148–149.

15. Lessor, "Social movements, the occupational arena and changes in career consciousness," 44.

16. This is exactly how time and motion theory is applied in the workplace. Each task is designated a fixed time value.

17. Playing pranks is a part of the profession. See Jack Santino, "A servant and a man, a hostess or a woman: A study of expressive culture in two transportation industries," *Journal of American Folklore* 99 (1986): 304–319.

18. I have yet to find a satisfactory explanation for why the UK system did not incorporate seniority. It may have been a combination of more antagonistic union-management relations and the fact that the vast majority of UK cabin crew flew international (and therefore longer) trips, meaning less choice was available to crew.

19. "Flight attendants complain about Burns' comment," *Billings Gazette*, October 26, 2005.

20. Shelley Coverman, "Role overload, role conflict and stress: Addressing consequences of multiple role demands," *Social Forces* 67 (1989): 965–982.

21. In a post-9/11 survey conducted by the AFA, 45 percent of respondents said they had dependents. Of these, 60 percent had children, 20 percent aging relatives or parents, and 20 percent both; 61 percent claimed to be responsible for their dependents on a daily basis. Heather Healy, interview. A 1997 study put the number of flight attendants with dependent care responsibilities at 55 percent; 43 percent had children under eighteen. Desrosiers and Emlen, "Airlines, flight attendants and dependent care," 10.

22. Judith Long Laws, "Work aspiration of women: False leads and new starts," in *Women and the Workplace,* ed. Martha Blaxall and Barbara Reagan (Chicago: University of Chicago Press, 1976), 35.

23. Balancing work and family has spawned its own cottage research industry in recent years. See, for instance, Anita Garey, *Weaving Work and Motherhood* (Philadelphia: Temple University Press, 1999); Angela Hattery, *Women, Work and Family* (Thousand Oaks, CA: Sage, 2001); Barbara Schneider and Linda Waite, eds., *Being Together, Working Apart* (Cambridge: Cambridge University Press, 2005); and Joan Williams, *Unbending Gender* (New York: Oxford University Press, 2001).

24. This is not to suggest other workers have it easy. For example, see Blanche Grosswald, "'I raised my kids on the bus': Transit workers' coping strategies for parenting," *Journal of Sociology and Social Welfare* 29 (2002): 29–50.

25. There are parallels here with the night-shift nurses Anita Garey interviewed, where women continued to support a construction of motherhood through being "around" when they *are* needed. Anita Garey, "Constructing motherhood on the night shift: 'Working mothers' as 'stay-at-home moms,'" *Qualitative Sociology* 18 (1995): 415–433.

26. Harriet Presser observes how families where parents are engaged in shift work attempt to arrange their schedules to minimize child care costs. Harriet Presser, "Shift work among American women and child care," *Journal of Marriage and the Family* 48 (1986): 551–563.

27. Split-shift parenting, or tag teaming, is an increasing phenomenon in the United States in general. See Laura Pappano, "Tag team," *Working Mother,* August 2001, 44–48.

28. Angela J. Hattery, "Tag-team parenting: Costs and benefits of utilizing nonoverlapping shift work in families with young children," *Families in Society* 82 (2001): 419–427.

29. Hattery, *Women, Work and Family.*

30. Desrosiers and Emlen, "Airlines, flight attendants and dependent care," 15.

31. There is a methodological point here in the sense that those I interviewed are, inevitably, the "success" stories. Those workers who could not cope fell through the cracks and off the radar screen when it comes to research. To my knowledge, neither carriers nor unions track former workers and their reasons for leaving.

32. As Hochschild puts it, "In this new model of family and work life, a tired parent flees a world of unresolved quarrels and unwashed laundry for the reliable orderliness, harmony, and managed cheer of work." Arlie Russell Hochschild, *The Time Bind* (New York: Metropolitan, 1997), 44. Hochschild's conception of work as haven has not been without its critics. See, for instance, William Bielby, "Firm commitments," *Contemporary Sociology* 27 (1998): 32–34.

33. Sara Ruddick, "Care as labor and relationship," in *Norms and Values,* ed. Joram G. Haber and Mark S. Halton (New York: Rowman and Littlefield, 1998), 15.

34. John Gillis, *A World of Their Own Making: Myth, Ritual and the Quest for Family Values* (Cambridge, MA: Harvard University Press, 1997).

35. Matthew Wald, "Nothing but gray skies . . . ," *New York Times,* March 6, 2006.

36. Edna R. Fiedler, Pam Della Rocco, David J. Schroeder, and Kiet T. Nguyen, *The Relationship between Aviator's Home-Based Stress to Work Stress and Self-Perceived Performance* (Oklahoma City: Civil Aeromedical Institute, Federal Aviation Administration, 2000).

37. "Stress and Flight Crew," http://www.theairlinepilots.com/medical/stress andflightcrew.htm, December 27, 2005.

38. The training group was for commercial flight attendants wanting to convert to corporate flying. All were current flight attendants at U.S. airlines. Held at Alteon Headquarters, Long Beach, California, January 24, 2005.

39. Cindy Krischer Goodman, "Traveling moms need Olympian organizational skills," *Miami Herald,* January 18, 2006.

40. In their study of Australian flight attendants, Jupp and Mayne argue that "attendants who were to separate from their partners on tours of duty also experienced increased distress during the 12 hours or so before departing on tours." J. Jupp and P. Mayne, "Flying apart: Separation stress in female flight attendants," *Australian Psychologist* 27 (1992): 157.

41. Hochschild, *The Time Bind,* 3.

42. Goodman, "Traveling moms need Olympian organizational skills."

43. Heather Healy, interview.

44. Volpe, "Study of flight attendant subculture," 9.

45. Hochschild, *The Managed Heart,* chap. 7.

46. Ibid., 110.

47. See, for instance, M. P. Filby, " 'The figures, the personalities and the bums': Service work and sexuality," *Work, Employment and Society* 6 (1992): 23–42.

48. See, for instance, Gilles Deleuze and Felix Guattari, *Anti-Oedipus: Capitalism and Schizophrenia,* trans. Robert Hurley, Mark Seem, and Helen Lane (Minneapolis: University of Minnesota Press, 1983).

49. Volpe, "Study of flight attendant subculture," 11.

NOTES TO CHAPTER 3

1. Details of the crash come from flight attendant Kaye Chandler's Web site, www.twaflight843.com.

2. The first officer was piloting the aircraft at the time and turned control over to the captain, who had precisely one second to decide whether to abort takeoff.

3. A similarly successful evacuation occurred in July 2005 when an Air France A340 skidded off the runway when landing at Toronto. All 297 passengers and twelve crew were evacuated. Fire destroyed the A340.

4. "Factual report of investigation," unpublished report, National Transportation Safety Board, Office of Aviation Safety, 1992.

5. Associated Press, "Ex-TWA workers say goodbye to American," April 30, 2003.

6. This division breaks down along traditional gender lines. As sociologist Nicky James argues, "There exists a distorting, divisive conceit through which men are associated positively with rational thought and action while women are negatively associated with emotional reaction. This false distinction facilitates a

gender division of labor through which men's labor is understood to be central to the creation of value, while women's work is considered peripheral." Nicky James, "Emotional labor: Skill and work in the social regulation of feelings," *Sociological Review* 37 (1989): 39–40.

7. Robert Besco, "Flight attendants: Aviation's under-recognized safety resource," *Flight Safety Foundation: Cabin Crew Safety* 26, no. 2 (1991): 2.

8. In the 1970s, flight attendants placed "being a safety agent" first when ranking activities associated with their jobs in terms of importance. They placed "cocktail service" last. Mary Carylene Stuckey, "The Determinants of Occupational Cynicism among Female Flight Attendants" (master's thesis, Southern Methodist University, 1977), 47.

9. Corylee Spiro and Elizabeth Harwell, *Cabin Pressure* (New York: St. Martin's Press, 1989), 182.

10. Joann Kuzma Deveny, *99 Ways to Make a Flight Attendant Fly—Off the Handle!* (Edina, MN: Beaver's Pond Press, 2003), 1.

11. Such concerns merged with a growing occupational health movement. See Lessor, "Social movements, the occupational arena and changes in career consciousness," 44–46.

12. Pat Friend, interview.

13. Bomar and Bankston, *Birdie,* 158.

14. Barry, "Femininity in Flight," 187n79.

15. Even carriers with good safety records, such as Hong Kong's Cathay Pacific, refuse to discuss the matter. Stephen Barlay, *Cleared for Take-Off* (London: Kyle Cathie, 1994), 35.

16. Ironically, the increase in crash survivability due to better-built airplanes makes flight attendants more critical for passenger safety, according to the NTSB. National Transportation Safety Board, *Flight Attendant Training and Performance during Emergency Situations,* Special Investigation Report, NTSB/SIR-92/02 (Washington, DC: NTSB, 1992).

17. Volpe "Study of flight attendant subculture," 11.

18. Atle Dyregrov, Anders Skogstad, Odd Hellesoy, and Liv Haughli, "Fear of flying in civil aviation personnel," *Aviation, Space, and Environmental Medicine* 63 (1992): 834.

19. Rebecca Chute and Earl Weiner, "Survey of flight personnel focuses on safety implications of intracrew communication," *ICAO Journal,* June 1996, 11.

20. "Strategies target turbulence-related in injuries to flight attendants and passengers," *Flight Safety Foundation: Cabin Crew Safety* 36, no. 1 (2001): 3.

21. "10 percent flight attendant injury rate higher than construction (8.8 percent), mining (4.8 percent)," *Transport News,* June 16, 2000, www.transport news.com/Articles/127440.

22. "Strategies target turbulence-related in injuries to flight attendants and passengers," 2.

23. Nattanya Andersen, *Broken Wings: A Flight Attendant's Journey* (Coquitlam, BC: Avia, 1997), 59.

24. These details are taken from the official NTSB report summary, www .ntsb.gov/ntsb/ brief2.asp?ev_id=20001208X07126&key=1.

25. Dyregrov et al, "Fear of flying in civil aviation personnel," 834.

26. Carol Boyd and Peter Bain, "Once I get you up there, where the air is rarified: Health, safety and the working conditions of airline cabin crews," *New Technology, Work and Employment* 13, no. 1 (1998): 24.

27. Rebecca Chute and Earl Weiner, "Cockpit and cabin crews: Do conflicting mandates put them on a collision course?" *Flight Safety Foundation: Cabin Crew Safety* 29, no. 2 (1994): 2.

28. Omar Barayan, "The case for upgrading cabin crew status," *Flight Safety Foundation: Cabin Crew Safety* 25, no. 5 (1990): 2.

29. Southwest encouraged new cabin crew to sit in the cockpit on trips to see how pilots worked. Delta, meanwhile, incorporated flight attendants into its Crew Resource Management (CRM) programs. See Anders Skogstad, Atle Dyregrov, and Odd Hellesoy, "Cockpit-cabin crew interaction: Satisfaction with communication and information exchange," *Aviation, Space and Environmental Medicine* 66 (1995): 841–847.

30. Given the sensitive nature of this subject, I have changed the name of the city destination and withheld both airline name and flight attendant's alias name.

31. Lawrence Salinger, Paul Jesilow, Henry Pontell, and Gilbert Geis, "Assaults against airline flight attendants: A victimization study," *Transportation Journal* 23 (1985): 66–71.

32. Blake Morrison, "FAA seldom punishes violence," *USA Today,* December 5, 2001.

33. Andrew Thomas, *Air Rage: Crisis in the Skies* (Amherst, NY: Prometheus, 2001), 23.

34. Mark Gottdiener, *Life in the Air: Surviving the New Culture of Air Travel* (Oxford: Rowman and Littlefield, 2001), 94–95; "FAA, pilots and flight attendants propose measures to reduce passenger interference with cabin crews," *Flight Safety Foundation: Cabin Crew Safety* 32, no. 3 (1997): 1.

35. Statement of Captain Stephen Luckey, Chairman, National Security Committee, ALPA, to Subcommittee on Aviation Committee on Transportation and Infrastructure, U.S. House of Representatives, June 11, 1998, http://cf.alpa .org/internet/tm/tmo61198.htm.

36. Claire Williams, "A pain in the neck: Passenger abuse, flight attendants and emotional labour," *Journal of Occupational Health Safety—Australia, New Zealand* 16 (2000): 434.

37. T. J. Ballard, P. Romito, L. Lauria, V. Vigiliano, M. Caldora, C. Mazzanti, and A. Verdecchia, "Self-perceived health and mental health among

women flight attendants," *Occupational and Environmental Medicine* 63 (2006): 37.

38. Hochschild, *The Managed Heart*, 171–172.

39. Taylor, "Stewardesses, stereotypes and air rage," 9.

40. Hochschild, *The Managed Heart*, 110–111.

41. International Transport Workers Federation, *Air Rage: The Prevention and Management of Disruptive Passenger Behaviour* (London: ITF, 2000), 3.

42. Ibid., 17.

43. Morrison, "FAA seldom punishes violence."

44. Ibid.

45. Ibid.

46. Ibid.

47. BBC News, September 1, 1998, http://news.bbc.co.uk/1/hi/uk/162805.stm.

48. International Transport Workers Federation, *Air Rage*.

49. Angela Dahlberg, *Air Rage: The Underestimated Safety Risk* (Aldershot, UK: Ashgate, 2001), 143.

50. Quoted in Ralph Nader and Wesley Smith, *Collision Course: The Truth about Airline Safety* (Blue Ridge Summit, PA: TAB Books, 1994), 87–88.

51. Telephone conversation with Lonnie Glover, APFA safety spokesperson. July 14, 2005.

52. "Growing pains at Valujet," *Business Week*, May 15, 1995.

53. Thomas Lawton, *Cleared for Take Off: Structure and Strategy in the Low Fare Airline Business* (Aldershot, UK: Ashgate, 2002), 140.

54. Jane Goodman, "ValuJet: The roots of a tragedy," *Flightlog*, Winter 1996, 6–7; Michael Fumento, "Flight from reality: The ValuJet cover-up," *New Republic*, October 7, 1996.

55. Aviation Safety Protection Act, H.R. 3187, U.S. House of Representatives Committee on Transportation and Infrastructure, Subcommittee on Aviation, Washington, D.C., July, 10, 1996, 24.

56. Ibid., 13, 46.

57. Ibid., 47.

58. Barry Glassner, *The Culture of Fear: Why Americans Are Afraid of the Wrong Things* (New York: Basic Books, 1999), 197.

59. On particular problems faced by shift workers, see C. Czeisler, M. Johnson, J. Duffy, E. Brown, J. Ronda, and R. Kronauer, "Exposure to bright light and darkness to treat physiologic maladaption to night work," *New England Journal of Medicine* 322 (1990): 1253–1259.

60. Sakari Suvanto, Markku Partinen, Mikko Harma, and Juhani Ilmarinen, "Flight attendants' desynchronosis after rapid time zone changes," *Aviation, Space and Environmental Medicine* 61 (1990): 543–7.

61. M. Vejvoda, A. Samel, H. Maass, N. Luks, A. Linke-Hommes, M. Schulze, L. Mawet, and H. Hinninghofen, "Untersuchunger zur Beanspruchung

des Kabinpersonals auf transmeridianen Strecken" (unpublished manuscript, German Centre for Air and Space Study, Cologne, 2000), 1.

62. Arne Lowden and Torbjorn Akerstedt, "Sleep and wake patterns in aircrew on a 2-day layover on westward long distance flights," *Aviation Space and Environment* 69 (1998): 596–602.

63. Written testimony of Cheryle Leon, President of Association of Professional Flight Attendants, and on behalf of the Coalition of Flight Attendant Unions. Flight Attendant Duty Time Limitations (102–3), hearing before the Subcommittee on Aviation of the Committee on Public Works and Transportation, House of Representatives, 101st Cong., 1st sess., on H.R.14, to amend the Federal Aviation Act of 1958 to provide for the establishment of limitations on the duty time for flight attendants, March 13, 1991, 169.

64. "American Airlines flight attendants discuss the dangers of fatigue with members of congress," APFA Press Release, April 21, 2004.

65. Dave Guerriero, "Duty time limitations: Is it 14 or 15 hours?" http://www.afausairways.org/mec/dutytime.html.

66. A. Hagihara, K. Tarumi, and K. Nobutomo, "The number of steps taken by flight attendants during international long-haul flights," *Aviation, Space and Environmental Medicine* 72 (2001): 937.

67. P. Reynolds, J. Cone, M. Layefsy, D. Goldberg, and S. Hurley, "Cancer incidence in California flight attendants (United States)," *Cancer, Causes and Control: CCC* 13 (2002): 317–324.

68. F. W. Cope, "Idiopathic menstrual disorders in airline stewardesses: A possible origin from solar radiation of heavy magnetic particles," *International Journal of Biometeorology* 25 (1981): 219–221; R. Iglesias, A. Terres, and A Chavarria, "Disorders in the menstrual cycle in airline stewardesses," *Aviation, Space and Environmental Medicine* 51 (1980): 518–520; Elizabeth Whelan, Barbara Grajewski, Emily Wood, Lorna Kwan, Mimi Nguyen, Teresa Schnorr, Edwin Knecht, and James Kesner, "Feasibility issues in reproductive biomonitoring of female flight attendants and teachers," *Journal of Occupational and Environmental Medicine* 44 (2002): 947–955.

69. Paul Scholten, "Pregnant stewardess: Should she fly?" *Aviation, Space and Environmental Medicine* 47 (1976): 77–81; Rafael Aspholm, Marja-Liisa Lindbohm, Harri Paakkulainen, Helena Taskinen, Tuula Nurminen, and Aila Tiitinen, "Spontaneous abortions among Finnish flight attendants," *Journal of Occupational and Environmental Medicine* 41 (1999): 486–491. Also see J. Cone, L. M. Vaughn, A. Huete, and S. Samuels, "Reproductive health outcomes among female flight attendants: An exploratory study," *Journal of Occupational and Environmental Medicine* 40 (1998): 210–216.

70. Boyd and Bain, "Once I get you up there," 19.

71. "10 percent flight attendant injury rate higher than construction (8.8 percent), mining (4.8 percent)," press release posted on risk analysis Web site,

Riskworld, June 16, 2000, at www.riskworld.com/pressrel/2000/00q2/pr00a180 .htm.

72. Press release issued by AFA at http://www.afanet.org/legislative/default .asp?id=13.

73. "Flight attendants file suit against federal agencies," AFA-CWA press release, September 19, 2005.

74. "Report says emergency training for US cabin crew sometimes deficient," *Flight Safety Foundation: Cabin Crew Safety* 27, no. 5 (1992): 1.

75. Pat Friend, interview.

76. J. G. Ballard, book review of Robert Wohl, *The Spectacle of Flight: Aviation and the Western Imagination, 1920–1950, Guardian Weekly,* June 3–9, 2005, 26.

77. "Cabin crews must capture passengers' attention in predeparture safety briefings," *Flight Safety Foundation: Cabin Crew Safety* 35, no. 4 (2000): 1.

78. Independence Air press release, Dulles, Virginia, June 14, 2004. In fact research suggests that passengers do not pay attention during safety briefings because they are unaware how important they really are. If anything, such briefings should be far more serious. See Sue Knight and Nick Butcher, "Planning prevents conflict between cabin service and safety," *Flight Safety Foundation: Cabin Crew Safety* 34, no. 6 (1999): 5.

79. A synopsis of safety recommendations suggested flight attendants should display "appropriate eye contact and body language should reinforce the spoken message" and "personal enthusiasm for the subject during every safety briefing," neither of which seemed prevalent on Independence Air. "Cabin crews must capture passengers' attention in predeparture safety briefings," 10.

80. Independence Air home page, http://www.flyi.com/careers/default.aspx.

NOTES TO CHAPTER 4

1. Alex Waterfield, "Hooters Air is flying high," www.azcentral.com/php-bin/clicktrack/print.php?referer=http://www.azcentral.com, November 8, 2005.

2. Internet discussion forum "Airlines with attractive flight attendants," at http://www.airliners.net/discussions/aviation_polls/read.main/65081/a#50 (accessed on November 15, 2005).

3. Loe, "Working for men at the intersection of power, gender and sexuality," 399–421.

4. Jeremy Boren, "One man's Hooters vacation," *Pittsburgh Tribune Review,* February 28, 2005.

5. Jeff Sonderman, "Will new approach fly?" *The Times-Tribune* (Scranton), October 23, 2005. Airport subsidies to airlines are not unusual. Tallahassee Airport recently subsidized Air Tran for two years to the tune of more than $3 million, and the airline discontinued service one year after the subsidy elapsed.

6. "Hooters Air weighs London flights," *Myrtle Beach Sun News,* August 6, 2005.

7. Ibid.

8. For a discussion of this evolution, see Rosemarie Tong, *Feminist Thought: A Comprehensive Introduction* (Boulder, CO: Westview Press, 1989).

9. Shulamith Firestone, *The Dialectic of Sex* (New York: Quill, 1970); Mary Daly, *Beyond God the Father* (Boston: Beacon Press, 1973).

10. Whether gender inequality is best analyzed through patriarchy or capitalism (or both) is a major debate for feminists. See, for example, Anna Pollert, "Gender and class revisited; or the poverty of 'patriarchy,'" *Sociology* 30 (1996): 639–659. Journals such as *Body and Society* and *Gender, Place and Culture,* both launched in the mid-1990s, illustrate how, "from being under-researched and under-theorized, the body has now become central." Kathryn Backett-Milburn and Linda McKie, "Constructing gendered bodies," in *Constructing Gendered Bodies,* ed. Kathryn Backett-Milburn and Linda McKie (New York: Palgrave, 2001), xvii.

11. Michel Foucault, *Discipline and Punish,* trans. A. Sheridan (New York: Vintage, 1977), 201.

12. Naomi Wolf, *The Beauty Myth* (New York: Anchor, 1992).

13. Melissa Tyler and Philip Hancock, "Flight attendants and the management of gendered 'organizational bodies,'" in *Constructing Gendered Bodies,* ed. Kathryn Backett-Milburn and Linda McKie (New York: Palgrave, 2001), 35. See also Melissa Tyler and Pamela Abbott, "Chocs away: Weight watching in the contemporary airline industry," *Sociology* 32 (1998): 433–450; Melissa Tyler and Steve Taylor, "The exchange of aesthetics: Women's work and 'The Gift,'" *Gender, Work and Organization* 5 (1998): 165–171; Steve Taylor and Melissa Tyler, "Emotional labor and sexual difference in the airline industry," *Work, Employment and Society* 14, no. 1 (2000): 77–95.

14. S. Bordo, "Anorexia nervosa: Psychopathology as the crystallization of culture," in *Feminism and Foucault,* ed. I Diamond and L. Quinby (Boston: Northeastern University Press, 1988), 87–117; Judith Butler, *Gender Trouble* (New York: Routledge, 1990).

15. Doris Lessing, *The Summer before the Dark* (New York: Knopf, 1973), 60, 62.

16. In the 2004 remake, the character played by Nicole Kidman complains, "These women are like deranged flight attendants."

17. Blanc, Digo, and Moroni, "Psychopathology of airline stewardesses," 187.

18. Barry, "Femininity in Flight," 512.

19. Quoted in Lessor, "Unanticipated Longevity in Women's Work," 132; emphasis in original.

20. Kolm, "Women's Labor Aloft," 254.

21. Dooley, "Battle in the Sky," 124.

22. Before she was hired at "Bazooms," Loe had to sign a form accepting that, "In a work atmosphere based upon sex appeal, joking and innuendo are commonplace." Loe, "Working for men at the intersection of power, gender and sexuality," 400.

23. Kane, *Sex Objects in the Sky*, 28.

24. *National Reporter*, November, 1965, 7, quoted in Dooley, "Battle in the Sky," 118.

25. Kolm, "Women's Labor Aloft," 233.

26. Barry, "Femininity in Flight," 509.

27. Dooley, "Battle in the Sky," 122.

28. Cobble, *The Other Women's Movement*, 210.

29. Barry, "Femininity in Flight," 552.

30. Kathleen Barry, "Pink-collar feminism in full bloom: Flight attendant activism in the 1970s" (paper presented at the annual conference of the British Association of American Studies, Cambridge, UK, April 2005).

31. Dooley, "Battle in the Sky," 127.

32. Batey, *Asian Branding*, 120.

33. It was the first airline to sign up for the A380 superjumbo, soon to grace the skies with some 700 passengers.

34. Stephen Holloway, *Airlines: Managing to Make Money* (Aldershot, UK: Ashgate, 2002), 112.

35. Justin Doebele, "The Engineer," *Forbes*, http://www.forbes.com/business/global/2005/1226/034A.html, December 26, 2005.

36. Rohit Deshpande and Hal Hogan, "Singapore Airlines: Customer service innovation," *Harvard Business Online*, July 22, 2003.

37. Dean Visser, "Singapore Airlines flies on charms of its 'girls' into more crowded skies," *Advertising Age International*, Special Issue: Asia, October 1997, 9.

38. Louis Kraar, "Flying high with the 'Singapore Girls,'" *Fortune*, June 18, 1979, 132.

39. David Forward, "Super Star: Singapore Airlines adds sparkle to Star Alliance," *Airways*, August 2000, 42.

40. Batey, *Asian Branding*, 121.

41. Edward Said, *Orientalism* (New York: Vintage, 1979).

42. Peter Pae, "Carrier aims to stay above rivals," *Los Angeles Times*, March 25, 2006.

43. Batey, *Asian Branding*, 121.

44. Evi Mariani, "It's not easy being an SIA Singapore Girl," *Jakarta Post*, May 5, 2005.

45. Murray Hiebert, "A nice girl like you," *Far Eastern Economic Review* 158, no. 49 (1995): 79.

46. "Singapore Airlines: A nice girl like you," Belgian video documentary.

47. Hiebert, "A nice girl like you," 79.

48. Ibid.

49. International Transport Workers Federation, *Civil Aviation Review,* 1997, 15.

50. S. Cheng, "Cathay wants to unseat Singapore as pacesetter in passenger service," *Advertising Age International,* October 1997, 9; recruitment page, Cathay Pacific, www.catheypacific.com/insidecx/careers/body_attendant.html.

51. "Chastity as job prerequisite," *Fortune,* June 29, 1992.

52. Jim O' Rourke, "Crew baby rule has union up in arms," www.smh.com .au/cgi-bin/common/popupPrintarticle.pl?path=/articles/2004/01/10.

53. Emirates Air recruitment page, http://www.emiratesgroupcareers.com; Qatar Airways application guide, http://www.qatarairways.com/?jobsearch& section=cabincrew.

54. Blyton et al., *Contesting globalization.*

55. Singapore Airlines: A nice girl like you."

56. Shane Enright, International Transport Workers Federation, Civil Aviation Section, and Sarah Finke, Women's Section, joint interview conducted by author, London, August 15, 2000.

57. Stephen Linstead, "Averting the gaze: Gender and power on the perfumed picket line," *Gender, Work and Organization* 2 (1995): 192–206.

58. Shane Enright and Sarah Finke, joint interview.

59. "The global fight against airline sexism," *Flightlog,* Summer 1997, 7.

60. Hooters Air home page, http://www.hootersair.com/about/advantages/.

61. Susan Spano, "Hooters Air gimmick appears to be just skin deep," *Los Angeles Times,* June 1, 2003.

62. Waterfield, "Hooters Air is flying high."

63. "Vigilance in aircraft galley and service procedures preserves margin of safety," *Flight Safety Foundation: Cabin Crew Safety* 34, no. 1 (1999): 1.

64. Continental Airline home page, http://www.continental.com/company/ career/flightattendant.asp.

65. Southwest Airlines home page, http://www.southwest.com/careers/flight_ attendant.html.

66. Dooley, "Battle in the Sky," 112.

67. Ibid., 314.

68. Ibid., 326. Carol Pollard noted how many of her interviewees used the term "parent-child management" to describe relations with the company. Pollard, "Sky Goddesses," 74.

69. UK workers report similar experiences of eating disorders and stress over weight checks. See Tyler and Abbott, "Chocs away," 444.

70. I have changed the airline and city in this story and removed the flight attendant's alias.

71. Kathleen M. Barry, "Lifting the weight: Flight attendants' challenges to enforced thinness," *Iris* 38 (1999): 54.

72. In 1980, a divided U.S. Court of Appeals for the Fourth Circuit found in favor of Eastern Airlines' grounding of a flight attendant after the thirteenth week of pregnancy; a year later, the Ninth Circuit Court supported Pan Am's decision to ground workers as soon as they found out they were pregnant. See Nielsen, *From Sky Girl to Flight Attendant*, 96–98.

73. Dooley, "Battle in the Sky," 344.

74. Lessor, "Unanticipated Longevity in Women's Work," 123.

75. Tyler and Abbott, "Chocs away," 440–441.

NOTES TO CHAPTER 5

1. John Van Maanen and Stephen R. Barley, "Occupational communities: Culture and control in organizations," *Research in Organizational Behavior* 6 (1984): 295.

2. Robert D. Putnam, *Bowling Alone* (New York: Simon and Schuster, 2000). Hochschild, in *The Time Bind,* argued that work and home had become inverted in terms of both relaxation and levels of social capital. On the development of workplace rituals cementing "family-style" management, see Charles Jandreau, "Social rituals and identity creation in a middle class workforce," Working Paper 014–02, Emory Center for Myth and Ritual in American Life, Atlanta, 2002. The family metaphor in the workplace is not new in itself—especially in the South, companies have used it for at least 100 years.

3. As Kolm observes, flight attendants even shared similar geographic backgrounds. At American Airlines, in 1941, three states accounted for one-third of the entire stewardess corps of more than 275. Kolm, "Women's Labor Aloft," 95–96.

4. Flight attendant Marjorie Howe, quoted in ibid., 81.

5. Rozen, "Turbulence in the Air," 105.

6. Murphy, "Managing 'Nowhere,'" 60.

7. Heather Healy, interview.

8. Ibid.

9. Cobble, *The Other Women's Movement,* 210.

10. "Betty," quoted in Phillip Neil Quisenberry, "Glamour and Glitter: The Social Construction of Enviable Careers" (master's thesis, University of South Florida, 1992), 36.

11. Murphy, "Managing 'Nowhere,'" 116–117, 136.

12. Carrie Leigh Haise and Margaret Rucker, "The flight attendant uniform: Effects of a selected variable on flight attendant image, uniform preference and employee satisfaction," *Social Behavior and Personality* 31 (2003): 565–576.

13. Ibid., 572.

14. Barbara De Lollis, "Airlines hope new fashions make financial statement," *USA Today*, July 8, 2005.

15. Alexandra G. Murphy, "Hidden transcripts of flight attendant resistance," *Management Communication Quarterly* 11 (1998): 522.

16. Ibid.

17. Hochschild, *The Managed Heart*, 7.

18. Lessor, "Unanticipated Longevity in Women's Work," 208.

19. Ward, *The Essential Guide to Becoming a Flight Attendant*, 95–96.

20. Rich, *Flying High*, 71.

21. Hochschild, *The Managed Heart*, 25.

22. Terri Ballard, Laura Corradi, Laura Lauria, Clelia Mazzanti, Giulia Scaravelli, Federica Sgorbissa, Patrizia Romito, and Arduino Verdecchia, "Integrating qualitative methods into occupational health research: A study of women flight attendants," *Occupational and Environmental Medicine* 61 (2003): 163–166.

23. Whitelegg, "From smiles to miles."

24. Arlie Russell Hochschild, "Smile Wars," *Mother Jones* 8 (1983): 36.

25. Hochschild, *The Managed Heart*, 105–106.

26. Ayn Rand, founder of the school of objectivism, through her novels *The Fountainhead* and *Atlas Shrugged*, seemed to reduce every human interaction to a calculated ego-boosting operation.

27. Cas Wouters, "The sociology of emotions and flight attendants: Hochschild's *Managed Heart*," *Theory, Culture and Society* 6 (1989): 117. See also Sharon Bolton and Carol Boyd, "Trolley dolly or skilled emotion manager? Moving on from Hochschild's *Managed Heart*," *Work, Employment and Society* 17 (2003): 289–308.

28. Bolton and Boyd, "Trolley dolly or skilled emotion manager?" 298.

29. Petzinger, *Hard Landing*, 465.

30. Mark Blacklock, "US unions fight back," *Airline Business*, December 1993, 16.

31. Gwen Ifill, "Strike at American Airlines; Airline strike ends as Clinton steps in," *New York Times*, November 23, 1997.

32. *Newsweek*, December 6, 1993.

33. Petzinger, *Hard Landing*, 466.

34. Judy Mann, "Coffee, tea and solidarity," *Washington Post*, November 26, 1993, E3.

35. Petzinger, *Hard Landing*, 467–468.

36. Sandra L. Albrecht, " 'We are on strike!' The development of labor militancy in the airline industry," *Labor History* 45 (2004): 113.

37. Del Jones, "Strike Gives Industry the Shivers," *USA Today*, November 23, 1993.

38. Mann, "Coffee, tea and solidarity."

NOTES TO CHAPTER 6

1. Brighton was famous for its *two* piers. The East Pier is the main pier, while the West Pier stood derelict since 1975. Part of it collapsed into the sea in December 2002 before a fire ravaged what was left four months later.

2. Scholar Afra Botteri distinguishes between "distance-oriented flights" and "exit-oriented flights." Flight attendants prefer the former, which are often international, because they are "not only more interesting but they provide flight attendants with more autonomy within the rules and standards established by the organization." The latter, short-haul, multidestination routes, by contrast, resemble "work on an assembly line." Afra Botteri, "The Occupational Status of Airline Flight Attendants" (master's thesis, Concordia University, 1979), 150.

3. Lessor, "Unanticipated Longevity in Women's Work," 59.

4. Linda McDowell, *Gender, Identity and Place* (Cambridge, UK: Polity Press, 1999), 206.

5. Massey, *Space, Place and Gender.*

6. Dolores Hayden, *Redesigning the American Dream* (New York: Norton, 1984).

7. Gill Valentine, "Women's fear and the design of public space," *Built Environment* 16 (1990): 288–303; Mona Domosh and Joni Seager, *Putting Women in Place* (New York: Guilford Press, 2001).

8. Hanson and Pratt, *Gender, Work and Space.*

9. Roselaub Coser, "Stay home, little Sheba: On placement, displacement and social change." *Social Problems* 22 (1975): 470–480.

10. Whitelegg, "From smiles to miles."

11. Berman, *All That Is Solid Melts into Air.*

12. Quoted in Christine Yano, "Airborne dreams: Japanese American flight attendants and the development of global tourism" (paper presented at the University of Hawaii, November 30, 2005), 20.

13. Hanson and Pratt, *Gender, Work and Space,* 20.

14. Bratt, *Glamour and Turbulence,* 20–22.

15. Rich, *Flying High,* 25.

16. Domosh and Seager, *Putting Women in Place,* 118.

17. Young, "Throwing like a girl," 147.

18. Drew Whitelegg, "Places and spaces I've been: Geographies of female flight attendants in the United States, *Gender, Place and Culture* 12 (2005): 257.

19. Japanese American flight attendants joining Pan Am from 1955 onward also embraced foreign cities enthusiastically. Yano, "Airborne dreams," 9–10.

20. Nielsen, *From Sky Girl to Flight Attendant,* 102.

21. Rich, *Flying High,* 22.

22. Daniel Boorstin, *The Image* (Harmondsworth, UK: Penguin Books, 1962); Jameson, "Postmodernism."

23. Lessor, "Unanticipated Longevity in Women's Work," 60.

24. Ray Oldenburg, ed., *Celebrating the Third Place* (New York: Marlowe, 2001).

NOTES TO CHAPTER 7

1. Research at the Center for Everyday Life at UCLA suggests that in dual-earning couples, the mom returns home before dad 72 percent of the time. Panel presentation by Elinor Ochs, Emory Center for Myth and Ritual, "Myths of the Family" Conference, Emory University, March 31, 2006.

2. Ballard et al., "Integrating qualitative methods into occupational health research," 164.

3. Chad Childers, "Dating the Flight Attendant," http://cannibal.mi.org/~chad/dating_the_fa.html.

4. Volpe, "Study of flight attendant subculture," 12.

5. See, for instance, M. J. Saxton, J. S. Phillips, and R. N. Blakeney, "Antecedents and consequences of emotional exhaustion in the airline reservations sector," *Human Relations* 44 (1991): 583–602.

6. Ballard et al., "Integrating qualitative methods into occupational health research," 164.

7. J. K. W. Morris, R. C. Taylor, D. Clark and K. McCann, "Oil wives and intermittent husbands," *British Journal of Psychiatry* 147 (1985): 479–483.

8. Rita Rigg and Martin Cosgrove, "Aircrew wives and the intermittent husband syndrome," *Aviation, Space and Environmental Medicine* 65 (1994): 654. The authors conducted research in Hong Kong and freely admit that the perhaps peculiar dynamics of the ex-patriot community there may reduce their findings' usefulness when applied to other countries.

9. Jupp and Mayne, "Flying apart," 157

10. Ballard et al., "Integrating qualitative methods into occupational health research," 164.

11. Rich, *Flying High,* 57.

12. Ballard et al., "Self-perceived health and mental health among women flight attendants," 37.

13. Leslie A. MacDonald, James A. Deddens, Barbara A. Grajewski, Elizabeth A. Whelan, and Joseph J. Hurrell, "Job stress among female flight attendants," *Journal of Occupational and Environmental Medicine* 45 (2003): 706.

14. Harriet Presser, "Shift work and child care among young dual-earner American parents," *Journal of Marriage and the Family* 50 (1998): 133–148.

15. Diane E. Levy, Gary L. Faulkner, and Richard D. Dixon, "Work and family interaction: The dual career of the flight attendant," *Humboldt Journal of Social Relations* 11. no. 2 (1984): 78.

16. R. C. Barnett and Y. C. Shen, "Gender, high- and low-schedule-control

housework tasks, and psychological distress," *Journal of Family Issues* 18 (1997): 403–428.

17. Francine Deutsch, "Halving it all: The mother and Mr. Mom," in *Families at Work: Expanding the Bounds,* ed. Naomi Gerstel, Dan Clawson, and Robert Zussman (Nashville, TN: Vanderbilt University Press, 2002), 129.

18. Gillis, *A World of Their Own Making.*

19. See, for instance, Marshall Duke, Robyn Fivush, Amber Lazarus, and Jennifer Bohanek, "Of ketchup and kin: Dinnertime conversations as a major source of family knowledge, family adjustment and family resilience," Working Paper 26, Emory Center for Myth and Ritual in American Life, 2003.

20. Seventy-seven percent of dual-earning families eat one dinner together a week. Elinor Ochs, "Myths of the Family" panel presentation.

21. Deutsch, "Halving it all," 130.

22. The airplane in question was an Embraer EMB 120 Brasilia. Nine of the 29 passengers were killed when ASA Flight 529 crashed near Carrolton, Georgia, on August 21, 1995, en route from Atlanta to Biloxi.

NOTES TO CHAPTER 8

1. Barbara S. Peterson, *bluestreak* (New York: Portfolio, 2004), 113.

2. http://www.unitedafa.org/cmt/gv/loc_emails.asp. See also Steve Daniels, "Errant email sparks latest UAL labor row," http://www.chicagobusiness.com/cgi-bin/news.pl?id=18883 (both accessed on March 10, 2006).

3. Daniels, "Errant email sparks latest UAL labor row."

4. David Leonhardt, "Costs are important, but revenue is crucial," *New York Times,* December 6, 2002.

5. Jeff Bailey, "United Airlines plans to hire 2000 flight attendants," *New York Times,* November 11, 2005.

6. "United Airlines receives tremendous response to flight attendant recruitment, suspends applications," press release, United Airlines, November 16, 2005.

7. Bailey, "United Airlines plans to hire 2000 flight attendants."

8. Story on United on Market Place, WABE Atlanta, April 3, 2006.

9. Doug Cameron, "Lean and mean," *Airline Business,* October 1992, 50–53.

10. Thomas Kochan, Andrew von Nordenflycht, Robert McKersie, and Jody Hoffer Gittell, "Out of the ashes: Options for rebuilding airline labor relations" (unpublished paper, Massachusetts Institute of Technology), http://web.mit.edu/airlines/www/conferences/DC-2003/documents/08-DC2003-kochan2.pdf 2003.

11. Jon Bonné, "Airlines still struggle with paths to profit," MSNBC www.msnbc.msn.com/id/3670292/ December 12, 2003.

12. Delta Air Lines, *Finding a Better Way: Quick Reference Guide for Delta Flight Attendants,* 2003, 19, internal in-flight services pamphlet.

13. Ibid., 17.

14. According to Lakoff, "cognitive models derive their fundamental meaningfulness directly from their ability to match up with preconceptual structure. Such direct matchings provide a basis for an account of truth and knowledge." George Lakoff, *Women, Fire, and Dangerous Things* (Chicago: University of Chicago Press, 1987), 303.

15. APFA hotline message from President Tommie Hutto-Blake, http://www.apfa.org/public/hotline/072205.html, July 22, 2005.

16. IAM questions and answers, http://www.iamd1142.org/fa/Contract2005/QA.htm#33, January 11, 2006.

17. "United concealed that changes to retiree health care were likely," AFA-CWA Press Release, March 18, 2004; Matt Kempner, "Flying under Chapter 11: Delta pensions could be at risk," *Atlanta Journal-Constitution*, September 18, 2005.

18. Russell Grantham, "Delta to overhaul pension plan," *Atlanta Journal-Constitution*, November 19, 2002.

19. Susan Clarke, "Changes may shrink nest eggs," *Orlando Sentinel*, January 5, 2003.

20. In fact, 9/11 helped the airline "discover its brand identity," according to one member of its marketing team. Jonah Bloom, "Sky-high marketing excellence," *Advertising Age*, http://www.adage.com/news.cms?newsId=36736#, December 12, 2002.

21. Wynbrandt, *Flying High*, 159.

22. Peterson, *bluestreak*, 113.

23. Jonathan Tasini, "Airline employees up in the air," *Houston Chronicle*, November 27, 2004.

24. Out of respect for privacy, I shall not disclose on which flight attendant Web site this appeared.

25. Peterson, *bluestreak*, 115–116.

26. Kristen Corey, Deborah Galvin, Marcia Cohen, and Alan Bekelman, "The impact of the 9/11 attack on flight attendants: A study of an essential first responder group" (unpublished paper for Association of Flight Attendants, Washington, DC, 2003).

27. Francine Parnes, "For flight attendants, stress comes with the job," *New York Times*, August 12, 2003; Barbara De Lollis, "Job stress beginning to take toll on some airline workers," *USA Today*, December 2, 2004.

28. MacDonald et al., "Job stress among female flight attendants," 703.

29. Philippa Gander, De Nguyen, Mark Rosekind, and Linda Connell, "Age, circadian rhythms, and sleep loss," *Aviation, Space and Environmental Medicine* 64 (1993): 189–195.

30. Kristen Tagami, "The lure of open skies," *Atlanta Journal-Constitution*, January 5, 2005.

31. "Industry is rebounding, FAA says," *Air Transport World,* March 26, 2004.

32. Flight Safety Foundation editorial, "Flight attendants who work alone need specialized training at regional airlines," *Flight Safety Foundation: Cabin Crew Safety* 33, no. 3 (1999): 2. Of course, some regional airline fliers—as at least two told me—enjoy flying alone and do so by choice.

33. JetBlue in-flight crew recruitment page, https://jetblue.recruitmax.com/ ENG/candidates/default.cfm?szCategory=jobprofile&szOrderID=14092&sz-CandidateID=0&szSearchWords=&szReturnToSearch=1.

34. "Airline makes trolley dollies swim for their jobs," *Ananova,* www .ananova.com/news/story/sm_1537361.html, September 15, 2005.

35. Chancal Pal Chauhan, "Shape up or ship out, A-I crew told," *Hindustan Times,* December 14, 2005.

36. "Aer Lingus staff memo acknowledged by airline," www.finfacts.com/ irelandbusinessnews/ publish/printer_10002677.shtml, July 20, 2005.

37. Mark Todd, "Cabin crew flying after victory over Virgin Blue," *The Age,* October 11, 2005; Michael Blackley, "Virgin Blue discriminated against older hostesses for 'young blondes,'" *Scotsman,* October 11, 2005; Julie Bourke, "Are we having fun yet? Age discrimination in recruitment," www.cch.co.au, October 12, 2005.

38. "Plane clothes investigation," *CNN Online News* edition, cnn.com/ 2006/TRAVEL/ 01/19/fashion.uniform/index.html, January 19, 2006.

39. Russell Grantham, "Delta's Song all tuned up for battle," *Atlanta Journal Constitution,* November 9, 2003.

40. Cate T. Corcoran, "Runway fashion," *Slate.*

41. "Song to be folded into Delta lines," *CNN Money,* October 31, 2005.

42. This story was passed on to me by someone well connected with United.

43. Ellen Heuven and Arnold B. Bakker, "Emotional dissonance and burnout among cabin attendants," *European Journal of Work and Organizational Psychology,* 12 (2003): 93.

44. Ibid.

45. This letter made the rounds on the flight attendant message boards, but its content—and sense of outrage on the part of flight attendants—was picked up by the national media. See Joe Sharkey, "Coffee, tea and fatigue: Airline job loses its allure," *New York Times,* April 20, 2004.

46. Manik Mehta, "Flight attendants' jobs are being outsourced to India," *Bernama,* September 11, 2005.

47. Monarch Airlines recruitment page, http://www.flymonarch.com/cnt/ careers/cabincrew.asp.

48. Arthur Miller, *Death of a Salesman* (Harmondsworth, UK: Penguin Books, 1949), 112.

49. Toni Inglis, "Nursing the trends," *American Journal of Nursing* 104, no. 1, Suppl. (2004): 28.

50. Susan Trossman, "What do credentials mean to you?" *American Journal of Nursing* 102, no. 5 (2002): 71.

51. Mary Smolenski, "Playing the credentials game," http://community .nursingspectrum.com/MagazineArticles/article.cfm?AID=22004.

52. Ann Cary, "Certified registered nurses: Results of the study of the certified workforce," *American Journal of Nursing* 101, no. 1 (2001): 44–52.

53. Rupert Jones and Jeevan Vasagar, "Welcome aboard your easyJet flight: Now would anyone like to help with the trolley," *Guardian,* July 1, 2006. To clarify, the company was asking for applicants, not suggesting that passengers start working immediately.

54. John Gillie, "Alaska Airlines seeks quitters," *News Tribune,* June 29, 2006.

55. "Hong Kong cabin crew action day to end forced retirement," International Transport Workers Federation, Press Release, May 26, 2006, http://www.itfglobal.org/news-online/index.cfm/newsdetail/797; News in brief, http://www.flug-revue.rotor.com/FRNews99/FR990110.htm.

Selected Bibliography

Andersen, Nattanya. *Broken Wings: A Flight Attendant's Journey.* Coquitlam, BC: Avia, 1997.

Baker, Trudi, and Rachel Jones. *Coffee, Tea or Me? The Uninhibited Memoirs of Two Airline Stewardesses.* New York: Bartholomew House, 1967.

Ballard, Terri, Patrizia Romito, Laura Lauria, Vincenzo Vigiliano, Massimiliano Caldora, Clelia Mazzanti, and Arduino Verdecchia. "Self-Perceived Health and Mental Health among Women Flight Attendants." *Occupational and Environmental Medicine* 63 (2006): 33–38.

Barry, Kathleen M. "Lifting the Weight: Flight Attendants' Challenges to Enforced Thinness." *Iris* 38 (1999): 50–54.

Batey, Ian. *Asian Branding: A Great Way to Fly.* Singapore: Prentice Hall, 2002.

Blyton, Paul, Miguel Martinez, John McGurk, and Peter Turnbull. *Contesting Globalization: Airline Restructuring, Labour Flexibility and Trade Union Strategies.* London: International Transport Workers Federation, 1998.

Bolton, Sharon, and Carol Boyd. "Trolley Dolly or Skilled Emotion Manager? Moving on from Hochschild's *Managed Heart*." *Work, Employment and Society* 17 (2003): 289–308.

Boyd, Carol, and Peter Bain. "Once I Get You Up There, Where the Air Is Rarified: Health, Safety and the Working Conditions of Airline Cabin Crews." *New Technology, Work and Employment* 13, no. 1 (1998): 16–28.

Bratt, Aimée. *Glamour and Turbulence: I Remember Pan Am 1966–91.* New York: Vantage, 1996.

Chute, Rebecca, and Earl Weiner. "Cockpit and Cabin Crews: Do Conflicting Mandates Put Them on a Collision Course?" *Flight Safety Foundation: Cabin Crew Safety* 29, no. 2 (1994): 1–8.

Cobble, Dorothy Sue. *The Other Women's Movement.* Princeton, NJ: Princeton University Press, 2004.

Dahlberg, Angela. *Air Rage: The Underestimated Safety Risk.* Aldershot, UK: Ashgate, 2001.

Douglas, Deborah. *American Women and Flight since 1940.* Lexington: University Press of Kentucky, 2004.

Gillis, John. *A World of Their Own Making: Myth, Ritual and the Quest for Family Values.* Cambridge, MA: Harvard University Press, 1997.

Hanson, Susan, and Geraldine Pratt. *Gender, Work and Space.* New York: Routledge, 1995.

Harvey, David. *The Condition of Postmodernity.* Oxford: Blackwell, 1989.

Hattery, Angela. *Women, Work and Family.* Thousand Oaks, CA: Sage, 2001.

Heuven, Ellen, and Arnold B. Bakker. "Emotional Dissonance and Burnout among Cabin Attendants." *European Journal of Work and Organizational Psychology* 12, no. 1 (2003): 81–100.

Hochschild, Arlie Russell. *The Managed Heart.* 2nd ed. Berkeley: University of California Press, 2003.

Kane, Paula. *Sex Objects in the Sky.* Chicago: Follett, 1974.

Kolm, Suzanne Lee. "Who Says It's a Man's World? Women's Work and Travel in the First Decade of Flight." In *The Airplane in American Culture,* edited by Dominick Pisano, 147–164. Ann Arbor: University of Michigan Press, 2003.

Lefebvre, Henri. *The Production of Space.* Trans. Donald Nicholson-Smith. Oxford: Blackwell, 1991.

Lessor, Roberta. "Social Movements, the Occupational Arena and Changes in Career Consciousness: The Case of Women Flight Attendants." *Journal of Occupational Behavior* 5 (1984): 37–51.

Lett, AlexSandra, and Harold Silverman. "Coffee, Tea and Dignity: Knocking Down Employment Barriers 37,000 Feet Up." *Perspectives: The Civil Rights Quarterly* 12 (1980): 4–11.

Lovegrove, Keith. *Airline: Identity, Design and Culture.* London: Laurence King, 2000.

MacDonald, Leslie A., James A. Deddens, Barbara A. Grajewski, Elizabeth A. Whelan, and Joseph J. Hurrell. "Job Stress among Female Flight Attendants." *Journal of Occupational and Environmental Medicine* 45 (2003): 703–714.

Marx, Karl, *Capital,* vol. 1. Trans. Ben Fowkes. Harmondsworth, UK: Penguin Books, 1976.

Massey, Doreen. *Space, Place and Gender.* Cambridge: Polity, 1994.

McLaughlin, Helen. *Footsteps in the Sky.* Denver: State of the Art Press, 1994.

Moles, Elizabeth, and Norman Friedman. "The Airline Hostess: Realities of an Occupation with a Popular Cultural Image." *Journal of Popular Culture* 7 (1973): 305–313.

Murphy, Alexandra G. "Hidden Transcripts of Flight Attendant Resistance." *Management Communication Quarterly* 11 (1998): 499–535.

Nielsen, Georgia Panter. *From Sky Girl to Flight Attendant.* Ithaca, NY: ILR Press, 1982.

Omelia, Johanna, and Michael Waldock. *Come Fly with Us! A Global History of the Airline Hostess.* Portland, OR: Collectors Press, 2003.

Petzinger, Thomas. *Hard Landing*. New York: Random House, 1995.

Rich, Elizabeth. *Flying High: What It's Like to Be an Airline Stewardess*. New York: Stein and Day, 1972.

Rozen, Frieda. "Technological Advances and Increasing Militance: Flight Attendant Unions in the Jet Age." In *Women, Work and Technology*, edited by Barbara Drygulski Wright. 220–238. Ann Arbor: University of Michigan Press, 1987.

Spiro, Corylee, and Elizabeth Harwell. *Cabin Pressure*. New York: St. Martins Press, 1989.

Taylor, Steve, and Melissa Tyler. "Emotional Labor and Sexual Difference in the Airline Industry." *Work, Employment and Society* 14, no. 1 (2000): 77–95.

Thomas, Andrew. *Air Rage: Crisis in the Skies*. Amherst, NY: Prometheus, 2001.

Tong, Rosemarie. *Feminist Thought: A Comprehensive Introduction*. Boulder, CO: Westview Press, 1989.

Tyler, Melissa, and Pamela Abbott. "Chocs Away: Weight Watching in the Contemporary Airline Industry." *Sociology* 32 (1998): 433–450.

Tyler, Melissa, and Philip Hancock. "Flight Attendants and the Management of Gendered 'Organizational Bodies.'" In *Constructing Gendered Bodies*, edited by Kathryn Backett-Milburn and Linda McKie, 25–38. New York: Palgrave, 2001.

Whitelegg, Drew. "Cabin Pressure: The Dialectics of Emotional Labour in the Airline Industry." *Journal of Transport History* 23 (2002): 73–86.

———. "From Smiles to Miles: Delta Air Lines and Southern Hospitality." *Southern Cultures* 11 (2005): 9–29.

———. "Places and Spaces I've Been: Geographies of Female Flight Attendants in the United States." *Gender, Place and Culture* 12 (2005): 251–266.

Williams, Claire. *Blue, White and Pink Collar Workers in Australia*. London: Allen and Unwin, 1988.

———. "A Pain in the Neck: Passenger Abuse, Flight Attendants and Emotional Labour." *Journal of Occupational Health Safety—Australia, New Zealand* 16 (2000): 429–435.

———. "Sky Service: The Demands of Emotional Labour in the Airline Industry." *Gender, Work and Organization* 10 (2003): 513–550.

Wolf, Naomi. *The Beauty Myth*. New York: Anchor, 1992.

Wouters, Cas. "The Sociology of Emotions and Flight Attendants: Hochschild's *Managed Heart*." *Theory, Culture and Society* 6 (1989): 95–123.

Index

About the Author

Drew Whitelegg is director of special projects at the Emory Center for Myth and Ritual in American Life at Emory University (MARIAL). He holds a Ph.D. in geography from King's College, London. He is a member of the editorial board of the *Journal of Transport History* and of the executive committee of T2M, the International Association for the History of Transport, Traffic and Mobility.